POTSHOTS AND SNAPSHOTS

things that made us

By many hands
Edited by Peter Morton

Copyright: Peter Morton 2019
Third Printing 2021
ISBN: 978-0-6450901-2-3

CONTENTS

Part 1 Animal tales

A dark and stressful night
John Granger — 1

Snake stories
Peter Morton and Phillip Stain — 4

Snakes in the South East
Peter Morton — 8

A serious snake story
Bevan Roberts — 11

The day we stalled the eagle
Robin Dutton — 17

Gentle Labradors
Peter Morton — 21

The princess and her lady-in-waiting
Leonore Morton — 28

Part 2 Bikes plus

Bloody sand
Peter Morton and Geoff Whitehead — 39

The Baron and his lady
Peter Morton — 44

Motor cycles and me

Greg Jenke   49

How I became a Jaguar man

Bob Kretschmer   57

That's what parents are for

Marg and Bob Kretschmer   65

Part 3 Fishing

Bensbach a barra man's dreamtime

Bob Hutchinson   75

Game fishing adventures, Mark 1

Peter Morton   83

Game fishing adventures, Mark 2

Peter Morton   86

Lawdo goes fishing

Colin Gamble   90

Part 4 Gambling

The curse can be a blessing

Peter Morton   93

Gambling

Peter Morton   95

Part 5 Jobs and the tasks of others

A rural medical career

Jonathon Newberry   101

Bob the public servant, Story One

Bob Hutchinson   105

Bob the public servant, Story Two

Bob Hutchinson   109

Driver licence stories

Steve Ballard   114

The Barn

Colin Gamble   120

How did we get into this mess?

Steve Ballard and Peter Morton   123

Part 6 Jobs I fancied

A would-be politician

Peter Morton   138

By appointment to HRH Prince Charles

Peter Morton   143

Part 7 Ken Martin

Ken Martin, sculptor

Ken Martin and Peter Morton   145

Part 8 Crazy things we have done

Jerker and the doctor man

by themselves   158

The saga of the Stains and us

Mortons and Stains   169

Part 9 Outback stories

RMW: the sale of his first boots

Peter Morton   182

Troopy

Gillian Harris   187

Fitzroy Crossing

Peter Morton   194

La Grange Mission, the Watts and us

Chris and Ann Watts, and Peter Morton   199

The Mount Leonard saga

Peter and Leonore Morton   207

Part 10   A pot pourri of other tales

Quiz nights

Peter Morton   215

From Minniecrow to Ascot

James Paltridge   219

A long way to Wanilla

Shaun Kurovec   223

Peter Harvey PhD

by Peters Morton et Harvey   227

Return Journey

Rory Barnes   233

The day I nearly met Peter Morton

Robin Dutton   239

The day my brother shot me

Robin Dutton   244

The hessian bag revolution

Peter Morton   248

Part 11   The sad reality of life sometimes

A strange and even scary tale

Peter Morton   253

An unforgettable night and person

Peter Morton   256

Gerry Allen

Peter Morton   260

Lad had a hobby

Steve Ballard   265

Part 12 The wonderful but sometimes sickening world for girls

Little girl's shoes

Peter Morton — 268

She matters

Jenny Podorozhnaya — 276

Sisters and the silent messenger

Peter Harvey — 278

Part 13 Travel

A day to forget became unforgettable

Terri Christensen — 288

Bob and the twitcher chick

Bob Hutchinson — 292

Divining: myth or magic or madness?

Bob Hutchinson — 300

Doug Wade's knee

Peter Morton — 303

It started with a hat

Peter Morton — 307

Memories of Streaky Bay plus

Peter Morton — 313

The day I got on the wrong ship
Robin Dutton   317

Part 14   Is a SOB my least favourite character?

What is a son of a bitch?
Peter Morton   320

Part 15   Woolongong dreaming

Dad's new car
Colin Gamble   325

The coach, part one
Colin Gamble   329

The coach, part two
Colin Gamble   331

The rock
Colin Gamble   334

Part 16   Ulysses would have had them

The story of the Linsells
Ruth Linsell and Peter Morton   337

The Contributors   351

DEDICATION

This book is dedicated to our other halves because they surely helped to make us who we are.

INTRODUCTION

I have recently written an autobiography about my life and times as a doctor in outback and rural Australia from 1969 to 2015 except for six months at the RAAF Base in Edinburgh in South Australia.

Inevitably, when writing an autobiography, distractions come about something interesting but not germane to the narrative at the time. I noted these distractions.

Friends became interested and were also keen to record aspects of their lives for their children and grandchildren.

That simple beginning blossomed into this book; an anthology of 60 tales by me and 22 other authors.

I know all the authors, some for a short time and others for decades. I respect and admire the talents of them all.

These tales can be told at a camp fire, at a dining room table or read in bed. Few are about medicine.

I have tried to classify them and that has been imprecise at best.

I hope that they are seen to be funny, whimsical, interesting, informative, adventurous, motivational, ribald, thought provoking, exciting and to recognise achievements.

Several are sad, reflecting the reality of life and two are gut wrenching about a problem that is front and centre in our world today.

The group has grown and the enthusiasm has increased. There is an air of excitement and I have received stories literally up the last few hours before the deadline.

Last but certainly not least thanks to my fellow writers. Many writers were unsure, reluctant, shy and anxious but were brave enough to "have a go".

I hope it will all be worth it when you and your loved ones see the finished product in a book. Thank you for having a go and joining in.

PM

Part 1 Animal Tales

A DARK AND STRESSFUL NIGHT

By John Granger

One of my earliest memories of veterinarian practice at Port Lincoln happened at Koppio, 30km north of home, on a truly dark and stormy night. I had to stitch up a gelding that had gone through a barbed wire fence. After examining the cuts by torchlight, it was obvious the horse would need to be anaesthetised so that I could clean and suture the deeper tissues and the skin itself.

In those days we knocked horses out with a barbiturate anaesthetic and then kept them asleep with a sterile mixture of chloral hydrate, Nembutal and magnesium sulphate dripping from a glass bottle connected by a rubber tube to a needle in their large neck vein.

I rigged this up and asked the horse's owner to hold the bottle in position. I showed him how to double the tube between his fingers to control the anaesthetic liquid running into the vein while I did the necessary suturing.

After about twenty minutes I asked him, "How are you getting on, Fred? If the bottle of anaesthetic is getting too heavy maybe someone else can hold it for you, but please keep that rubber tube closed." The owner replied. "Don't worry John, it is not heavy." My heart took a few unscheduled beats. He had not kept the rubber tube blocked and the entire bottle of anaesthetic had run into the horse!

The horse was not dead, but it certainly was not about to

wake up! I left the farmer at 11 pm, having suggested the horse be kept warm with rugs and that he contact me with any queries.

The next day I had a full day TB testing cattle 200 km away. The farm where I left the horse, like many, did not have a telephone, so I heard nothing, but I was very concerned about the horse. A few days later I received a message saying that the horse was fine, but that he had not got up until about 11.00 am the next day!

We were very lucky! The horse could have died or have suffered nerve damage from being down for so long. In today's world what I did was quite unsatisfactory, probably litigious, but in those days this was the only way we could get the job done. The soft muddy yard we worked in was probably less likely to put pressure on the nerves of a horse lying on his side for over twelve hours. Dry firm ground would have been less forgiving.

The maintenance anaesthetic we then used is probably no longer on the market as there are now newer short acting agents available that are much safer.

Horses now are often taken to a veterinary facility where well qualified veterinary nurses assist and where safer gas anaesthetic machines are used and where there is good lighting and protection from the rain and hot sun, for both man and beast.

The reality though is that many horse owners cannot afford the "Rolls Royce" treatment, or there may be no facility of this sophistication nearby, or they may not have a horse float, or, for one reason or another they may want their horse attended to on their own property.

It seems inevitable that country practice will still involve a veterinarian with his or her bag of instruments and an even bigger bag of tricks called experience.

The help of a handy farmer or neighbour to hold things like torches and umbrellas will be necessary for the foreseeable future.

I had a lot of fun, satisfaction and some wonderful experiences and I met some amazing people, but I confess I do not miss the long hours and the worries. This type of practice is for a young vet!

SNAKE STORIES

By Peter Morton and Phillip Stain

There are many yarns about snakes in the bush and here are a couple.

I was Medical Superintendent of the Alice Springs Hospital for six weeks around 1990 and for a treat my wife Leonore and I decided to visit Glen Helen, an old homestead turned into a nationally famous restaurant.

It is an hour or so from Alice Springs at the western end of the magnificent MacDonnell Ranges. We had our daughter Sarah aged seventeen and our sons eleven-year-old Tim and nine-year-old Peter with us.

We all had a swim in the nearby Finke River, said to be the oldest river in the world and then got ready for dinner.

The restaurant was the original lounge and dining room so it was not big. Each of the five or six tables had a different matching set of Dalton China, which was a nice touch.

I made it quite clear to the children to leave us in peace. I gave Sarah some money and took them to the open bar and eating area. I noticed a couple of ringers, as cowboys are known in Australia, sitting at the bar with big hats tilted back and high heeled boots hooked onto the stool rails.

I returned to the dining room and had my first sip of a gin and tonic and sighed with pleasure. Soon I heard "Dad" in a whisper. Tim was at the doorway. He had done what he was told and his feet were not in the dining room but his head and shoulders were. He was clearly upset and then I heard the chilling words "There is a snake in the bar."

I will never forget the scene. Fortunately, it was funny. Sarah had backed Peter against the wall and was keeping him safe.

The barmaid was sweeping a large and very pretty python along the floor calling it by name and telling it not to be naughty and to go outside, which it did.

The super cool ringer dudes were standing on top of the bar looking very uncool indeed. I returned to the dining room to enjoy a delightful and top-class meal with Leonore.

The second episode was about 1984 at our Coffin Bay beach shack and involved our great friends Philip and Chris Stain.

I will let Phil tell the story.

Chris and I met in the early 1980s and I soon found out that her best friend was Leonore Morton, the wife of my old schoolmate Peter Morton.

We duly spent a Christmas with them at Coffin Bay. It was great to catch up with Peter and his parents who were also staying there.

One day Peter, his Dad and I went fishing. At the time I had a very bad knee from a football injury when I was 17 but avoided throwing myself over board with the anchor because I still had good balance.

When we returned to our moorings Mr Morton suggested that Peter and I clean the fish while he got us a beer from the shack. Naturally, having been away for a few hours, I asked after Chris when he returned.

Mr Morton replied that she and Leonore were all right and added that "They were killing a snake or something".

After we had a beer or two we wandered up to the shack and heard the story. The girls were doing the washing in an old tin laundry when a snake appeared. Chris tried to hit it with a broom as the snake was doing its best to escape through a hole. She then pushed the broom handle into the hole and jammed the snake. Leonore was sent to get something to kill it and returned with a bread knife. Chris then sawed the snake in half. The front half of the snake wriggled out through the hole.

I was very concerned about the snake escaping, particularly as Chris seemed worried. I was a city boy whereas Chris had been raised on farms. She knew all about guns, camping, fishing gear, campfires and snakes and I knew very little about any of those things and I must say I felt a bit inadequate.

Chris then asked Peter whether the snake would live. Peter said something like "Of course it wouldn't. It is a living animal and you cut the bloody thing in half"

Chris was still not happy so went to a higher authority. She called her Dad, the patriarch of the clan, who agreed with Peter. Things were now in order.

Next morning Peter answered the phone and was trying not to laugh. He hung up and told us that it was Chris's Dad on the phone and that he had been reassured by the experts at the Adelaide museum that the snake would not live.

Two nights later, when it was dark, Peter's daughter Sarah whispered to her Dad that there was a snake by the car. Chris was quick to grab a shovel but, in deference, passed it to me to do the manly thing. It made me feel good actually, but that feeling soon passed. I beat hell out of the snake only to realise by the fog of stinking muck and bits of it in my hair and on my hands that it was the front half of Chris's victim very, very dead.

This was a wonderful holiday. We married soon after and

together with Peter and Leonore have had some outrageously good times in the past 30 odd years, some of which may find their way into print but many will not!

In conclusion I did find out that the reason the snake was killed was that it was a potential risk to all, particularly the children, as it was so close to living areas.

SNAKES IN THE SOUTH EAST

By Peter Morton

Like most city people I had no experience of snakes when I first spent time in the south east with my school friend Dick Bagshaw.

Quite often I went there to study and while Dick and his Dad were working I had many cups of tea and chats with Mrs Bagshaw, who had quite an effect on my view of the world and particularly country lore and customs.

We got on very well, maybe because we were likely blood relatives. Her mother was a Morton whose kin came for Ayrshire where my great grandfather and his antecedents were born.

Anyhow, I got to know about her fear of snakes and that was something else we shared.

One day in the early 1960s I was studying at their house and she went into a bedroom. The next thing I head was a blood curdling scream of SNAAAAAKE. I rushed towards the door as she rushed out. As we entangled she yelled something that I took to be "There is a snake under the bed".

Doing my best John Wayne act, I grabbed a .303 rifle. They are a powerful weapon and the Australian Army's choice of rifle from the Boer War in 1902 until the Vietnam-War, when they were replaced in about 1960. I found a bullet somewhere, loaded the rifle and entered the bed room. It was a small room and I had to get down on my hands and knees to look under the bed, which I did with great trepidation.

And there it was. A bloody great Tiger Snake looking like

he was heading for a hole to the outside. Mrs Bagshaw did not want it to get away and come back when there was no resolute gun-slinger nearby, so she told me to shoot it.

Timing is everything in life. A.303s has a hell of a kick and is quite long and must be held firmly, ideally against the shoulder. These requirements were hard to meet collectively by a 190cm person sharing a small room with a snake, a bed and a very scared lady. Somehow I got sorted and was just about to shoot the last 20cm of the snake that was disappearing out the hole when a hand grabbed the rifle and the owner of the hand, one Richard Kent Bagshaw, said "Goodness me old chap what are you doing?" and "Did you know that the wall is fibro and the .303 would have made a hell of a mess". He added that he and his father had parked their car next to the wall the day before alongside a gas cylinder. He then said "Please eject the bullet, leave the bolt open and hand me the rifle butt first". Timing sure was everything.

Sadly the family had to sell the place two or three years later and moved to Avenue Range, 20-30 km south in 1965 or 66

Dick continued his habit of working two jobs by running their own farm and managing their old property that they sold to a Ron White from Adelaide.

I was again studying, this time at their new house, and went to work with Dick one day to give him a hand with something.

We were having lunch when Mr White and a friend from Adelaide, expectedly, arrived at a gate a few hundred metres away. His mate opened the gate and then grabbed a shovel and started beating the hell out of the ground.

He and Mr White looked around and then put something in the back of the ute they were driving.. I assume that they were looking for us, but we were sitting on the ground under a tree eating our lunch so were probably invisible.

Eventually they drove over and parked near us and we had a chat and drink of water.

In the course of the conversation, Mr White asked Dick if he would get a particular pair of pliers from the tool box.

He ambled over to the ute, opened the tool box and said "Bloody snakes everywhere this year", picked it up by the tail, cracked its head off and threw the body into the bushes. He then picked up the wanted pliers with his left hand and passed them to Mr White.

Paul Newman's Cool hand Luke had nothing on my mate Richard.

A SERIOUS SNAKE STORY - THE REAL DEAL

By Bevan Roberts

The story really begins when as a small five or six-year-old I realised that we had a farm in our family.

The farm was unnamed and I have no idea how big it was only that it was way, way down a dirt road at Hallett Cove a seaside settlement, not even a village, five or six miles south of Glenelg. There was only one road and a train line that provided some kind of connection with the outside world.

There was no electricity but papers and The Australian Women's Weekly came by the train. They were rolled somewhere by someone and thrown from the train to be collected by the kelpie dogs who fetched and returned them, to the farmhouse, a half mile up the hill from the train track.

There was a telephone with the mouthpiece fixed to a box that was attached to the wall. The earpiece was on a cord and sat in a cradle of sorts on the side of the box. It rarely rang but if it did, Hilda owned the answering role. So small was she, that she engaged the assistance of another box to stand on to reach the mouthpiece.

There were two houses known as the Farm House and the Old House. Both were made of local stone. The Old House was quite small and probably was originally a workman's cottage. There were stables and haysheds, a woodheap with snakes and always animals. I loved being allowed amongst the working horses. My lasting love of horses began here.

A team of, I imagine fifteen, all with names. A huge roan fellow called 'Boxer' had the softest muzzle and a temperament to match.

We often collected coal that had been thrown off the coal tender immediately behind the locomotive, on the tight turns of the line as it skirted some pretty steep gullies. Coal was shared by the finders, in our case my dad and myself and Uncle Albert the Farmer.

We took our share home and were heroes as it gave out a noticeably greater heat than wood in our open fire place in the lounge.

Uncle Albert, Aunty Hilda and Keith and Elsie their children from my mother's side lived on the farm.

Albert was fearsome and old. Hilda tiny and while I suspect Keith and Elsie were well into their thirties, neither was married. They were all however happy, happy people.

Keith had been to war and there was a large coconut from New Guinea that sat way up high on top of the dresser. It came down every visit for a shake and discussion about its future.

At school I had become a pal of a "pommie" kid called Andrew Panter. His Dad was out here working at the Weapons Research Establishment at Salisbury or the nearby RAAF Base. He was most likely a boffin but everything about those facilities and the Woomera Testing Range was very hush- hush at the time.

Andrew lived at Somerton, with his mother and dad and younger brother Howard. It was a short ride from our place at Warradale.

In 1955 we were both in grade seven at the Scotch Junior School in Adelaide and in the September School Holidays, Blondie (as he was nicknamed because of his fair hair) and I planned a rabbiting trip to the Farm.

I rode my bike to Somerton and we walked along the beach to Brighton and caught the train to the Hallett Cove Station. From there we walked to the farm. Hilda and Elsie were there, Albert and Keith were not.

After a look around, cool drinks and sandwiches we were off to do some rabbiting. A shovel, spade to dig out the burrows and a bag or two from the shed at the Old House was all we needed. A feed would soon be on its way.

We walked along the ridge road in front of the house and then beyond, where the road stopped. Then down into and across the gully and its trickling creek and up the other side. We were probably a mile from the farmhouse.

I walked through the gate with Blondie trailing a short way behind. Probably 10 paces into the paddock I felt what I thought was a grass seed in my left sock. Looking down it was not a grass seed but a large brown snake between my legs having completed a bite and now moving quickly on. The two puncture marks just above my shoe line on my heel confirmed the worst.

We were both Cub Scouts and had been through the drill of what was required.

I tied a tourniquet, made from two knotted handkerchiefs, around my leg above the knee and then began to cut the area with sharp shale that was lying about and Blondie went for help.

My guess is that probably fifteen or twenty minutes passed, before the beige Hillman, with Elsie and Andrew aboard arrived at the end of the road and I walked through the gully towards the car. I was almost there but from the shock and the push up the gully I could no longer see.(*This is a recognised effect of brown snake envenomation. Ed)*

I was taken to Doctor Owen Bowering at Brighton, well known Doctor for the Glenelg Football Club and thereby assured of fame and patient flow.

The cutting that I had done had produced some bleeding, but Owen's scalpel slice produced a real flow.

There was no anti-venom at the surgery, so the next step was to the Adelaide Children's Hospital. Elsie drove the Hillman with purpose, Andrew provided encouragement and support. Sight had returned.

The Hospital was expecting us and there were many injections of all kinds. I now had a rapidly rising temperature.

No doubt my Mum and Dad had been informed somehow and I recall them being there later in the evening. Things blurred and time mattered not to me. I learned later that on the second day they were told that it might be a good idea to expect the worst. My temperature had reached 106 and things must have looked grim. Mum said to me later, "Your face was blown up and tight like a ball."

I survived. My foot needed a skin graft and all in all I was in hospital for all of the third term, missing lots of good stuff that being at the top of the Junior School promised. It was however a mighty adventure.

Fielders Ward, named for the Bookmakers who had donated considerable funds to the Hospital, was my home.

Nurses came and went. Sweeney was one of my favourites and another June Lendon became the Flower Queen of Adelaide during my stay and I still see her daughter from time to time.

Blondie returned to England at the end of second year in

1957 aged almost 14. We did not see each other until 2013, when we picked up on a friendship that was built on much more than just the snake story.

He had become an engineer and ultimately the global head of an enormous British building company, Wimpey's. He remains one of the Queen's men and is a simply fantastic person. His little brother became an Impresario of note, with theatres in London, New York and Sydney.

Albert and Hilda lived long lives and never really changed; Keith worked hard until he passed on. Elsie married a bonzer fellow Murray King but their love was cut short when he had a heart attack and died. Elsie lived to be 101 and every time we saw each other we talked about the snake and Andrew's run for help.

The snake of course was caught, by Albert, but finished in too many pieces to be preserved as a souvenir. I have a couple of scars and a story to tell.

Bevan is my first cousin and I well remember visiting in hospital but not that he was so sick. What I do remember was just how much discomfort he had from the sliced heel that had been skin grafted when he played football and cricket and rubbed the skin raw. A brave lad indeed. It is a cautionary tale as to what might have happened. The take home message is that boots and thick socks should be worn, or at least thick socks, when in the bush or on farms. Brown snakes have highly dangerous venom but a poor biting mechanism that is effectively grooves on the front of its fangs so even socks may stop envenomation.

No more cutting snake bites, using tourniquets, or washing wounds so that the area can be swabbed and the venom identified. A bandage is applied firmly from the foot or hand to the top of the limb. There should be a bandage in everyone's kit Ed

THE DAY WE STALLED THE EAGLE

By Robin Dutton

My wife Judy and I arrived in Woomera in January 1973. We had a house in Boorong Street that we chose because it was scheduled for redecorating that year. This was a good thing, because the cracks in the wall were quite extensive. You could see into the garden through one of the wider cracks in the laundry wall. In April we went on holiday to Queensland and it was arranged that the house would be repainted in our absence. We carefully chose the colour scheme, being a very pale cream for all the walls, and an olive green for the doors and architraves. Imagine our surprise when we returned three weeks later, late at night, to find that all the walls were olive green and the doors were cream. When I complained the following day, I received an apology, but was informed that we would have to live with the colour scheme, as it was not scheduled for repainting for another seven years. The only consolation was that the weekly rental was only $5.79, whereas we were collecting the princely sum of $21.00 per week for our house in Rose Park, Adelaide

If you were into sport, Woomera at that time was a great place to live. I played competitive squash and took up gliding during my time there. There were many pros and cons to the sport of gliding in Woomera. The gliding conditions were exceptional, thermals were strong and easy to find. However, for about one hour's actual flying time, you had to assist for the rest of the day, and the weather was HOT! During my first flight, the instructor asked me if I would like to experience some aerobatic manoeuvres. Oh yes, I replied, and I was hooked.

Another time we found a thermal with two wedge tailed eagles soaring, so we joined them. One of them was soon soaring alongside our inner wingtip. My instructor said; "Watch this" and very slowly began to reduce speed. The eagle adjusted his wingtips and stayed with us for a while. You could see the eagle spreading its wingtip feathers further and further as we almost reached stall speed. Suddenly the eagle tumbled out of position, at which point the nose of our glider was pushed down to regain speed. The eagle came back for more and stalled a second time.

It was an experience during my first solo flight a couple of months later that convinced me to go back to sailing. Together with water skiing, they had been my main sporting interests for a few years after we arrived in Australia. Early in that flight I found a very strong thermal, locked on it and started climbing. I was climbing faster than the instrument's maximum of 32 feet per second. It was a very tight thermal, so I had the glider cranked steeply with the nose down. Most people imagine that gliding is a nice quiet sport, but it is not. If you are circling, cranked right over, you have to keep the nose down in order keep the speed up, otherwise you risk stalling the inner wing. So long as it is noisy, you are OK. It is when it goes quiet that you are in danger of stalling. Anyway, I went up very quickly to about 10,000 feet before levelling off then and enjoying the flight back down. At that point I realized that each of my flying instructors had assumed that the other had put me through the drill of extricating the plane from a spin stall. Wrong! I had never done it but knew the theory, so I would probably have been alright.

During the two years that I was in Woomera, record rainfalls were experienced. There were 23 inches in 1973 and 22 inches the following year. Most of the salt lakes were full of water. Judy took a flight in a Fokker Friendship over Lake Eyre and at an altitude of 3,000 feet no land could be seen. In February 1974, at a marine shop in Adelaide, I came upon a red second hand Hobie 16 catamaran that had been in the water only three times. I decided there and then that this would be safer than gliding!

The following weekend, a very strange sight was seen coming into Woomera, a Hobie 16 catamaran being towed. I got permission to sail on Lake Koolymilka, which when dry was the home of the Koolymilka Football club. I have photographs of my boat sailing in 16 feet of water between the goal posts and past the gable roof of the Koolymilka FC changing shed. The editor of this book gave copies of these photographs to legendary football coach, Neil Kerley, who's first coaching job, was with this club.

Within weeks there was a twenty-foot trailer sailer and a couple of other boats sailing on the lake. Mid-year we were asked to relocate to Shell Lagoon. By the end of the year we had half a dozen boats, sailing and racing.

Towards the end of 1974, I found an advertisement in the Commonwealth Gazette seeking a site Engineer for the soon to be constructed Lae International Airport at Nadzab in PNG. I asked Judy how she would feel about that, and she replied with another question "How would you feel about a divorce?" Luckily for me, she came around to my point of view, and in February 1975 we moved to Port Moresby, prior to moving to Lae a couple of months later. The Commonwealth Government paid for the Hobie Cat to be shipped to Lae, so for a year I had the fastest sailing boat in PNG.

LABRADORS ARE GENTLE BUT NEVER UNDERESTIMATE THEM

By Peter Morton

Sometime in 2017, I was having a cup of tea with my farmer mate Noel with my Labrador lying at my feet. We had laughed at the way she was cowering in the presence of his tiny Tenterfield Terrier and Kelpie sheep dog.

Noel came from the high country in NSW but has been farming on Eyre Peninsula for 50 years. He looked pensive for a time and then said "You know I love dogs and Labradors are considered one of the best but they can be bloody bad sheep killers and you know what happens to dogs that kill sheep on farms".

This confirmed something a Rod MacLeod told me in the mid-1960s at Wentworth in NSW. My first Labrador and I were in his ute and I asked why he had a pistol in the glove box. He replied "We are close to Wentworth and town dogs kill our sheep and Labradors are the worst offenders".

This made me think about my experiences with dogs, and particularly Labradors.

The first dogs I remember were Peter and Jock, father and son Blue Heelers who used to travel in the boot of my uncle's car and although other people were always careful with them, I played with them happily when I was five or six years old.

During my childhood we had several small dogs culminating with Terry an Australian Terrier when I was nine or ten.

I loved, walked and played with him but deep down I

wanted an Alsatian and even wrote to Rin Tin Tin, the Alsatian dog actor, and proudly displayed his photograph in my bedroom.

Mum and Dad knew a Mr and Mrs Clarke who lived near the Morphettville race course in Adelaide who owned a magnificent Alsatian named Kim and for years I used to take him for walks.

I must have been 14 or 15 and with my mate, Ian Chappell, who became and still is a household word in Australian cricket, took Kim for a walk in the sand hills at West Beach in Adelaide. There was a track leading to the beach and a shack where Martha the feared and mysterious pig lady lived. Her willingness to shoot annoying boys with her shotgun was legendary.

My mate asked me about her and all I could tell him was that she was an odd sort, virtually a hermit and she raised pigs for food and maybe sold some. One day I saw her fishing off the shore so that was another source of food. There were plenty of hares around that area and it was only a few hops to the Adelaide Airport, where I remember seeing them from the road and aircraft windows in the 1970s.

Her real story was shrouded in mystery, but she did it tough. Probably where she came from was even tougher. We both had good throwing arms and landed a salvo of stones on Martha's roof. Out she came with a banshee yell, waving a shot gun and in an unmistakeable scream told us to, "Get to buggery out of it or I'll put a bullet in your bloody arses".

She scared the hell out of us alright, so we fled with the dog as fast as we could across some black dirty looking stuff that was the end product of the sewage processing. It was softer than it looked, resulting in smelly, dirty boys and dog.

I have always thought this was a funny thing to do but now I am bitterly ashamed that two boys, and I was the leader, who lived in nice homes with all comforts, plenty to eat and with loving parents should treat this poor woman so unkindly and nearly deleted the story just prior to editing. Let it be a mea culpa.

Perhaps Martha or the patron saint of pig ladies retaliated with the bizarre actions later of Kim the dog that could have seriously injured me or even worse.

Ian and I went to our separate homes and I took Kim into our back yard and let him have a drink and roll around.

He seemed happy but when I bent over to put on his lead to take him home, he snarled and launched himself at my throat from a distance of 40-50cm. I reacted very quickly and shoved my forearm so far into his mouth he couldn't bite. Fortunately, I was six feet tall at the time, which may have been important. He relaxed and I walked him home. Maybe he was only 50% serious but he certainly wasn't playing and it was the last time I took him for a walk. It erased the dream I had of having an Alsatian.

For the next few years Terry was my doggy mate and footy team mascot in a jumper Mum knitted him. But one winter he was not well and we feared it would be his last.

I suggested to Mum and Dad that we forget the Alsatian but one of those Golden Labradors would be good and they agreed. I only knew about Golden Labradors but soon realised that the photograph of Mum's father as a gamekeeper in Wales with a shot gun over his right shoulder had a black Labrador sitting next to him.

With the name Jason firmly in mind I found a litter of black Labradors and grabbed one, before Mum and Dad changed their minds, and indeed named him Jason. It was in 1963 or 64 and I must have had a job somewhere because I paid 40 pounds/80 dollars for the puppy. Mum said "Fancy paying all that money for a black dog," but she soon came to love him as much as I did.

Terry soon let this interloper know who was boss. A year or so later we played host for a few days to a bitch in season that was to be mated with Jason. Terry was in dog heaven. He was a middle-aged chap and every morning, when let out, he would scramble around the bitch's head, foot, tail, or wherever trying to have his way with her. He would then collapse and sleep for the rest of the day. She seemed faintly amused and Jason took no notice.

But the morning after Jason and the bitch were mated Mum let Terry out the back door and Jason erupted and grabbed him by the head and maybe would have killed him if Mum hadn't slammed the door on him and yelled.

Terry spent the day trembling on Mum's lap with a rug over him and being plied with eye droppers of brandy and aspirin. Next morning the object of his lust had gone so he growled at Jason and nipped him to set matters right again. He lived for another five or six years, probably because of the mental and physical stimulation of keeping Jason in order.

Jason and I were great mates and he would sit under my desk while I studied, surfed with me and was even mascot for The Queen Elizabeth Hospital Football team. We were inseparable. He always travelled to the south east with me, where my farmer mates teased me about him being a sook who was afraid of sheep dogs.

One day things changed. Jason was being yapped at and taunted by three sheep dogs and one must have bitten him. Boy did he sort them out. Later that day we visited a neighbour who also had sheep dogs.

To Jason these dogs were just more bloody pests, so he was after them and chased the three or four onto the roof of an old car and kept them "treed" for some time. Telling this story reminds me of the Kenny Rogers song "Coward of the county".

A more serious incident took place at Moana beach south of Adelaide. Jason was sitting between my car and another gazing out to sea when a big Alsatian attacked him from behind without warning. Somehow he managed to recover and give the Alsatian a fair scragging.

I was scared stiff actually. I did not like dogs fighting and I thought he was in real trouble. When the owner of the other dog rushed up to rescue him I said something like "Better keep your dog away mate he might get hurt next time". The fact that I was pale and shaking did detract from my cool warning.

The last story about the fighting Jason took place in the Broken Hill Hospital. When I left home to work at Broken Hill, Jason was getting old so Dad offered to keep him and on a planned trip to Sydney left him with us in Broken Hill.

One night my wife Leonore was working at the hospital as a nurse and looking after a particular patient and I was waiting in the doctors' lounge with Jason. I was not on call but worried about that patient.

This was justified as he had a cardiac arrest. The alarms

loudly rang so I tore up the stairs and of course Jason followed and took great umbrage with all these people jumping around and yelling, with his mum and dad in the middle, perhaps in danger, so he attacked the oxygen cylinder.

Just kidding, but he did run into the room and slipped on the polished floor and knocked over the oxygen cylinder before Leonore spirited him out.

Cardiac arrests are dramatic events and I wonder if anyone involved remembers a large black creature running in and being dragged out. No one would believe them anyway!

The next story took place about 10 years later in Warrnambool and involved Jason's son, also called Jason.

The next-door neighbours had an Alsatian and Red Setter and one day they bailed up Jason on the footpath. He behaved in a way I had never seen or heard about before or since. Jason was clearly very frightened and this must have released some genetic response from his wolf ancestors.

He had his hindquarters almost on the ground protecting his genitals and abdomen. His shoulders were hunched and his elbows pushed out to the side protecting his chest and throat. He was quite still except for his head that was swinging from side to side, close to the ground with his neck muscles tense.

The Alsatian was serious but the Red Setter was his normal dopey self and must have thought it was all good fun because he got close enough to Jason's swinging head for Jason to bite his foot which made him yelp and run away. The Alsatian joined him and Jason relaxed.

Labradors are used by police and the military and are very loving and gentle, trustworthy dogs but they are also big, courageous, strong and do not like being bitten.

By the way, we now have our seventh black Labrador, a female named Phryne after the television character in *Miss Fisher's Murder Mysteries.* We got her because as were looking for a cute, dark haired, sexy female to have puppies. She was mated to a golden dog and all the pups were golden as well, but captivating!

One of these puppies are owned by our elder daughter in Sydney and another by my good mate John Granger, now in Adelaide who wrote the first story in this book so our visits have an extra pleasure seeing our grown-up puppies.

THE PRINCESS AND HER LADY IN WAITING - FOREVER TOGETHER

By Leonore Morton

The anticipation and excitement about the arrival of our sixth Labrador was something special as we had been without a dog for a few years. We missed the companionship and also planned to breed top quality pups.

As we left the kennels, in the Adelaide Hills, with this little black bundle nestled on my lap I could tell she was very special and looked forward to many hours loving and training her. We named her "Lexi" after the kitchen wench in the popular TV series Monarch of the Glen.

She settled into her new home relatively easily and started sleeping in the bathroom, then the laundry and finally quite happily on the back verandah.

She was soon betrothed to Remus a beautiful, big, strong yellow Labrador owned by good friends Dianne and David Nightingale. He and our new puppy were bred by Gladys Hand, at Mount Barker.

To keep us even more on our toes our daughter Kirstin had just given birth to Jackson our first grandchild and came to stay with us from Sydney for six months because her husband Andrew, a soldier, was deployed overseas the day after Jackson was born. Kirstin and son came well prepared with baby equipment, a television set to her exacting standards and her dog, Bonny, a mixture of many breeds that combined to produce a very sweet dog.

Bonny was a very welcome mate, carer and teacher for

Lexi and they got on extremely well. Kirstin declared that Lexi was the Princess and Bonny was , Lady Bonny, her lady in waiting. Every day they played until both were exhausted. Bonny wanting some peace and quiet from the pesky pup would find a quiet spot in the garden to sleep and Lexi would drop wherever convenient to power nap.

The months passed quickly and despite some digging and chewing that we minimised by burying chicken wire in appropriate places Lexi settled in well. She was a fast learner and I was thrilled with her response to sit, stay and come. Both of us were working full time so every minute was precious. While preparing dinner I would go into the garden and run her through her paces to sit, come for a treat, stay and to retrieve a ball.

She relished this play and affection after long hours of being alone.

Peter used "Jackson" as a command for her to eat and much to my horror I pictured Lexi attacking Jackson but Peter reassured me that would not happen and it did not. She learnt this quickly as would any Labrador when food is involved and would sit patiently waiting for the word. In years to come our son Peter and his wife Patricia were looking after Lexi. Peter came in from work and asked why she was sitting, drooling in front of her untouched food bowl. Patricia said "I gave her the command Patrick"! We were amazed she had been so faithful to our training. Patrick is our second grandchild!

Lexi soon grew into a beautiful well-proportioned dog with a good square head and tail like an otter that are requirements for an ideal Labrador. She played like any puppy and had an endless supply of toys. Often, we would arrive home to find the backyard scattered with "snow" from yet another cuddly toy she had annihilated. There was one toy she especially liked, a purple grape with green "ears and large white eyes". We were never sure what the attraction was but it stayed with her forever-and we still have it.

To breed any pedigreed dog, registration with the Canine Association and numerous veterinarian tests and X-rays are needed for sire and dam.

When all this was done and she was a suitable age her playmate, Remus, became her mate and the countdown started.

We had bred pups before and were quite relaxed. I kept her well exercised. Peter made a whelping box under the verandah. I collected newspapers for the delivery and Lexi remained quite calm although she was enormous. Dianne and David visited often and there was much speculation as to how many pups she would have.

I was at work when labour started. Dianne was at hand and Peter was able to get home. The first pup arrived and Lexi, utterly bewildered, sought refuge in the broad bean patch and showed no interest in her first born, a black male. After some persuasion she came out and we introduced her to her puppy. From there it was plain sailing. Nine healthy pups were delivered. Five black and four golden now called yellow.

Naturally we were very excited with Lexi's efforts and bragged about her nine pups. Unfortunately this resulted in unsought advice on feeding. I must admit that I was anxious about a young mother managing such a large litter so I rang Gladys Hand, Lexi's breeder and asked her opinion. Her advice was, 'Feed her what I told you and let nature take its course," and that is exactly what happened. Lexi took to motherhood like the proverbial 'duck to water' and all the pups thrived.

Life became very busy. Lexi was given large, nutritious meals of milk, cereal and fresh meat, on demand—Nirvana for a Labrador!

We were up early each morning to feed her, clean the whelping box, replace the newspapers and then go to work. I would rush home at lunch time to check mother and babies. While Lexi was feeding her pups it was relatively easy as she kept them meticulously clean and very rarely left them. Then we received instructions from Gladys to gradually introduce water then food.

The diet she used was 'natural' and very complicated. Breakfast consisted of various portions of oats, bran, honey and milk to be mixed in individual bowls.

Dinner was nine or ten items added to meat such as chopped carrot, parsley, garlic and cayenne pepper and then another meal at supper time. Some pups were faster than others so it was a race to check that each one got their share and that they didn't pinch their neighbours. We did manage to get a photograph of them all feeding from individual bowls with the help of five other people. Next job was clean up! All pups flourished. Mother and grandparents were slightly frazzled to say the least.

Peter had fenced off an area on the back lawn where we put a kennel our builder friend knocked up. The pups would play vigorously on the lawn then retreat to the kennel to cuddle up together for the essential sleeps. Mum was temporally separated from them during the day then let in to feed them at night.

At six weeks they were weaned. It was amusing to see Lexi give up the job of feeding her babies. She was extremely thin, even in her face and her coat had lost its shine. One day she decided it was time to stop being a "mum". She wanted to act as the teenager she was and play with her children rather than feed them. She frolicked around the garden dodging around and jumping over the pups who sat around gaping at their mother who was behaving in such a weird way.

Now we had to sell the puppies. There was a lot of paper work to ensure each puppy was registered with the Canine Association.

The six-week visit to the vet was somewhere between an ordeal and fun. Mother and nine pups were examined, vaccinated and wormed. We arrived with all in tow, literally. The surgery cat met us at the door completely oblivious of the dog, took the lead of one of the pups in his mouth and walked off with the pup in tow towards the front door. Mother was not pleased and let said cat know.

Remus's owner had the pick of the litter and chose the best yellow male for his son. Our son Tim wanted a black male that he named Barney. One day a family of dad, mum with a baby and two-year-old arrived to choose their pup to join their Samoyed dog at home in a relatively small yard. If I had been more experienced I would have declined the sale. As it turned out I met the man some months later to find out they had sold the pup on to people who had bought one of the other pups so it ended well.

Peter took the largest black male, the last to be sold, to

Adelaide and delivered him to a man in a car park he had arranged to meet. Peter must have shown some concern. The man quietly said "You don't have to worry about me mate I have just put down my diabetic Rottweiler. I have tested his urine every day for five years to work out the dose of insulin I had to give him". He had found a good home.

Peter had arranged a job with the Australian Army in Darwin starting in January 2003. I had been working full time with the Australian Red Cross and was granted leave of absence. The process to move was huge. We found tenants for the house, put the contents into storage and headed for Darwin on December 30th with Lexi who had regained her youthful figure and shiny black coat.

A rule we had for all our dogs was that they travelled on the floor of the front passenger seat. Lexi followed this implicitly, even when we were not in the car. I was tired of having a thirty-kilo dog sitting on my feet so for this long trip I decided it was time for the family dog to be relegated to the back seat in a harness. This really put Lexi's nose out of joint and she sat up and stared at the back of Peter's head for hundreds of kilometres during this and many other journeys.

Darwin was an entirely new experience for us and our dog. The first health problem with her were 'hot spots' which were angry looking sores on various parts of her body hidden by her fur that had to be shaved exposing the entire sore which was treated with antibiotics and antiseptic solutions. We became experts as they recurred. Cane toads had not come to Darwin but crocodiles were ever present and we had to keep our eyes open walking on the beach as they often attacked dogs.

It was hot in Darwin and Lexi always slept outside. One night, after an alarming electrical storm, I checked her only to find her curled up on the house step, the highest ground, with water flooding the patio so on this occasion I let her come inside. She had not barked or shown any fear of the thunder which accentuated the fact of Labradors as gun dogs, being very tolerant of gunfire and other loud noises.

Our house backed onto the Darwin Golf Course and made for very pleasant but hot daily walks. A luxury, or even a necessity, of the house was a swimming pool that was wonderful after the daily walks. Lexi would go straight into the pool to cool down, swim a couple of laps, then come out and shake triumphantly. I knew it upset the chlorine balance of the water and the amount spent weekly at the local pool shop increased but we made allowances for our special girl.

Another favourite pastime was to chase frilled neck lizards in the garden but somehow she would pull up just before she ever reached them. I was told that they were worm infested so I am sure that is what put her off!

Peter's work hours at Roberson Barracks were from 7.00am until 4.00pm which was a change from the hours he had worked for the previous thirty odd years. It was a novelty to be home so early, have a swim and then relax with a beer and Lexi giving him her full attention. She learnt very quickly from a wink to 'fetch' a peanut he had thrown into the garden.

We travelled a great deal, many times to national parks, that meant boarding kennels for Lexi. One kennel owner in particular was very friendly. Lexi was in season so the owner allocated her a far corner next to an old girl who would keep her company. When we picked her up she was not in her kennel but in the lounge room of the main house. Her personality was so infectious that she captured this man's heart who allowed her to play with his own dog.

This dog, maybe a Labrador sheep dog cross developed an intense dislike of crocodiles when the owner was working at a crocodile farm in Broome. He confronted a very nasty gent, who had killed his mate a week or two before. The croc attacked the dog from the other side of the wire mesh of his pen. His jaws slammed shut and jammed in the wire somehow. The dog looked at the captured crocodile with a smug and satisfied look and bit the crocodile's nose at which the crocodile recoiled and left a tooth on the ground outside the wire.

The tooth looked quite fetching on a chain worn around the kennel owner's neck. Undoubtedly he had trouble separating it from the dog!

At one stage we looked after Barney, our son's dog and Lexi's son. They were good friends and enjoyed the swimming pool.

Lexi came into season and as Barney was not de-sexed I hired a 'bitch's box' like those in the 'Footrot Flats' stories but a more sophisticated version made for Northern Territory conditions and feral dogs. It was elevated about a metre from the ground, spacious and secured with double layers of toughened wire where Lexi stayed out of reach of Barney and any stray dogs.

The previous season I had brought her inside. Our house was open plan and was hard to isolate her. One day after an outing I found Princess Lexi sleeping very comfortably on our bed with her head on a pillow. I had forgotten to close the bedroom door and she took the opportunity for a comfortable sleep with the luxury of an overhead fan.

When our time in Darwin ended, we went to Gladstone Queensland for a year and eventually returned to Port Lincoln in 2007. All was wonderful. We were back in a temperate climate with our large garden for Lexi to enjoy. Tim and his wife Lisa had moved to Whyalla and provided a wonderful stop over on our trips to and from Adelaide. Once again Lexi and Barney were united. They were very happy until food got between them. On one occasion Lisa had to break up a very vicious fight that broke out in their small laundry. Blood was drawn and Lisa was quite shaken, even though she had been brought up with big dogs and was an expert in that type of situation. Tim calls her 'the dog whisperer'.

Lexi was very fond of her and would sit very close to her whether she had just arrived or was about to leave. This was the beginning of her dislike for travel. When we were about to leave on yet another trip she would sit with dogged determination by our back door and only the temptation of a biscuit would lure her into the car. This was a very clear message to us she was over travelling particularly on the back seat.

In 2010 Tim and Lisa moved to Nhulunbuy in the Northern Territory. It was a huge move and there was no temporary accommodation for Barney. Naturally we offered to look after him. They both settled in and with the exception of eating separately there were no problems. Getting into the car was sorted easily. Barney would jump in first onto the front seat floor and then Lexi would wriggle her way in and both dogs were happy with my legs draped over them.

We had many walks along the beach each dog rushing into the water to retrieve a ball. Barney would beat Lexi in the water because he could run further in the water than her but Lexi could out do him on land. They went everywhere with us but when we flew to Adelaide to buy a new car we left them in the local kennels where they had been before.

We arrived home late on Sunday evening too late to pick up the dogs. Next morning we received an urgent call from Mel, the kennel owner saying Lexi had collapsed please come quickly.

We arrived at the kennels to see Lexi being carried out to a car to be taken to the Vets. She did not look well. On arrival we were met by the Vet saying they had done what they could but Lexi had passed away from a twisted stomach. We were devastated. She was eleven years old and extremely fit and certainly we were not prepared for her passing. We felt immediate guilt for not getting home earlier, but would we have noticed her condition late at night? It was a very sad moment as we stood stroking her soft black velvet like ears. The only saving grace was we had Barney to take home and still have a black Labrador with us.

I decided very quickly to have her cremated so she could be close to us just a little longer. She was indeed a very special friend who delighted us in many ways in particular her love of life and devotion to us.

That year we celebrated Christmas at Coffin Bay with all family members present. Kirstin and her family were travelling from Sydney when dear Bonny became very sick and died much to the sorrow of the family in particular

Patrick. She was cremated and the Princess and Lady in Waiting were laid to rest under a tree at our beach house in Coffin Bay.

Part 2 Bikes plus

BLOODY SAND

By Peter Morton and "The Duke" Whitehead

My wife and I will have lived in rural or outback Australia for 50 years in 1969 and half of our lives has been spent in Port Lincoln.

We have done a lot of camping and fishing and I thought I had found a way to get every vehicle, boat and camper we have owned bogged in sand. About six months ago I found another way while driving a vehicle in sand dunes the day before the tyres were to be replaced. Consequently, they had very little traction. Fortunately, I had chucked some wood, a shovel and a bloke who had spent 10 years in the Northern Territory as a surveyor in the car so all ended up OK.

Writing this reminds me of a trip we made from Cocklebiddy on the Eyre Highway due north to Rawlinna on the east west railway and to then Warburton and Docker River in some very tough and lonely country.

I ran over a knife that had fallen from a vehicle and it speared the driver's side back tyre.

I jacked up the car and removed the wheel nuts and our son, who was four or five, reached over the tyre to help Dad. I grabbed him and pulled him away from the wheel. A split second later the jack fell over and the car fell onto the tyre that stayed upright and supported the car. I hate to think what could have happened to his hands.

About a year ago in 2017 that son, his wife, their two

children and another couple joined us on a trip to Alice Springs via the Binn's Track through the Simpson Desert parallel with the dunes.

A car was bogged; it wasn't me, thankfully, but it was someone with the same surname.

I pulled off the track, unhooked the camper and moved in front of the bogged car and hooked on a chain. I was just about to drive off slowly to tighten the chain before putting any pressure on it when another vehicle came along and a chap stopped to help.

He was most upset that I was using a chain explaining that they were dangerous and that "He was an engineer and chains could break and hurt people". He suggested I use a snatch strap. I did this and successfully pulled the other car out of the sand after he kindly draped a damper over the strap. His was the only other car we saw that day in 300-400 km.

About two years before, between Birdsville and Windorah, it poured with rain and my mate following could not get traction in the mud. I had attached a chain to the rear of my Heaslip Camper and to his 4WD Ute that was pulling a 20-foot caravan, dragging those 30-40km to our destination and, indeed sanctuary, so I was very impressed with my chain.

When we returned to Port Lincoln after the Binn's Track trip I needed something fixed on my car so went to see my mate Geoff "The Duke" Whitehead at his workshop in Edinburgh Street.

He is a very popular mechanic and holds court every morning on the footpath. Women with Mercedes sports cars, farmers with utes, V12 E type drivers, caravans and their owners, the odd boat, doctors, lawyers, young women with cars, the lame and the blind, women with kids and others from near and far gather to hear his words of wisdom - including me.

He was raised on a farm, has fished and dived as an amateur and professional. He is the local Royal Automobile Association (RAA) man so has extricated many types of vehicles from the beaches and sand hills of lower Eyre Peninsula.

Here is what he had to say about chains and snatch straps in a letter he wrote to me.

"Peter, I have had breakages and lucky escapes from injury with both. I was called to rescue a heavy truck badly bogged in mud off the edge of a road. My 4WD was too light to attempt this but there was a bogey drive 20-ton truck nearby we hooked onto the bogged vehicle with a rated chain.

Unfortunately, the adrenaline fuelled young driver of the recovery vehicle accelerated with a slack chain and promptly snapped it in two. It whipped like a snake, but luckily along the ground. It narrowly missed onlookers and did no damage to the vehicles".

The driver was immediately educated about his wrong doing and the recovery was achieved with a pre-tensioned chain.

"The other experience was at a treacherous surf beach where, after a very successful diving trip, we beached our boat to dry load on its trailer after several large waves had dumped water into the boat.

I hooked a snatch strap from my 4WD to the boat and with a little slack in the strap I took off cautiously but only moved the boat a little way. The owner of the boat told me to reverse closer to the boat and "gun" the car more that I had done before. I did this reluctantly and the result was that I pulled the eye and a section from the dive boat and sling shotted the debris and shackle into my tail gate, punching a hole in the metal."

Once again this could have been worse. "The lesson is to weigh up the strength of the attachment points and when using a strap use a mat, rug, several towels or a hessian bag with a shovel or so of sand tied at the top and draped or tied over the mid- point of the strap as dampers. Things that look like saddle bags with lead in them are also available. If the strap breaks and starts to slingshot it will mute it and cause ravelling of the strap, lessening the possibility of damage.

Peter, these are two first hand experiences of misuse but, used correctly, both can be used for retrieving vehicles. Chains are better where a steady drag is required and the towing vehicle can gain traction, but for bogged vehicles where little traction is available snatch straps with dampers certainly can be invaluable."

"I was interested when you told me that your friend who has worked in the outback on cattle and sheep stations all his life has always used chains and never seen one break. Our mutual friend Noel has seen chains break several times but only under extreme conditions much like my situation."

So it is chains for towing and many recoveries and snatch straps for beach or anywhere else where traction is difficult and use dampers. Something our son suggested was to tie the snatch strap from the tow vehicle tow ball to the passenger side of the bogged vehicle which should lessen the risk to the driver.

"The Duke's" answer to this was to have a direct pull in a straight line and to not use the tow ball itself as it can break from the tow bar and become a lethal missile. The snatch strap or chain should be attached via a rated shackle to the towing hook on the car or remove the tow ball and attach the shackle to the tow bar.

"The Duke" went on to say "This means it is necessary to carry a spanner or Stillson to remove the tow ball but this is not a bad thing because tow balls can loosen on occasions" and added "All passengers and rubber-neckers should be 30 metres away as there are serious forces involved in all this and things can go wrong".

This article started out to be taking the "mickey" out of myself and others for getting bogged but it sort of changed into a story about how extricating a car from sand can be quite dangerous.

Hopefully, someone may use the knowledge to safely salvage a bogged vehicle.

THE BARON, HIS LADY AND OTHER LOVES.

By Peter Morton and Bob Kretschmer

MOTOR BIKE MAN

Leonore and I met Bob and Margaret Kretschmer in the early 1980s when they moved to Port Lincoln soon after us.

Bob is a Naval Engineer. He was born and educated in Port Pirie and later Whyalla and the United Kingdom. His father was an engineer at the smelters in Port Pirie and Bob spend endless hours in the shed at home with his father developing what became formidable mechanical skills.

Margaret was a member of the very successful Nicholson family who had several sheep stations south of Whyalla and was educated in Adelaide. They both are descended from families who arrived in South Australia in the first 10 years of settlement something of which they are very proud and are active in the relevant Pioneers' Association.

Travellers through the area may notice a faded sign "Long Sleep Plain". This refers to the place where Margaret's father and fellow Scot, Perce Baillie, an historian from Port Lincoln, had a ferocious but ultimately losing battle with some Teacher's whisky on a long ago camping jaunt. *The Editor is delighted to inform the reader that this has been repainted.*

Bob has had a long love affair with motor cycles from his last year at primary school in 1951when he had a ride on a Royal Enfield 350.

In 1957 he moved to Whyalla and began a technical traineeship at the BHP shipyard. In 1958 he acquired his first bike a Norton ES2. In 1960 he bought an MG TF that stayed in a shed when it rained and two years later an MG A and later again an MG B. In 962 he took up parachuting but thought it was too dangerous so decided to race motor bikes and bought a 500 Manx Norton!.

He rode in various events with a degree of success in South Australia and Melbourne. In 1965 he heard the siren's call for bike riders, the Isle of Man TT, so sold everything and off he went to the UK and in no time at all got a job, a flat, another Norton ES2 and a riding mate Taffy Evans.

Bob and Taffy rode all over the place in England and had a ball but he was offered an excellent job back in Whyalla so home he went early in 1967 preceded by one of the last two Greeves Silverstone 250cc road racers ever made. He also bought a Triumph TR4A AND met his future wife Margaret and carted her around the South Australian motor cycle circuit.

Bob has a wonderful way of seeing the world and I quote from an article he wrote, *"In 1969 Marg and I decided to get married with a short engagement as a formality. To establish some sort of partnership balance, I collected Marg's engagement ring one Saturday morning and a Bultaco 250 Matador trials machine for me (Oh really!) for the same amount of money on the same day."*

He later moved up to a Bultaco Sherpa 250 that was also used for trials and scrambles.

It is interesting that his willingness to join or start groups of like-minded people and initially or later become a leader is first mentioned in Whyalla where he was the first president of the Whyalla MCC. This willingness to be involved and help others has been and still a big part of his and Margaret's life.

But things didn't stand still for long. In 1974 Bob accepted a job offer in "The famous Malta Ship Repair Dockyard." Before leaving Australia he bought and stored a BSA M21 he still rides and in Malta a Yamaha 125 for commuting.

Bob founded a new club and was the president and rode "sponsored Suzuki 125 and 250cc machines for "Australia" in the scrambles with some success."

He made an amazing find of a BSA WD M20 bike that had been sealed in an underground garage since the war. He plans on passing this on to Andrew, his son, with instructions that it is not to be restored.

Then it was a move to England, the purchase of a new Mick Andrews replica Suzuki 250 cc trials machine, joining another Motor Cycle Club (MCC) and being made president.

After eight years it was time to go home and take up a position at the Port Lincoln Shipyard in 1981 and later to set up as a private marine surveyor that lasted until his recent retirement.

He duly bought a Hawke sidecar for the M21and it has been in five Bay-Birdwood Rallies.

Guess who was on the committee of the vehicle restorers club in Port Lincoln until he and Margaret moved to Adelaide in 1997?

THE BOB WE KNEW

As mentioned above we met Bob and Marg in our early days in Port Lincoln and it happened that a Chris Stone and I with several others brought a game fishing boat made of wood at that time.

Bob surveyed this, left it in his back yard on blocks, helped us look after the engine, rub it down, paint and anti-foul it and with Chris remove the keel that resolved a nasty habit of the boat broaching in a following sea.

He also came to Kangaroo Island on a trip once and I have written about that elsewhere.

Bob and Marg are truly a gentleman and a lady. They both dress well and have excellent taste and high standards in everything they do. Bob has never worn a baseball cap. By the way I do not recall hearing Bob swear in any serious way. Those things mean something and were probably why I nicknamed him "Baron Von Krutchmore."

Our paths have separated since they have left Port Lincoln and also we have spent many years out of South Australia in recent times but we still keep in touch and the response of Bob in helping with these tales is typical.

They both devote a huge amount of time to organisations to do with quilting, motor cycles and vintage cars and other groups. They have a huge network of friends, new and old and unlike many of us ensure that they keep in contact with them and offer help in some way when necessary.

Oh yes they do not mind the odd lunch with each other or friends.

I really admire Bob and Marg. Bob can do all sorts of things with his hands, imagination and mind that I cannot. For the life of me I do not know why he does not understand the meaning and role of trumps in card games. Marg says he is bit slack on remembering the details of her shopping instructions—thinking of more important things like carburettor settings I suppose.

Last but not least Margaret and Bob have suffered

setbacks in their lives that would have destroyed many marriages, or worse, but they have endured.

I have heard Bob say many times "Well you just get on with it." And that is exactly how they have lived their lives.

I have met many special people in my professional and social life who have exhibited courage and tenacity in their personal lives and Bob and Margaret are very high on that list –Salute!

MOTOR CYCLES AND ME

By Greg Jenke aka "Jerker"

Ever since my older brother took me for a ride on his first bike, a Royal Enfield, I have had a fascination with motorcycles. It was uncomfortable sitting on the tank but I was smitten. Soon after my sixteenth birthday I bought my first motorcycle.....well a Lambretta scooter anyway!

It took me to school and was a great source of enjoyment for my friends who thought it was hilarious for two or three of them to pile on the rear carrier to make it wheel stand or "wheely" as it is better known. Great for fun, not so good for Lambretta scooters and their owners.

The scooter soon gave way to a "real" motorcycle, or at least as real as a student could afford...a CZ 175. A what? I hear you ask. Well I didn't know either but I was told by the owner of Murrays Motorcycles in Gawler that there was no better scramble bike. That may be so but I wanted a cool sounding, look good sort of chick magnet bike. The CZ 175 is none of those things. It was made in Czechoslovakia and looked like it, with only one exhaust pipe which sounded pathetic at best.

My CZ holds the dubious honour of being involved in my very first accident on a bike. An inpatient car driver not wanting to go as slow as a single cylinder, 175cc, smoke billowing excuse for a bike from behind the iron curtain, decided to overtake me as I executed a turn, hit the car, fell off with my helmet grazing his tyre as he went past. Fortunately, only my dignity was damaged.

Enter Mr. Holloway my year 12 biology teacher who just happened to race motorcycles and also just happened to have his street legal race bike for sale. I took the bait and test rode his Kawasaki 500 Mach 3 which had been "tricked up" for racing. Oh my god...that is an understatement. This thing was lethal, particularly as the revs got to 4000 rpm which was its "powerband," a code word for launching down the road at breakneck speed. It was then I realized another anomaly of the Mach 3 Kwakka, it doesn't stop all that well. Truly a dangerous machine but just the chick magnet I needed, or so I thought and I bought it from my teacher who seemed somewhat bemused that I actually turned up for biology class and not the orthopaedic ward.

My best friend Paul who was also besotted by two wheels had bought his first bike, a rather dilapidated Triumph 650. It looked like crap, leaked oil, but it sounded magnificent. Mine on the other hand went like a cut snake but sounded like the CZ on steroids but with more smoke. I had to wait until Paul started his bike and rode off through the adoring fans who would then disperse and allow me and my smoke billowing, lawn mower sounding bike to sneak off. At least one saving grace was that the Triumph may have sounded fantastic but it was very unreliable and more often than not it wouldn't start despite Paul's attempts to kick it into life. Karma I thought.

It wasn't long before most of my friends acquired motorcycles, or was it that they were my friends because they had bikes? Anyway, we were leaving school and starting work or study and bikes were the common denominator. The Honda 750 4 became the bike de jour and most of us had one except for a couple of recalcitrants who had lesser beasts but secretly wished they had a Honda 750. The sweet exhaust note of the Honda was enough to stir us into a collective frenzy. One guy who invariably rode his bike full throttle up a nearby hill to allow the sound to echo through surrounding streets did so in the knowledge that he was sending a group of teenage boys into raptures.

Good times were had by all in the group who became very close friends through the many riding trips we shared in those early years. The bikes came and went. I eventually traded the Honda for a forgettable Yamaha triple and then to its big brother, the Yamaha 1100 shaft drive.

This bike had a huge physical presence, was a joy to ride and very, very powerful. A couple of mates and I decided to ride to Cairns from Adelaide a trip of over 6500 kilometres there and back. It was quite an adventure and I was the only one that returned unscathed although I did get a flat tyre about 40 kilometres from home and had an ignominious return through the streets of Gawler with the bike on dad's trailer! The other two guys had crashed en-route, one had hit a pig and whilst not badly hurt, riding their rather bent machines all the way back was not recommended.

The next episode halted my motorcycling for the next 24 years notwithstanding a couple of stupid antics along the way.

Our group met at my parents' house in Gawler one Saturday night to ride together to a party at Williamstown 40 kilometres away. There were two bikes "two up" in the group including my own. The party progressed until one of our group and his pillion decided they wanted pizza and took off on the bike down the Williamstown-Gawler road to get one. The rest remained having had quite a bit to drink although one guy followed later. He returned with the horrifying news that our mate had hit a tree and had been killed and his pillion had lost his leg.

That news was shattering to our group who up until that point had only experienced the joys of motorcycling. We thought we were 10 feet tall and bulletproof.

For me that night only got worse but I didn't realize the full extent until later. My dad was a volunteer ambulance driver and he was on call that night. The call came in that a motorcycle and pillion had crashed, one dead. Dad had watched us leave home that night and knew that I had a pillion passenger. I still get goose bumps when I think of the torment my dad went through driving to the scene of an accident in full expectation that he was going to get his son. He didn't tell me until sometime later that he drove that night through uncontrollable tears.

I sold my bike not long after that night not entirely because of the accident but also because I was going to travel around the USA and I needed the money. That was 1980 and except for a couple of really stupid episodes when I rode someone else's bike drunk, I didn't even contemplate getting another bike for 24 years.

I was returning from my usual Saturday morning attempt at golf in Coffs Harbour and drove past a motorcycle shop that was advertising test rides on the new Triumph range. For some inexplicable reason I was interested. This was mid 2004 and I hadn't even thought about bikes for over twenty years but here I was walking into the bike shop to enquire about a test ride. *Male menopause perhaps? Ed*

I am not sure whether it was curiosity or some calling but I fronted the salesman, told him that I was an experienced rider and could I go for a ride? I was told I had to book but a spot was open at 4.00pm. I was so delusional that I went home asked my eldest son Sam, 15, if he wanted to come for a ride and somewhat bemused, he agreed.

We both arrived for a ride for the salesman to inquire if we had helmets, jackets, boots etc.? Of course we didn't and had not even thought about it so we had to hire everything we needed. The salesman was starting to wonder just how experienced I really was.

I had hardly ridden in 25 years but the moment I sat on that bike I was smitten all over again. We had a very enjoyable experience together and I was again in the hunt for a motorcycle.....I didn't buy the Triumph!

I bought an ST2 the first of several Ducati's from a friend of a friend and as a consequence I was accepted into another likeminded group of motorcyclists who became close friends.

The 2005 Ducati Turismo was a tour around Tasmania and my first real trip since buying the ST2 a few months earlier. Sam was keen to go with me and Leanne whilst probably secretly dreading the thought said she was happy for him to be on the bike with his dad. So off we went on our motorcycle adventure from Coffs Harbor to Tasmania via the Spirit of Tasmania from Sydney.

The trip was fantastic. The camaraderie of our small group in the context of about 300 other Ducati enthusiasts, brilliant roads, great scenery but for me it was sharing such a great experience with my son.

You don't get too many opportunities to bond with your son like I did on that trip but to have six to 8 hours a day for 10 days of his undivided attention, through our helmet intercom was gold! Better still he had made a playlist of music, one of his songs and then one of mine. To this day my appreciation of his music and his of mine endures.

Two years later in the 2007 Turismo, from Noosa to Port Macquarie. I repeated the experience with our other son, Bryn who like Sam was about 15 at the time of the 2005 Turismo.

The result was the same. A great experience and bonding opportunity. It also gave the boys something really cool to say at "show and tell". They had been somewhat on the outer at school but that soon changed when they mentioned the Turismo experiences and they soon became very much part of their groups. That was special for Leanne and me to witness.

Above and beyond the wonder of the experience with the boys was my gratitude and admiration for Leanne's total faith in me to ensure they came to no harm even though she herself didn't want to go anywhere near the bikes....in fact she was petrified of them. I had tried on numerous occasions to lure her onto the bike but she steadfastly refused because I didn't ride slowly enough and that I was unsympathetic to her fear about the bike.

By now I had two Ducati's, a 998 and the ST2 which soon gave away to a number of Ducati Multistrada's a bike more conducive to comfortable touring than the ST2 had been and definitely more so than the race bred 998 which was very much a "me" bike. It wasn't until the second of the three

Multistrada's we have owned that another life changing breakthrough was made.

We had just moved to the Gold Coast from Coffs Harbor when we were visited by our good friends, the Thompsons who rode their Ducati, two up, to see us. After throwing the whole guilt trip at her about them being guests and her not joining in etc., Kathryn finally convinced Leanne to come for a ride with us on the back of my bike. Not unconditional of course, with the speed I was allowed to go being the main one. The tightening of her grip on my waist was the tell-tale sign that I was probably going over 60kph. Nonetheless it was a breakthrough. So much so that by the end of the ride I was doing considerably more than 60 and she was very, very chatty on the intercom.........so chatty in fact, I had to tell her to be quiet a couple of times so I could concentrate!

From that ride on, our life has changed. Most Sunday mornings we ride the bike for a coffee or breakfast run and sometimes even further. We have been on a Turismo together and she thoroughly enjoyed the whole experience including riding with a larger group and everything that goes with that including new friendships.

But it was our recent trip to Africa that demonstrated how complete the transition was from someone who didn't want to go near the bike to someone who is prepared to take risks on a bike because they enjoy it so much.

Such was our trip from Cape Town, in South Africa, through the Western Cape, Namibian deserts and the Okavango delta in Botswana finally finishing at the magnificence of the Victoria Falls in Zimbabwe. We travelled 4000kms in 17 days with 15 other bikes ridden by people from a number of countries: USA, Ukraine, Italy, Switzerland, Germany, Austria and the UK.

The ride wasn't easy two up. The deserts of Namibia were a challenge and just trying to stay upright in the sand, corrugations, gravel, dust from trucks etc. took a lot of concentration. Never was this so evident than when an Oryx (gemsbok) was running alongside parallel to the bike only a few feet away but whilst Leanne was marvelling at the sight I didn't even see it as I was concentrating so hard. Then there was Botswana with totally different obstacles to test you: potholes you could lose a Volkswagen in, cattle and goats near the villages running in front of you and trucks broken down right in the middle of the highway!

But all of that pales into insignificance when you ride into a herd of elephants! On one occasion we stopped to marvel at a few elephants eating on the side of the highway only to then realize that the other half of the herd was on the other side of the road and insisted that they crossed to road to join their mates—we sat still for a frightening but exciting 10 minutes as they passed within a few feet of us.

And guess what –the next trip for us both is on the drawing board.

HOW I BECAME A JAGUAR MAN

By Bob Kretschmer

Becoming a Jaguar Man

I was one of the inaugural members of the Port Lincoln Vehicle Club and in 1995 I started to think about a car to restore. I looked at several vehicles over the next few years without knowing what I wanted so success eluded me.

Marg and I ran a private Marine Surveying Consulting & Claim Investigation company and in 1997 we moved to Adelaide to further this business..

An old motor cycle racing mate, now a keen member of the Chrysler Restorers Club with a 1924 Dodge Bros Ute called me to advise that one of his fellow Club Members wanted to sell an 'early Jaguar'.

During a business trip to Adelaide in 1995 I 'inspected" a 1 ½ L Jaguar sedan in very poor condition but mostly complete.

I agreed to buy it without having any real comprehension of what was involved.

My brother agreed to dismantle it in Adelaide while Marg and I began the process of moving house contents & business from Port Lincoln to Adelaide during September 1997.

I joined the Vintage & Veteran Motor Cycle Club and rode regularly while I attended the long, difficult & expensive project of 100% Jaguar restoration.

It did not take me long to realize the Jaguar was a 1939 build SS Jaguar 1 ½ L Built by SS Cars Ltd in July 1939 with a1946 Jaguar engine.

In 1998 I joined the sub-group of the Jaguar Drivers Group of SA for people dealing primarily with cars that had push-rod operated engines vehicles like mine. Those members inspired and helped me then and now and it also was a new and pleasant social experience for us both.

The Rebuild

As I mentioned above the car was a mess in every respect and I took 10 years to get it running with help from SS Register members.

Bruce Fletcher was my technical advisor who also did the wiring & windows plus other guidance. Bob Lynch reproduced the new dash front panel while Ross Gogler restored some instruments.

Basically I finished with a pretty good & technically sound vehicle.

I had the motor & gearbox over-hauled by a mechanic who moon-lighted at his home.

The first time I ran out of money, Marg offered me a loan provided she chose the paint colour. Why anybody would send a black car with bone interior to Australia defies my logic.

I bought many different spray cans of paint that Marg vetoed so we jointly visited every new car showroom in the eastern suburbs of Adelaide. One day she spotted a beautiful Bentley painted 'Silver Tempest'.

"THAT IS IT" she announced, no further visits, no further discussion, end of subject. I am now proud of her choice despite it not being an original SS Jaguar colour but that seemed fair.

Apart from a different paint colour & upholstery the vehicle is close to bolt-perfect but I have no intention of 'showing' it.

Trials & Tribulations

The 2007 Tri-State Border Run for SS, Mk1V & Mk V vehicles to Bathurst in was coming up & I announced that I would be taking the SS Jaguar. *'You are mad, you are stupid'* etc. was the advice I generally received. I had only driven it around the block twice and it was neither finished nor road-worthy but I managed to wangle a 3-day permit to drive in the Rally at Bathurst.

I borrowed Bruce Fletcher's dual axle car trailer. The combined weight was too much for our Ford Falcon sedan so we used our son's Mercedes 420 SEL sedan.

Off we went with Bruce and his wife Anne following.

We stopped near Renmark to check the load and I saw that the Jaguar sun-roof had gone – bugger! Could not think of any else thing to say, Marg was supportive by keeping quiet, thank you.

Moving right along-

First over-night stop at Balranald using Marg's nightdress taped over the roof 'hole'.

Next day just a few km. short of Hay the LH rear wheel of the trailer came off – bugger!

Marg telephoned Bruce & Anne who fortunately were still at Hay.

Marg found the wheel in the scrub but the hub bolt threads were damaged so I removed the opposite side wheel & crawled along on one axle into Hay where Bruce had already arranged a repair place.

In 35 minutes Bruce & I had changed the offending hub & wheel, re-fitted the other side wheel with help from the owner's dog, which closely watched the operation, purchased a full spare wheel & set off for West Wyalong our second overnight stay without further difficulty.

On the Saturday morning we had our usual Static Display in The centre of Bathurst and I noticed the engine temperature was rather high and later the engine nipped-up (started to seize) at the entrance to the motel, but I was able to coast inside the boundary fence. No more motoring for this Border Run, bugger! Marg was supportive again!

The Rally Program included a run around the famous Bathurst Race Track & Marg & I drove the Mercedes instead.

Back in Adelaide after I had removed the grill & radiator, Bruce Fletcher noticed that the outside of the fan pulley was rotating but not the inner drive shaft to the water pump, i.e., no coolant circulation.

The mechanic who had rebuilt the engine had the pump impellor vanes welded AND fitted the impeller not checking at the time if the thing would actually rotate. Bugger!

I rebuilt the pump myself and it has been good since.

During a Club Run early 2008 I could not get second gear & there was a terrible noise from the engine at idling speed.

With the next Border Run to Broken Hill in November I decided to pull the combined engine & gearbox out.

The mechanic had omitted to fit a special thrust washer in the gearbox. Bugger!

The problem of noise was poor fitment of the camshaft chain drive sprocket to the camshaft end plus a non-approved chain by my mechanic. Bugger!

Bruce helped me fix all that but there was an additional problem in that some of the valve stem heads had 'worn' into the ends of the rocker arms making accurate measurement of the clearance impossible. I found later that the mechanic had simply refitted the rocker gear as he found it. Bugger! I fixed all that and re-installed the engine & gearbox over a period of 2 months.

Off we went to Broken Hill for the 2008 Border Run.

By that time I had an obsession with engine temperature & had fitted a long- stemmed gauge obtained from Weber BBQs to measure the inside temperature of the roast meat during cooking. I have a radiator cap with a hole in the centre through which I inserted the gauge stem into the coolant flow from the engine. Whacko.

I found that the engine would happily run at 80 deg. corresponding to *Roast Pork* on the gauge.

Do you reckon I copped it from people like Bob Lynch & his merry men with me running the engine on *roast pork!*

There were many other problems which I progressively coped with but it was a very expensive, frustrating & disappointing start to Jaguar motoring.

Marg has been stoic during the ongoing saga. Thank you again with a cherry on top.

The Better Fun Years

Since Broken Hill, we have taken the little car to six SS Register Border Runs and together with local club runs have clocked over 10,000 miles.

Post-Build Improvements & Modifications

I mentioned above that the restoration build included a 1946 Jaguar engine.

At the 2009 Mildura Border Run I happened to come across a 1939 SS 1 ½ L engine with engine Number just a few away from the original, near complete but in very poor condition which I bought for $500.

(The car was built by the SS Cars Ltd. Coventry in June 1939 and shipped to Australia in August that year. *Jaguar* was the model signifying the first all-steel bodies after the earlier coach-built/timber-framed bodies.)

I had that engine totally machined in Melbourne but rebuilt it myself over the next few years. Bruce helped me with the valve and ignition timing.

Early 2012 Marg contracted a serious ear balance problem and found travelling in the SS Jaguar upsetting.

I tried altering the front springs, rear springs, overhauling the Luvax-Girling lever-arm shock absorbers, had complete suspension analysis by Pedders, changed the damper oil several times & fitted new radial-ply tyres, but all to no avail.

Having spent so much money on the SS engine I decided to test domestic financial harmony again by buying a Toyota Celica steel-case gearbox which entailed chassis modifications.

To help me I bought a hydraulic scissor-lift which folds flat & lives under the car. A new hydraulic engine removal crane also helped.

The trip to Port Lincoln was the last for Marg with the balance problem so I researched shock absorber technology.

I was not happy with Pedders special big machine & continued searching until I heard about *SupaShock* at Magill.

In December 2014 I went to see them. As an engineer I was blown away with the level of engineering technology.

They treat each car as a project and the MD Oscar Florinotto gave me a quote to re-engineer the suspension. I did not have that amount of money readily available but they arranged a special finance package. OK I said provided the car will be ready for the 2015 All-British Day, it was.

Basically they discarded the Luvax Girling lever units & fitted their own specially designed, manufactured & tuned telescopic units.

For the purists please note that, not a single bolt hole or weld had to be applied to the chassis.

The system allows for complete reversal should that option ever be considered.

The end result is a much better car which now allows Marg to travel and to hand-sew in acceptable comfort. That seemed fair.

Reflections

Now that I have the vehicle in a reliable and presentable state, where do I go from here?

With the money spent and a fraction of the time involved, I could have bought a fully restored MG TF 1500 plus my original Triumph TR4 A in concurs condition with plenty of $ to spare.

I have inspected both of the above vehicles recently & they are currently available.

What does that suggest? A financial blunder with an SS

Jaguar 1 ½ L sedan as an asset for which there is very little demand and therefore little real value.

Most of the 1 ½ L models in SA are for sale without buyers but I am heartened that there are two currently being restored, one in Qld. and one in Vic. both of which I am helping with surplus parts to some degree.

The new Jaguars hold no special interest for me despite an appreciation of new technology, vehicles and modern life.

I will however continue to support & enjoy the JDCSA with my little 1 ½ L until age takes over.

PS: I re-purchased my original Triumph TR4A in November 2017 which has been beautifully restored.

THAT'S WHAT PARENTS ARE FOR

By Margaret and Bob Kretschmer

To paraphrase a Barry Humphries character, "This is so Margaret and Bob I could have wept" – there is a wealth of information in and between the lines. Ed

In 2000 our son Andrew had recently left Perth after a stint in the Tanami Desert for a 2-year appointment in Uganda. While not particularly interested in motor vehicles he had taken a particular interest in our 1939 SS Jag rebuild project and enjoys showing to his friends.

A female workmate from Perth owned a 1967 Daimler Sovereign and decided to relocate to Adelaide last year and Andrew, apparently out of misguided sympathy for his father, purchased the Daimler.

Mileage meter showed about 72,000 m. Included with the purchase documents were Oct 2000 invoices for major services to the auto transmission & the engine.

For various reasons Andrew was not able to spend much time in Perth & due to his impending appointment overseas, let the registration lapse. As part of his salary package, the company employing him, agreed to finance the storage of his car in Perth.

That seemed unfortunate when it could just as easily be stored in Adelaide so that we could keep an eye on it and an agreement was made that Andrew would register & insure the car and we would go over and drive it back – our big holiday for 2001. Marg booked us on the Indian Pacific train.

I packed a tool kit & jerry can.

Ugandan telecommunications are erratic at best and the email system was not reliable. On the night before our departure, we received a telephone call from Andrew at 3.00 am primarily for the purpose of giving me instructions on how to start the car because under WA law, when an older vehicle is re-registered, it must be fitted with an electronic immobiliser.

The telephone connection was poor with every fourth word a beep but I thought I would manage a step-by-step procedure – he would leave his mobile telephone on all the time.

We need to say at this point, that with the rush to get away, Andrew left a heap of unpaid accounts which had been redirected to us and we subsequently redirected them to him the day of our departure per his instructions.

We had a pleasant trip on the train arriving in Perth on Sunday morning.

A friend (an XJ6 man) collected us & drove us to Claremont to collect the car. All four keys were found and the countdown procedure commenced – water, oil, connect battery – a fan came on somewhere so we knew that there was power. I noted the original ignition switch on the dashboard with matching key plus a steering lock & ignition switch on the steering column.

I have been unable to fix the pattern below but this is a surreal story just as Bob transmitted- it is so apt! Ed

Directions
Check small, slow flashing red light at
   bottom RH
corner of windscreen denoting
   immobiliser
deactivated.
Turn ignition on (I naturally turned both switches on)
Press RH upper button to energise immobiliser and activate normal ignition circuit
Note change in immobiliser light
Press starter button on dash

I could not find a RH upper button to press and tried everything else, even the dimmer switch for the lights on the floor without success and much annoyance.

Result – proceed with our host to North Fremantle for Marg & me to return in borrowed car plus drill as the new number plates were resting in the rear window, bearing in mind that we had a luncheon appointment in Fremantle.

Back on site

Secured front number plate

Rear one would not fit, so popped it back in the rear window

Repeated attempts to start without success – more annoyance

Marg said that it would be about 3.00 am in Uganda so let's telephone Andrew. Good idea, out with my mobile.

Telstra –"Sorry that Number is not connected" ---Bulls... -

he called us 3 days ago

Telstra Service Difficulties after four internal transfers. "Your call is important to us, please wait. For quality control and training purposes, this call may be monitored."

Bob – Expletive!

Eventually a nice lady advised ".... Service disconnected due to unpaid A/c" – I apologised for the expletive.

Good old Dad, out with the credit card $316.00 & 5 minutes later Service & International Roaming restored.

Ring ring, 4.00 am in Uganda, answering machine. Left rude message.

Marg said "Bob, you are always telling me that I have two left hands and that my problem analysis lacks logic, let me try."

Bob – "Oh all right then"

Marg gets in, presses everything in sequence – instant action!!!

Humid, flustered, we both need a drink – off we drove to Fremantle, met friend, champagne all round, plus a bottle of white between three with our lunch.

WA's drought broke at last and it started to rain, and rain, and rain.....

Took friend back to city – windscreen wiper operated but blades U/S, windows all fogged, can't get vent direct to on to window. Inside of all windows covered with dried lemonade or equivalent – very pretty.

Entering city – full RBT

Marg's seat belt clasp lost under her seat

No seat belts in rear, friend put her shoulder bag strap around her

Rear Number plate in window
Me some wine
RBT "move along sir"
Now really really raining – visibility extremely poor
Delivered friend to city hotel
Drove around the corner and ran out of petrol
Fortunately Don Evans had told me at the last Register Meeting that this model car has two fuel tanks, found the switch and watched with trepidation as the gauge needle moved just over the thickness of the 'Empty' mark.
Straight to service station, did not pass Go or collect $200.

<u>Monday</u>
Check spare tyre – flat
Noted battery is not correct size – correct one in boot.
Tyre U/S est 20 years old, wall cracked – new one required
Battery U/S   "   "
Fuel gauge drops visibly whilst driving around city
Purchase windscreen cleaner, anti-fog, internal & external, extra jerry can, fuses, spare belt for power steering –, none available for alternator, hose clips, engine oil, brake fluid, coolant, tape

Wettest July day in Perth on record –
Water in boot, water in rear seat foot well, water in parcel tray, water in glovebox, water in door pockets

<u>Tuesday</u>
Drove to West Swan to meet Bruce Fletcher's friends, Graeme & Prue Brown & to see their '37 SS 6 cyl car. GB is also currently restoring an XK 120. Morning coffee while Graeme

made arrangements for me to take car to his mechanic Dave Sullivan at Balcatta who is familiar with old Jags.

Discovered - top radiator hose u/s- piston in from carburettor dash pot damper had come off and was jammed in the suction chamber.

- all duly fixed

Nearby Auto Parts place – Can't get 50Amp glass fuses Can't get proper hose so purchased one that I could adapt

Wed 1 Aug

Marg, having taken over a carefully selected assortment of cassettes of music and stories discovered that Andrew had fitted a CD player so purchased two CDs for the trip home after visiting two shopping centres. Only one speaker worked and the machine will not eject CD!

Still wanting an alternator belt & 50 A fuses, I called into Levitt Industries just off the highway at Midland. Specialises in Jaguars Series 1 onwards

Dismantlers – stuff everywhere.

Can't get 50 A fuses – bought more 35 A

Levitt does not reckon the belt manuals are reliable so measures alternator belt in-situ & supplies one

For good measure we bought a 'litre' badge missing from the boot, plus a Jag 420 parts manual & finally set off for the trip home.

I had noticed that the engine stopped momentarily a couple of times – stupid SU carburettors I thought.

Fuelled up at Mundaring including 2 x 20 litre jerry cans & finally cleared the built-up area just after noon.

About an hour later I thought I saw a couple of small wisps

of smoke come up from around the steering column & a slight smell.

Stopped – bonnet up, noticed that oil dipstick was not in the special catch. Resumed – all seemed OK, maybe the smoke & smell were crank-case fumes from dipstick, sounded reasonable at the time.

The first fuel tank duly emptied and I switched over, but with some coughing & back-firing – settled down for easy motoring.

Not for long – several misfires

Must be air locks in the fuel system following the changeover, 5.30 pm

At 5.45pm the engine died and I pulled over, naturally on a bend, deep gutter, just getting dark

Head & side lights work, nothing else.

I can't see anything wrong.

Decision Time – now just dark

Marg will stay with car while Captain Courageous hitches a ride into town (42 kms west of Southern Cross)

I suggested that Marg try starting after ½ hr in case a ballast resister had overheated – no mobile coverage.

Luckily only a short wait for a ride to SC to the BP garage – telephone coverage

Telephoned RAC in Perth

Nice Rebecca returned call 10 minutes later to advise that my RAA membership had expired the day before. More blaspheming & expletives (my administration manager will need to come up with some very smart answers to get out of this one).

More talking – out with the credit card again.

Marg and I will be friends once more.

Eventually Jamie the 18 stone local mechanic arrived with his battered old Ford F150, with just a bucket seat for the driver. Tool box & wheat bag for me to lean against the petrol tank, plus an old pillow for Marg to sit on later should it be necessary to tow the Daimler.

Back to the car after 2 ½ hrs. 2 deg C.

During the trip back I described the symptoms. Reply "Have you fitted a @#$^* immobiliser?" "Yes, my son had been told that he had to for re-registration".

"Bulls... you do not have to for vehicles over 21 years old".

Anyway, my new mate looking very attractive with 4 days facial hair & the works befitting a bush mechanic, pulled out the immobiliser, broke open the cover, hot-wired a few things, bridged a few contacts with an old knife, stripped back a few more and presto – off we went, car running OK but noticed that the amp meter was showing discharge, whereas before the stop it been showing slight charge. Never mind, motel by 9.00pm. Restaurant officially closed but because of our situation, we could order if we went in straight away. All the locals plus a few fellow travellers somehow seemed to know of our plight.

Thursday

Drove the car to the repair shop. Time moves slowly in Southern Cross & our mechanic had had a few call outs during the night so same clothes but now with 5 days hirsute growth.

Out with immobiliser, re-check. All the functions appeared to be in order and without any evidence of over heat or fusions.

Marg & I explored Southern Cross on foot & returned an hour later. Mechanic announces - "Jeez youse are lucky, the immobiliser is OK so I repaired last night's cable carnage and noticed that while poking about, the ignition light came on, went off, on, off etc

Fault – loose blade terminal on the rear of the ignition lock/switch with melted plastic sheath & the original ignition switch is not connected"

THEN he held up the shredded alternator belt. Hence the meter discharge – clearly marked on the only non-shredded bit of belt "Jaguar". "No worries" said Captain Marvel, "I carry a spare belt, measured and supplied by WA's resident Jag specialist"

WRONG the belt is 50mm too long.

Never mind, the Jamie had a heap of belts on the floor in the corner behind some old 44 gal oil drums

½ hr later, one just too big, one just too small

SMOKO time in Southern Cross. Jamie ambled across the highway to another shed & duly returned with a belt that fitted.

In the process, we could see that the inside of the power steering belt was cracked. "Never mind" said I undaunted, "I have a spare one carefully selected by Marlow" (Perth's version of Rocca Bros).

PROBLEM The belt will not fit between the radiator & the fan auto turbo

My mate wanted to move the engine back, Marg did not have any pantyhose, so we replaced the old belt and bought a joinable, all-purpose red belt to carry as an emergency.

Out with credit card again. Ready to depart the service

station and I only just avoided a very nasty incident when I asked Marg if she wanted anything from inside – e.g. a sedative. Fortunately I was ignored (until we reached Coolgardie).

Finally departed Southern Cross, at 11.00am, with car running well. Stopped for lunch at Coolgardie, telephone coverage so called Andrew on direct line to the mine – he was just so proud that we were driving his Daimler home to Adelaide "The car is running perfectly" we said.

We had planned to stop at Caiguna but that would have meant that we would be driving at night so due to the late start, we only got as far as Balladonia – kangaroos everywhere.

After all of the above, we continued the journey to Adelaide without further incident. Cruised at 3000 rpm, estimated 90 kmh & covered 85km in the hour. Fuel consumption 15.1 litres/100 km or 18.7 mpg for the whole trip of 3,090 km.

Our job as parents, was to safely store & look after the Daimler and Andrew has encouraged us to use it as much as we wish so you may see us in it occasionally at Register outings.

Part 3 Fishing

BENSBACH A BARRA MAN'S DREAMTIME.
By Bob Hutchinson

Fishing trips are not always just about fishing. They can also be a rich source of new experiences, being embedded in different cultures and meeting new people.

On a recent trip to Papua New Guinea (PNG) I experienced all these things seeking to catch a metre plus barramundi by lure casting. The biggest barra, as they are universally known, I had caught previously in the Northern Territory was a respectable 93cm.

I had read a lot about the Bensbach River and Lodge and it seemed to be an ideal place to catch my dream barra.

I organised flights from Port Lincoln to Cairns and then by 12-seater twin engine plane to Bensbach. There was a brief stop at Horn Island, near Thursday Island in the Torres Strait, to take on fuel and then another brief stop at Daru Island in PNG waters just north of Thursday Island where we were processed through PNG customs. The Bensbach fishing lodge and river is on the southern side of PNG very close to the West Papuan border.

The Lodge has all the amenities needed for an enjoyable stay. There was a comfortable lounge and dining room and basic but adequate twin share rooms. 240-volt power 24 hours a day from a generator and some mobile telephone coverage. There are two flushing toilets and hot & cold showers in each wing of the guests' accommodation

Food was plentiful, varied and tasty. Breakfast was a

selection of cereals, toast and jam, fresh fruit, eggs, bacon, beans, chilled orange juice and tea and coffee.

Lunch was crumbed chicken legs, homemade bush meat pies, sandwiches, cake and bread rolls as well as tea, coffee or cold drinks all packed into an esky. I particularly enjoyed the homemade bread, wallaby rissoles and scrumptious venison pies made from local deer. The evening meal was always three courses and served in the dining room.

Everything was very clean and tidy including the grounds with well-kept lawns and lovely tropical flowers in neat garden beds. Each night before retiring we put our dirty clothes in a woven grass basket outside our door. They were collected, washed, folded and returned to our room while we were fishing the next day. There is a nice view from all the rooms across the lawns to the river's edge where we met the guides each morning.

The guides and cooking staff were from local villages and have onsite bunkhouse style accommodation. Sometimes two guides and/or grounds staff would travel several kilometres in their dugout canoes to their villages late at night for family and marital duties of all sorts and return early the next morning.

The guides are usually on duty for three continuous weeks and then have one week off. If they are not guiding there are other things to do at the Lodge.

Every day the guides are selected according to where we planned to fish. Some guides worked upstream others downstream from the Lodge as it is most important to be sensitive to their traditional boundaries. Each village headman or chief has to allow access to their traditional area and naturally they would want their own people guiding. This had all been negotiated prior to our arrival and a small payment had been made.

My fishing buddy Greg Jones from Melbourne and I were very happy with our guides, Uncle Neme and his two nephews, Cat & Isaac. Their boat handling skills, knowledge of the river and snags was excellent as was their ability to retrieve fouled lures above and below the water. In the seven days we were fishing I do not think we lost a lure to a snag.

Isaac had been away to Daru Island School for two years and could speak Aussie English as well as his Uncle but when we passed villages not surprisingly he and Cat spoke their own language as they sometimes did on the boat between themselves. One day I cheekily asked if they we talking about us and their giggles and eyes confirmed this.

Cat was softly spoken and very shy. They all had an excellent sense of humour. We had another angler on our boat one day who and farted frequently. Cat giggled and whispered saying "abdominal perfume" which cracked us all up.

The main way people get around is in dugouts and a family may have different size canoes to carry from one person to a whole family. Once I saw 17 people of all ages, two bicycles, two dogs, cooking utensils and other family belongings in one huge canoe. They were moving to a temporary camp away from the village but closer to their riverside garden that was a few kilometres away. These gardens are used for one season, then left to lie fallow for a year or longer. Many are under water during the wet season.

Depending on size it takes as little as a week to make a

canoe from the trunk of a paper bark tree and they have a life of five to seven years. Only hand tools are used and the finished canoe has very straight lines and is quite smooth inside and out. I ran my hand along the inside of one and there were no splinters.

The people also use the outer "paper" bark from the tree for wrapping food, cooking fires as well as roofing that they replace annually.

Each evening as we returned to the Lodge we would see women sitting quietly in their canoes fishing to supplement the evening's meal. It wasn't unusual to see young children paddling and playing in smaller dugouts,

There are crocodiles in the general area but none near the Lodge or villages as the villagers hunt them out for food.

On one trip in a small shallow inlet Uncle Neme showed us some bamboo poles about two metres long with a few metres of net attached to each one. He said that they are shared by many villagers and each person ties some strips of vegetation in a particular pattern to the pole to show others who is using the pole and net at any given time.

There is prolific bird life in these wetlands and jungle and we were told that almost 750 different species have been recorded—a twitcher's paradise.

Every day we would see deer, pigs and wallabies on the flood plains and they are hunted by the locals using traditional spears and bows and arrows. The hunters usually can sneak up on the wallabies but they try to drive the deer and pigs into the water where they are easier to spear or shoot with arrows.

Bows are made from bamboo as is bow string. For birds

they use multi prong arrow heads. Another way they bring down birds is to use throwing sticks similar to aboriginals in Northern Australia. It takes a lot of strength to draw and hold the bow as many of us found out.

Guns are strictly prohibited in the area. The only guns I ever saw were held by the PNG Defence Force soldiers on patrol looking for Indonesian poachers.

Greg and I were privileged to be invited by our guides to visit their villages. All were free of litter and the ground swept clean a complete contrast to the vast majority of aboriginal settlements in Australia that I have seen.

Each family had their own little garden area and produced yams, melons, sweet potato, bananas, corn and beans. Bright colourful flower beds were very popular lining boundaries between houses and along the walkways. Houses were bamboo framed with paper bark roofs and walls. Isaac introduced us to his father who had retired from guiding. Both father and son were very happy when I said Isaac had been well trained by his father and was an excellent guide. Isaac proudly showed us the frame work of his own house that was being built ready for his forthcoming wedding.

Cooking was done on open fires and nearly all houses had a raised bed in the sleeping areas. At night they would light fires under these platforms so the smoke would drive away the mosquitoes. I heard that it worked on the mosquitoes but harmed the villager's lungs and may have even led to early deaths.

I cannot recall seeing anyone smoking although it may be a Lodge rule that no smoking when guiding or staying at the Lodge. Betel nut chewing was also prohibited but the typical stained teeth associated with that practice were occasionally seen.

Alcohol was permitted for guests and there was a wet bar and lounge in the Lodge but I saw no evidence of alcohol consumption either in villages or Lodge by the locals. We had been told in our briefing notes not to give alcohol to the locals.

There were small bamboo walled compounds in the village where pigs and small crocodiles were kept, fattened up and then cooked and eaten perhaps for special occasions.

Village children were shy but highly amused at my silver-grey beard and delighted in gently tugging it and running off with squeals of laughter. The adults were shy by our standards but carried themselves with a quiet dignity and were most obliging in sharing information and allowing photographs. We always asked permission before taking any photograph and the villagers young and old loved seeing their images on the camera screens.

We were very privileged in being shown two graves. One was of a local man who had been trained in western medicine as a medical aide. On returning, he used a mix of modern and bush medicine to treat people but unfortunately he had died from malaria about a year previously.

The other grave was that of a white teacher who died of a heart attack.

They were both held in very high regard and their graves were fenced, had rooves and were in a very prominent location in the village. Both graves were very well maintained and we were told that several times a week fresh flowers were put on their graves. We did not see any graves of villagers.

to the fishing. There was a choice of up or down stream however the river level was high and upstream few snags were exposed and this made it difficult to fish for several reasons.

The fast-flowing current in the wet season often moves snags making navigation at speed hazardous. With the river high we sometimes had trouble getting the boat under fallen trees that were blocking our way. On the fishing side: barra fishing here is all about casting lures close to snags to tempt the waiting and hiding barra to strike at the apparent meal. If we couldn't see the snags it made it difficult to know where to cast. We did a day and half upstream for a few barra each day but nothing overly large so we moved downstream.

The boats of course were essential. They were all aluminium punts left over from World War Two. The punts were a bit leaky from fatigue, hitting snags and so on but still useable.

Outboard motors were all tiller steered Yamaha 40HP 4 strokes in good condition except for boat number three that was Greg's and mine and had air in the fuel line. The effect of having to frequently stop to clear it meant an extra two hours delay in getting back to the bar and tea. The problem was later identified as a poor coupling of the fuel line to the motor that was readily fixed after two trips.

On the morning of departure most of us left tackle and clothing to be distributed amongst the guides and housekeeping staff. Our bags and rod tubes were carried to the waiting plane and we said a sad goodbye to the wonderful people who made our trip so successful.

En route back to Australia we had to land at Daru again to

have our passports stamped and pay $15.00 departure tax. Australia then wanted a $55.00 arrival tax from each of us back at Horn Island, where Customs and Border Police went through our gear searching for prohibited goods. One in our group had a bow and arrows which were seized for treatment before being forwarded to him later.

And yes Greg and I ticked off the metre plus barra from our bucket lists thanks to the expert guiding and boat handling of Neme, Isaac and Cat.

GAME FISHING ADVENTURES MARK 1

By Peter Morton

My wife Leonore and our three children, soon to be four, moved to Port Lincoln at the end of 1979

Port Lincoln is well known as a fishing paradise for small fish such as whiting, medium size such as snapper, big like tunas and huge and dangerous White Pointer sharks. These sharks were legendary and I had read about Alf Dean who had caught many of them on rod and reel in the 1950s and 1960s, including one that was 1208kg or 2,664 pounds in 1959 near Ceduna. I also had read in a newspaper of one caught at Streaky Bay or Ceduna by some lunatics in a small boat who lassoed one with a rope and must have choked its gills somehow.

It was said to be 4500 pounds. My Uncle was a successful game fisherman and when I looked in the 1980s, he still had the South Australian record for a Mako shark caught outside Coffin Bay and I aspired to do this sort of fishing as well.

Soon after arriving we became friendly with Chris and Christine Stone, who ran a tackle shop and petrol station called "The Gas Catch" and started talking about game fishing and re-forming the Port Lincoln Game Fishing club. This eventually happened and was celebrated with the "Home of the White Pointer" fishing tournament.

Rolf Czabayski, who had a tackle shop in Adelaide and was keen on game fishing had a boat *Calypso* and invited Chris, me and Ian Phippard from Perth on a trip to the Neptune Islands south of Port Lincoln, an absolute hot spot for White Sharks.

John Taylor, a cray fisherman and diver, was also invited and was just the person for this sort of trip.

The trip was rough but exciting.

Most people would know that Matthew Flinders visited here and Coffin Bay in 1802, the first European to do so, naming Boston Bay, Points Donnington and Bollingbroke, Sleaford Mere, the Sir Joseph Banks Group of Islands and many other places after his native Lincolnshire in England, or people who had helped in his career such as Coffin Bay.

We passed by Memory Gove and Cape Catastrophe on our way through Thorny Passage on our west and on the east were Thistle, Taylor, Hopkins, Grindal and other islands named after the crew members who were lost when Flinders sent a boat ashore to look for water. It is always a moving experience to see these places and try and imagine what it was like in such a leaky, crowded ship so far from home. I suppose it was a little like the first astronauts.

We reached South Neptune Island in the late afternoon and it was even rougher in such open water where the next stop was Antarctica. We anchored in a little triangular cove with the nose of the boat only a metre or so from the rocks and hid from the southerly winds.

We had plenty of tuna scraps for bait and to attract the fish so we started running tuna oil into the water and very soon had a 1000-pound White Shark around the boat. John had tied a rope to a whole tuna and lowered it over the side. The water seemed to open as the shark, without the tiniest of splashes, came partly out of the water, grabbed the fish and then silently slid back. It was probably 600-800mm wide and I was so close I could have touched it; I certainly could see barnacles on its skin.

It was truly a magnificent creature and I had the first stirring of not wanting to kill such a wonderful creation of nature. It was too late, dark and dangerous to try to catch it so we left the tuna oil dripping and had tea.

After tea we had another real treat. John could play a guitar and sing really well. I have no idea of the names of the songs but they were all old English folk songs and he sang dozens of verses, all from memory. Perhaps his guitar was a good friend to him out in his cray boat when alone for long and lonely periods.

But all things come to an end. We had to maintain a watch as we were so close to the rocks. If the wind changed we probably would have hit them. That bit was easy but we also had to check that the tuna oil was running - not much fun in the pitch black from midnight until two whatever during my shift.

The boat had gaps just above the deck so water could flow in and out in the transom and the tuna oil bottle was outside the boat so it was a matter of looking behind the boat in the water. With just a torch any chance of night vision was lost while trying to keep that huge shark around the boat.

I found that sitting on the flying bridge about five or six feet above the water with a torch to see if tommy ruffs were swimming around the tuna oil was a perfect way to assess the state of play with the berley.

When it was light we caught tommy ruffs in a hand-held net by the dozens and they were all at least 20 cm long, the biggest I have ever seen. Meanwhile, the shark had long gone and I realised that I was glad that it had disappeared.

GAME FISHING ADVENTURES MARK 2

By Peter Morton

The aforementioned trip was exciting. It was nice to be out in the gulf where all sorts of fish could be caught and there were such wonderful land and seascapes.

It was not long before I, Chris Stone and some other people bought a game boat in Adelaide. It was not as flash as Rolf's by any means but it was roomy, comfortable with excellent fishing room and could sleep two in comfort, one in reasonable comfort and one on the floor.

It had a Volvo stern drive hooked up to a V8 marinised Chevrolet petrol motor that was very fast, appropriately named "Mako". We had sorted this out through Bob Kretschmer, a Port Lincoln marine surveyor, who had poked and prodded it and announced it was fit and well enough for us to buy.

Our friend Noel Linsell back loaded it from Adelaide Port Lincoln and we moored it in front of our house

The next day was to be a family and friends welcome to Mako. We had a little tender boat and I put this in the water and rowed to Mako, boarded her, checked things out, started the motor and headed towards the jetty where the gang were waiting.

Cars are not like boats. The biggest boat I had handled was 16-17 feet and this was getting towards being twice as big. As distinct from cars, boats vary much more in length and when boats get longer, they get higher, deeper, wider and heavier.

As I got closer to the jetty, despite going relatively slowly, it was too fast. With a 16-foot boat someone could put their foot out or grab a boat that is about to hit something but this unit was far too big to do that. I put it into reverse quickly and put power on, avoiding disaster. Everyone then boarded and we cast off.

I tried to head out to sea but the gears wouldn't engage because when I reversed the boat while it was still going forward I snapped something in the gear box. We were drifting and had to drop anchor about 40-50 metres away from the jetty and wait for rescue. That someone turned out to be Tom Shannon, a man who had put down our mooring who happened to pass by.

I cannot remember anything about how it was fixed. I was so embarrassed, guilty and ashamed I think my subconscious has suppressed the memory.

Anyway, things sorted themselves out and we had some great times on day and overnight trips to various places 20-30 miles away and caught our share of fish - but no White Sharks.

After the experience with Rolf I remember the first time we went chasing them at Memory Cove. I threw some berley in and unconsciously stepped back from the water thinking a shark would leap out of the water.

It was quite a thrill heading out to sea and we did have to pick up and practise some skills. It was not a female sort of boat. It was brash, tough and loud. We did not have an anchor winch so it was hard to pull up the anchor and unfortunately it was not practical for us to go out as a family other than around the harbor, as our children were not old enough to help physically. It was like going from a car to a fair size truck without power steering.

My biggest trip was to Kangaroo Island for a fishing tournament with "The Duke" Whitehead, a very skilled mechanic, and experienced fisherman and boat operator, Ray Bowley, a diesel mechanic, and Bob Kretschmer, a Marine Surveyor (as already mentioned), so we were well organised.

A trip of more than 100km needed navigation skills with instruments, a pencil and map, ability to handle a boat, thinking about the weather and operating a high frequency radio for which I had to do an exam. We were part of a bigger scene than usual.

We stopped at Wedge Island en-route overnight and made Kangaroo Island the next day. We achieved little in the competition but enjoyed ourselves very much, particularly at the sea food extravaganza on the last night.

On the way back to the boat I walked along the first floor of the motel units. There was a girl standing back leaning against the safety rail looking at an open door. As I excused myself to walk past she asked me for help. She had arrived late, dumped her gear in the room and ran off to tea but was sure she had shut her door.

Here was a chance to help the fair damsel so I walked into the room with her close behind, looked in the cupboard, kicked the divan and turned around and opened the bathroom door and got the shock of my life. She had hung a one-piece black jump suit in the shower alcove and it looked like someone had hung themselves. I jumped backwards, stepped on her foot and she screamed. I don't know what scared me more the apparition in the shower or her scream so it was back to the boat for therapeutic rum.

We left the next day and got a move on as there was some weather threatening. We anchored at the south eastern part of Thistle Island in Waterhouse Bay.

I set up my game fishing gear with double line and heavy wire and lo and behold hooked a big shark, maybe even a White Shark. I was impatient and tried to lift the shark instead of putting relentless pressure on it and broke the very heavy line, somersaulting backwards over the game fishing chair.

It must have been a sight and the guys were concerned that I had hurt myself but something happened I have heard about but never experienced.

Everything slowed down and I felt that I was completely in control of my movements and kept my head out of harm's way and landed like a gymnast, escaping unscathed.

Next day we headed home with some wonderful memories. I am pleased to say that we are still great friends with "The Duke" and of course the "Duchess" Gail and Bob and Marg Kretschmer. Bob I am pleased to say has contributed stories to this collection of tales and "The Duke" was an expert resource for the "Bloody Sand" story.

For a reason that has faded from my memory I started calling Bob "Baron" von Kretschmer in the early 1980s and still do. I would bet a sackful of pieces of eight that no one else in a little boat has carried a 'Duke" and a 'Baron" from Port Lincoln to Kangaroo Island and back!!!

LAWDO GOES FISHING

By Colin Gamble

Robert Lawton, Lawdo to his friends, was the epitome of manhood. He was six foot two inches, well built, blond-haired, with a ruggedly handsome face and a staunch friend to his mates.

His pastimes included rugby where he played second row for the Shamrocks first grade, and he rowed stroke in the A boat for the Wollongong Surf Lifesaving Club.

As a teenager he studied guitar at the Conservatorium of Music in Sydney and became an accomplished musician.

He was a character. In the 1960s he and three guitarist mates auditioned to back an American performer at Rushcutters Bay in the old Sydney stadium. The agent who booked them was so impressed he offered them the job.

As they were leaving he suddenly realised he didn't know their group's name. He yelled out to Lawdo "What's the name of your group mate?". Lawdo replied "The Skins".

When they turned up on the Saturday night there was the poster "FRESH FROM USA THE XXXXXXX BACKED BY THE FOUR SKINS This story was told by Lawdo so the truth of it is still being questioned.

As good as he was in those things his great love was fishing. Being from a coastal town he learnt his fishing skills from his dad. Later in life he was a coal miner and after going underground six miles into the escarpment he wanted nothing more than to go fishing off Bellambi bombora or bombie on his days off. Sometimes he used to take his mate

Goog Saunders with him. Goog was also a mate of mine but I never knew his actual Christian name. He was always Goog.

Goog was a good bloke when sober but a bloody pest when full which was most of the time. He worked as a caretaker at the local primary school and was also the first-grade manager of Shamrocks. First grade. That meant recording names on a list, nothing more. As was his nickname implied, he was the shape of an egg, short and round.

The real problem for Lawdo when he took Goog fishing was that he never caught any fish and complained to all and sundry that when Lawdo was catching fish he was ignored.

The truth is that Lawdo did look after Goog and tried to give him some fun by taking him fishing but Goog was always far too drunk to even bait a hook.

Every time Lawdo went to Goog's house, where he lived with his mum, to collect him to go fishing Goog would appear with an esky full of Resch's D A cans covered in ice and his fishing tackle. After he stowed this in the back he would get into the towing ute and open a can and start drinking it.

After many attempts to try to try to help Goog catch a fish Lawdo admitted that he always knew that Goog caught no fish because he was always too drunk and would eventually fall asleep in the boat.

This had to change so Lawdo devised a scheme so that his mate could catch fish. The solution was simple. No grog was to be drunk until the first fish was in the boat. When told of the new rule Goog reluctantly agreed to accept it. Lawdo knew Goog would try to ignore it but he would be firm.

The next Friday Lawdo started a run of 4 days off so what would be better than fishing off Bellambi bombie. Goog agreed to go next morning with the pick up at 5.30am. When Lawdo pulled up outside Goog's house he was relieved to see Goog was waiting just outside the front door. Goog put his esky and fishing box in the back of the ute and got into the front with a beer can in his hand. When Lawdo saw the unopened beer can, he reminded Goog of the new rule in case he had forgotten. "But I thought you were joking" replied Goog. "No way" said Lawdo.

As usual Lawdo reversed the trailer down the ramp just far enough to slide the boat off. Goog held the boat while Lawdo parked the ute and walked down the ramp to the boat.

In the bay there were many types of fish and one particular species was the flying fish. This fish is about the same size of a whiting and can become airborne by I imagine flapping its gills and can fly a distance up to 100 metres.

Just as Lawdo was about to get in the boat a flying fish flashed past his nose and landed in the boat.

"That'll do me" said Goog and grabbed a beer. Lawdo was so stunned he just looked to the heavens, and shrugged. And guess what Goog again returned pissed, poorly and piscatorially penurious.

Part 4 Gambling

THE CURSE CAN BE A BLESSING.

By Peter Morton

In 1967 I was doing obstetrics and gynaecology as a fifth-year medical student.

I was watching a betting system on horse racing, hypothetically, and it seemed to be working with small but frequent wins.

The day came to try it out with real money which coincided with a visit to Adelaide by some blokes from the country. One was with his girlfriend, now his wife of almost 50 years; let us call her Anna.

These visits usually involved the drinking of large amounts of beer and this was no exception. They had rented a flat at West Beach and I went there for lunch and later put the $10 on selected horses to win the daily double.

These were, say, horses number 2, 4, 6 in race 1 and 3, 5, 8 in race 2. To collect I had to pick the winner of each race.

I duly made the bet and thought I had lost as horse 3 won BUT I had reversed the numbers by mistake. Horse 3 won and in the other second race I now had horses 2, 4 and 6 to win and one of them did.

I may have won $10. It was so rare to have cash and or to eat chicken, so Anna and I drove up the Anzac Highway to buy a take away chicken with my winnings.

Near Morphettville race course two cars in front of us were dawdling so I accelerated between them. Just as I did this Anna grabbed her lower abdomen and gave a little cry, a yelp almost. I was distracted and lightly clipped the cars on my left and right.

Solution one was to accelerate, do a U-turn and head the other way. Mission accomplished. Reaction-oh hell. Drunk driving, leaving an accident and surely the victims would have seen my number plates.

Before we did anything I asked Anna what the trouble was. She explained that she often got mid cycle pain and it caught her off guard. Some women get this when they ovulate and it can be painful enough to mimic appendicitis. I knew all about this stuff in females because I had been studying it for three or four weeks. It even has a name-Mittlelschmertz

Solution two was to head for Glenelg police station and confess our, well my, sins and explain the reason.

This we did and were a bit anxious to say the least.

I explained to the young policeman that just before the accident my girlfriend had made a yelping sort of noise, clearly in pain and grabbed lower abdomen that and distracted me.

The constable listened intently to my detailed explanation of the cause of the problem. Meanwhile Anna stood stock still with her doe eyes cast down and lower lip trembling, never wavering.

He looked up sympathetically and said "Sorry about that, my girlfriend has trouble with the curse and stuff sometimes"

"We will let you know if we hear any more about it"

CASE DISMISSED-------------THE END

GAMBLING: CRAPS AT EXMOUTH AND RACES AT MARBLE BAR AND PORT HEDLAND

By Peter Morton

In 1969-70 I enjoyed horse racing and had some success in Broken Hill and Adelaide winning $2-3000, in today's money. This was just before we moved to Western Australia.

I also had some success during my time in Port Hedland tossing coins and dice and backing racehorses but the lesson I learnt about myself and gambling was the most important thing I took away from those days and has held me in good stead ever since.

I was sent to Exmouth as a locum for a week from Port Hedland. Exmouth was host to a United States Navy Base named after Harold Holt the Australian Prime Minister who was drowned in 1967 at Cheviot Beach in Victoria.

The job included July fourth when USA people celebrate Independence Day and they opened the Base to the Australian public.

There were various stalls and entertainments including a crap game in a corner somewhere. People took it in turn to throw a pair of dice. The person with the dice first makes a bet and then throws the two dice. The total of the two dice becomes their "point". To win, a player must throw their "point". If they throw a seven, the commonest total with two dice, then they lose.

It was all good fun and the young sailors were friendly and patient because everyone had to keep asking the rules. And then the ugly Aussie came along. He was hot with the dice and cleaning up big time but sadly he was also rude. He kept asking what he had to throw and when he got it he would say things like "No wonder you guys can't win in Vietnam, you can't even play this simple game." He spoke in a nasty way and the sailors were clearly getting very annoyed, as was I.

Apart from anything else we were guests so I was delighted and confess very surprised to separate this man from his money. I was the hero; everyone was really pleased when I "skinned" him but when I kept on winning, they were not so happy. Anyway, I soon lost a throw and everyone was happy except old ugly Aussie.

Later I heard about a race meeting in Marble Bar and that sounded rough, ready and exciting so off I went with my friend Dick Stedman the Mine Manager at Goldsworthy where I visited twice weekly to run clinics.

As was the custom in the North West they had well equipped nurses' quarters usually sparsely occupied with plenty of food so we were set for accommodation and meals. After unpacking we headed for the races.

We were looking around and an aboriginal man made a point of saying hello to me and reminded me that he used to work for me in Broome and was pleased to see me. I was somewhat puzzled as I had never employed anyone but the penny dropped when he told me he had done my gardening. This was a community service as he was a guest of Her Majesty at the time.

I do not remember much about the races except that one race was delayed when the starter decided he needed a wee so he dismounted from the starter's platform and headed for the bush. What he forgot was that people had binoculars so the bush he was hiding behind provided little cover. It was noisy dusty and fun. Marble Bar is famous for the hot climate. It is reputed to have had 168 days in a row of at least 100 degrees F or about 38 degrees C

One thing I do remember was the iconic "Iron Clad" pub, a galvanised iron building with a bar that was famous, small and packed.

Two up is often played after races but there was no room for an open area of floor to act as a ring. Someone would just toss a coin, catch it and put it on the back of his non tossing hand and people would make bets and money would change hands.

I did very well and remember having money in every pocket. In fact, I cleaned out the bar to the point where no one would toss with me.

I was on a roll and wanted to play proper two up so I asked a young policeman where the game was. He said he did not know and to ask the "Sarge" who was sitting at the end of the bar clearly in "his" place. This I did and was directed to a house with a palm tree in the front yard and next door to a most charming two-storey stone building in the main street that had been the mining exchange when Marble Bar was a thriving gold mining town in the late 1800s.

I knocked on the door and received an invitation to come in and walked down the short hallway drew the curtain and stepped into a room where two couples were eating dinner. I bet that they had a laugh about me next day.

To the Port Hedland races.

Every dry season, the southern winter, serial race meetings were held from north to south from Wyndham to

Carnarvon. Most of the horses were local or from nearby towns but there were horses from Perth as well.

At the Port Hedland meeting there were two from Perth named, let's say, "Darkie" and "Charlie".

This is a bit tricky but the story starts with a Calcutta. This is a function in association with an important race meeting to raise money for charity or other purposes and so enliven the atmosphere around the race meeting. The Calcutta is usually held the night before the races. The horses in the main race are auctioned and prize money paid to the successful bidders for the placed horses.

Apart from being fun and getting into the atmosphere of a special meeting it can be a way for serious punters to get better odds for a horse than at the track. Say there are twenty horses in a race and the club auctions them for an average of $50 per horse i.e. $1000 would be collected. The prizes might be $500, $250 and $150 for first, second and third with the club keeping $100. If a punter fancies a certain horse and the horse looks like starting at 2 to 1 and the punter wishes to bet $100 on it then he/she stands to win $200. On the other hand if he/she buys the horse at the Calcutta for $100 and it wins the punter would collect a profit of $400.

Now it gets interesting. "Charlie's" owners bought "Darkie" at the Calcutta so either "Charlie" is not good or well enough to beat "Darkie" or something else is afoot. I have no idea how I found out about that.

I duly went to the races on a Saturday but by the time the feature race was on I was broke. Punters often bet "on the nod" with bookies who know them. In other words they bet on credit and settle bets after the races.

I explained my predicament to a visiting specialist from Perth who was a racing man and he fixed it with a bookie for me to have a bet on credit. Now "Darkie" was 3 to 1 on in the betting which means three dollars has to be bet to win one dollar so I had bet of a $100 to win $33 which presumably was what I had lost. This was and still is by far the biggest bet I had ever made and was almost a week's wages and equivalent to $2000 at least for a Medical Officer in Port Hedland today.

I can remember waiting for the race and feeling sick. It all seemed too obvious and I was a sucker. Why did I think I was clever knowing about the Calcutta - maybe it was a "con.".

Anyway "Darkie" won and I went to collect my bet but as mentioned it was not available until the end of the meeting, but I could still bet using my winnings as credit. My nerves were ragged and I wandered around and looked at the horses in the next race where there was another odds-on horse running and a horse some reason I liked at 20 to one so I went back to my bookmaker and he had it at four to one and I had to bet with him. It won and the odds-on horse didn't.

Apart from a good story I found out how easy it would have been to borrow more money and I would have done just that and had $200 on "the nod" on the next odds-on horse that lost.

Reminds me of the advice to young men in those days; keep away from red heads in black underwear, don't play cards with strangers on trains and never back a horse that is odds on in Sydney.

The second day of the meeting was on the Monday and at the Calcutta for Monday's race "Charlie's" owners bought

"Charlie". By then I wanted nothing to do with special information, betting or anything else. I was the Medical Officer at the races and just wandered around.

The race duly started and "Charlie" was miles in front of "Darkie". When "Charlie" finished he was blowing foam from his nostrils and just after they passed the post "Charlie's" jockey fell off. "Darkie" later was awarded the race.

I re-wrote the above on 6/9/2017. On the previous Saturday I backed six horses and that included four winners. I won about $150 from a stake of $100. This was the biggest day's betting since Port Hedland by far where I gave myself such a fright when I realised what I might have done chasing my losses and I have never been in that situation again. It also made me realise what a mug's game it is to make so little from backing four out of six winners. I gave the $150 back the next week so that was a cheap lesson!

Part 5 Jobs and the tasks of others

A RURAL MEDICAL CAREER

By Jonathon Newberry

Rural Background

Rural background is the most frequently quoted determinant of a future rural career among health professional students. Needing a definition of rural background, government has come up with various time definitions and researchers have used these to explore the impact of the defined rural background. Five years seems to be the quantum. Continuity used initially has been superseded by cumulative years and pre-primary school time has been discounted as not having an influence. International research has of course not been bound by Australian government definitions. Despite this variation rural background remains the strongest association reported by surveys of existing rural practitioners and is seen as best predictor of a future career.

I find this to be a simplistic definition in need of a nuanced understanding.

My father was a teacher and as a family we moved every 4-5 years as dad chose different private schools jobs around Victoria. So I lived for two spells of 4-5 years in rural towns interspersed with two similar lengths of time in Melbourne. Fortunately for my career the last 4 years were in Melbourne, where I attended Dad's boys' school with a big focus on maths and science and gained entry to the Melbourne Medical School on the strengths of these subjects which are largely useless in a medical career.

Rural Interest

I would argue that *rural interest* is the background determinant of rural career choice and longevity. Early in my rural procedural career it was explained to me that "GPs who stay in the country have a passion /obsession" that keeps them there. Now as an academic I am embarrassed to quote a colleague and be unable to remember who said it; it may have been a wise competent GP from Benalla?

More recently another rural GP researcher colleague suggested there had been too many studies of why doctors don't stay in rural towns; he proposed we should study doctors who have remained in rural practice and ask what keeps you here? He planted vines, grew white wine grapes, worked hard at his PhD and kept working in procedural general practice to support his family and fund his passionate *rural interest*.

I learnt my procedural skills in anaesthesia and obstetrics in Great Britain, I learnt my GP consulting skills in Victoria, Scotland and from my career long mentor back in Victoria when I settled into rural GP. Where did I choose after training?

My wife and I chose a town where she had spent a large part of her childhood. It had a lake for my (life-long) sailing obsession and you could drive to the snowfields for a day's skiing in winter. Our children learnt to ride bikes safely, to walk in the national parks and to shy away from the demands of procedural rural practice.

Rural Academia

The rural doctor shortage led the Australian Government to create the Rural Medical Student funding for Medical Schools. Rural background, as above, was used as a determinant for selection into medical school and Rural Exposure was mandated for an academic year in the clinical years of the course. My mentor, by now a Professor of general practice in the University of Adelaide knew he needed a rural GP to run such a program and he knew I needed a change of pace.

Rural Clinical Medicine

Credibility among medical students depends on clinical ability and the ability to teach. The Australian governments funding enabled us to establish a multi-site Rural Clinical School around northern and western South Australia, initially I did this living in Adelaide. Our children were in high school through this time so, like me, they benefitted from the opportunity and diversity of a capital city high school coinciding with their father's career; just as I had done at the same age.

Credibility of the Adelaide Rural Clinical School was won and maintained by being in the country lots, dealing with rural clinicians to become teachers and continuing to practice only in rural towns. This also depends on lots of driving and regional airlines!

An academic career depends on research and writing for publication. The university and a number of research mentors have enabled that to be a productive part of establishing the credibility of the rural program among medical school academia.

Rural Interest (Again)

Same paragraph heading but this one contains the punch line.

I've spent 12 years as a rural located head of a Rural Clinical School; I've worked in a General practice here and in the local hospital, I've taught our medical students in the class room and in the consulting room. Some of them are now in rural practice because their rural clinical undergraduate time has been one of their influences. They haven't all had a rural background, although it remains spastically associated with current rural location.

I think they all have a *rural interest*, which we haven't measured, that has been the big unmeasured influence on their medical career.

Nearly forgot to say, when you're not at work, the sailing is great here.

BOB THE PUBLIC SERVANT – STORY ONE

By Bob Hutchinson

Many of the skits on TV or the internet about employment officers versus job seekers are very close to the truth in that there was a constant friendly competition between the two sides.

Until the 1970s, clients had to declare any casual employment since the previous visit to their Employment Officer. The answer was almost invariably "No" because they didn't want to lose any of their dole.

Now consider the following:-

In the early 1980s many locals were employed as extras in the film "Gallipoli" and were easily identified by their new "short back and sides" hairstyle and sunburnt ears, quite different to the long hair of the surfer era. For some strange reason none of those who we interviewed were successful at the auditions but could describe the filming in great detail.

There is a smell associated with seafood factories that permeates the clothes, skin and hair so job seekers would always change clothes before interview. It didn't mask the smell on their skin & hair though and when suitably prompted memories recovered remarkably.

One new and naïve junior employment clerk asked me how to assist a very attractive client who gave her address as "Cactus", a very well-known isolated surfing beach on the far west coast of Eyre Peninsula. Now these were the days where you had to try and place a client in jobs they had previous experience of, or had studied for. No she didn't want to leave her home address and her stated chosen profession was "stripper" or "hooker". I think we ended up getting her work in a shearing shed before she decided to move on.

Various health problems were given as reasons to decline job offers so we would ask for medical evidence if we were suspicious. One chap complained of a bad back and was always knocking back job offers so it was decided to refer him for a medical certificate describing his physical limitations. The resulting certificate was thrown on my desk with the comment "There you are I told you I had a bad back!" The certificate read along the lines of, "I have examined Mr X who complains of a bad back. I have thoroughly examined him and put him through a variety of exercises. My recommendation is that Mr X restricts himself to lumping no more than one bag of grain on each shoulder".

Mr X was not a good reader. Bags of grain weighed more than 50kg at the time.

One notable happy client was a chap who had just been fired from his engineer's job on a local fishing trawler. Because of the incident, chances of employment locally were not good but I found an opportunity for him in northern Australia as an engineer on a brand new trawler. He was unsure about relocating but I convinced him to do a telephone interview then and there. His face lit up and his grin stretched wider and wider as the interview progressed. He accepted the job over the phone. I asked him what changed his mind about relocating. "Easy I will be working with an all-female crew". His luck continued as his fares to relocate were paid by us. The old saying "Be careful what you wish for, you might get it," is always at the edge of my consciousness when I occasionally wonder how he got on.

At a Departmental conference one of my peers asked why we were asked to do so many reports and what use was made of them. The head honchos assured us that those reports were necessary and were always carefully considered.

My peer's response was that if that was the case then why didn't he ever receive feedback from his contributions as in every report he inserted a line similar to

"Minnie mouse loves being @#$%@# by Mickey Mouse" we all laughed except the bosses. I can't recall my peer getting further promotions.

One of my first bosses implemented flexi time way before it was the norm. His attitude was if you work hard, get the job done properly and under time then you could have that saved time off. One inflexible rule, we must always let him know.

One Monday morning Jim, a work mate, took off on a standard five-day rural trip. He worked long with minimal breaks and he returned to Port Lincoln late Thursday. He stored the car at his home and flew to Adelaide for the long weekend.

Big mistake made, he broke the rule and didn't tell our boss he had returned early. Our boss found out what happened when someone remarking that they saw Jim fly out.

The boss used the spare set of keys, picked up the work car and hid it. Nothing was said until a very sheepish worker asked the boss late on Monday if anyone had seen the government car. Some discussion followed but a lesson was learnt. Always obey the boss's rules.

One day I gave a good reason for head office to ring, something country managers tried to avoid at all costs. I had submitted a retrospective special leave application with the reason for leave being "Trapped at sea by bush fire".

Head Office wanted to know what games were I playing and what did I mean?

Easy, I was at Avoid Bay scuba diving and then visited my son on a cray boat where he worked when a bush fire started between Coffin Bay and Avoid Bay that closed the road.

With no way out the safest place was on the boat where we dined on cray and fresh fish and scallops.

The leave was reluctantly approved after they read about the bushfire in the newspaper.

What have I left out for another time? Being trapped in my office by a mentally disturbed criminal threatening to stab me with a knife; a boob flasher, being subpoenaed as a "labour market expert" in workers compensation cases, differences between working at Port Adelaide and more affluent areas of Adelaide and a few more if Peter ever decides to do another volume.

BOB THE PUBLIC SERVANT – STORY TWO

By Bob Hutchinson

Previously I wrote about the more humorous side of working in the Commonwealth Employment Service but there was definitely a very serious and even dangerous aspect.

Losing a job for whatever reason can be traumatic and it was vitally important that staff and I understood what losing a job can mean. Unless people have savings, or a secondary source of household income they will find it difficult to pay for essentials such as rent, mortgage, food and utilities and lifestyle will suffer. The amount of income support is calculated on the number of dependants, not previous earnings. A top-level executive would get the same the same unemployment benefits as an unskilled worker.

It was our job to treat all clients with respect and empathy and help them get back into the workforce as soon as possible. I was indeed fortunate that almost every staff member I worked with understood this and did their best to help.

Getting a client a job at any time is important but certain times are more important than others. I was walking to a café to have lunch one December day and an older lady approached and thanked me for recently getting her son a job. She cried when she told me he would now be able to buy his children Christmas presents. I thanked the lady but explained that I got her son the interview and as usual explained the interview process. I encouraged him to identify his strengths, weaknesses and what he could bring to the job. He won the job not me.

On the subject of timing the new State manager was with me and meeting that lady did me and the other staff no harm at all.

Older farmers often felt lost having to seek off-farm income during lean times. They perceived a lack of higher education as a major barrier but they did have many skills that they had acquired on the farm. Welding, carpentry, tyre fitting, machinery operation and truck driving were just a few of those skills they had. Employers generally liked employing farmers because of their skills and work ethic and it was usually easy to place them in a job particularly if they were prepared to leave their immediate location for a while.

I was indeed fortunate to have Phil Bush as State Director who was appointed when the state's staff morale was at an all-time low; the legacy of a highly disliked and disrespected previous Director. One of the first things Phil did was call all Managers into Head Office to explain what he expected from us.

After the initial introductory pleasantries he explained his philosophy and we almost cheered. Phil said if you have a deserving client but the guide lines give 99 reasons to say no, keep looking until you find a reason to say yes. That's what we are here for. If we were wrong all he said the most he would say was "You made a wrong decision," however if you didn't make a decision then he would say, "You failed as a manager". We were all happy with that and took the message back to staff. It was sad that his three-year term was up all too quickly.

An example of how he backed his staff was when I had

refused an application from a company to import workers. This was because they had not demonstrated serious efforts to recruit Australians for what were described at the very best as semi-skilled positions. The CEO of that company was not happy and contacted the Prime minister who contacted my Department's Minister who contacted the Head of my Department who contacted Phil Bush, the State Director. It sounds a bit like a Mr Bean or John Cleese skit but that is what happens with any complaints made to Ministers.

Phil asked me for a briefing paper that I quickly faxed to him. His private secretary telephoned me to relay Phil's question. Do I stand by my report? Yes I confidently responded and I was on the plane to Adelaide to attend a meeting with the State Director of Immigration, Phil and an angry CEO hoping to get me to change my mind. It would have been interesting if the CEO and I were on the same flight but it wasn't to be.

No one sat at this tense meeting and when the CEO threatened Phil with an avalanche of ministerial support Phil handed him a telephone and said for every one the CEO gets he would get two. No phone call was made and after the meeting, the Director of Immigration said he happily supported our decision as his overseas staff had found out that the "skilled experts" had only ever worked as labourers in rice paddies and had zero experience in the CEO's industry.

I had always believed that managers are paid for the hard tasks, not the easy. Staff should get the credit and managers should shoulder the blame to the public and hierarchy.

One day a staff member was unsuccessfully dealing with a noisy and disruptive client so I intervened and invited the client into my office. He was very agitated and irrational and for the next 90 long minutes threatened me with stabbing and a bashing. Every bit of training I knew about conflict resolution was dragged from the depths of memory in trying to keep this chap quiet and rational.

It got to the point where I was able to convince him to allow me to get a message to a fellow staff member. He had earlier threatened me if I touched my phone. I called in my deputy and asked him to cancel a fictitious appoint with a Graham Field who was the local well known police inspector. I hoped my deputy would understand what I was saying as all the staff knew my situation. Unfortunately it was almost an hour later when the penny dropped and my deputy realised that I needed police intervention.

I had no way of knowing if the police were coming. I continued to listen and talk with the client. Thankfully I eventually convinced him to leave with an appointment to see me the following day when I could spend whatever time was necessary to identify and resolve his concerns.

As he was walking out of building, two police rocked up and he immediately and unsuccessfully attacked them - not a wise or effective action. Thankfully I never did see him again and was told by police the next day that he had spent time in many of Australia's maximum security prisons and was well known for his violence and that very morning had assaulted a police officer at the station.

We all spoke about the incident, decided that we did the right thing, had a good laugh about my "coded message" not being immediately understood and got on with our jobs. Head Office reaction when told: nothing, no offer of counselling, duress alarms or even sympathy.

More proof that South Australia stops at the outer borders of the Adelaide metropolitan area.

DRIVER LICENCE STORIES

By Steve Ballard

I don't understand the hoo-haa over driverless cars. South Australia has tens of thousands of effectively driverless cars on the road most days.15-30% SA citizens, mostly blokes, should never sit in a car, let alone try to drive one.

In this State, to drive a powered vehicle is regarded as a right and a rite of passage.

Phooey.

One of the down-sides of working in medicine is that we are empowered, even mandated, to report those we consider medically unfit to drive to the Licencing Authority.

Many in the community regard this as legally acceptable dobbing; that is a "Doctor confiscating the person's licence".

Most of the characters in the following tales are long deceased.

The first story comes from an Orthopaedic surgeon colleague, who lived in Elliston with his Police Sergeant father in what was then an idyllic village, before it became attractive to the surfing community. (*His name was Reg and a good mate of my Uncle. I met him many times. Ed*)

The story relates that Dr T, the local doctor who was given to a certain bibulousness (*drank too much grog. I think!-Ed*) and on one occasion was caught by Sgt Menz. Long ago, before breathos, the policeman's word was enough and he is said to have taken Dr T's licence to drive

Not many days later, Dr T was called late at night by Sergeant Menz, to ask for a medical examination of a driver considered to have been driving under the influence of alcohol.

As an aside, the Police can and still do make such requests.

Dr T, whose sobriety at that time was not recorded, stated that as he did not have a licence to drive, the Police would have to pick him up from home.

So, that happened, and the licence reinstated. Bush Law? Who cares? (*Dr T's booze stories are legendary but he worked for 18 years in Elliston and on Eyre Peninsula from 1930-1964. Ed*)

Another story has a link to the Far North-West of SA.

Very early in my first year with the RFDS, a nurse and I had been flown to the thriving metropolis of Marla, a small opal mining town about 250 km south of the NT border, to provide our routine GP services. The nurse from Marla met us at the airstrip to drive us to the cupboard in the corner of the Police Station where we worked.

Driving on the gravel roads in Marla is like driving on marbles. Soon after we left the airstrip we encountered a vehicle travelling towards us. Intent on occupying the same bit of road he had not stopped at a blind junction.

Expert evasive driving by our driver averted a need to bring more RFDS resources to Marla. Typically laconic was the comment "...oh, that's old xxxx...he often does that. Not even certain his car has brakes." Bush Law? Not obvious.

Old xxxx had retired a few years before, and moved from Streaky Bay to Marla.

Reportedly a crusty cove at best.

I saw him a couple of weeks later, to...you guessed it... get his medical ticket to maintain his licence to drive.

I recognized him and was more thorough than usual, although he was manifestly unfit to be controlling 1500Kg boxes on wheels.... powered or not.

Slow in movement and very slow in cognition sums it up.

I advised him that I did not regard him as fit to drive, and my requirement was to advise the Licencing Authority.

His cognition was up to that and a round of abuse spewed forth.

As there were few realistic supports in Marla, he returned to Streaky Bay within days.

More recently I met a man who introduced himself as "Pig" at Mintabie, a dying Opal village, about 30km from Marla. He was about 70 and had bought the Mintabie Caravan Park and lived with his Mum. Why?

Pig had bad Coronary artery disease and was flown to tertiary centres several times when it got the better of him. At the time he was hale and hearty and took a shine to our GP registrar, though she brooked no nonsense from him.

Pig and his relatively well Mum struggled financially. He became convinced that he could regain a heavy vehicle licence and work for a mate in Alice Springs. I said no way. He politely disagreed and arrangements were made to have a formal cardiological opinion regarding his fitness to drive heavy vehicles. He could not accept that the conclusion was foregone.

Then he dropped dead one morning. Bush Law? Community just got lucky?

Then, there was "Old Jack".

Old Jack was a very tall chap with a tiny wife who became regulars in my Port Lincoln days.

Robust and stern but fair, he had been a Police Sergeant. He was that genuine rarity in medicine, with true asthma starting in his seventies, having not smoked, and returned to normal function with asthma medication.

As the years passed, this couple remained loyal, but Jack's cognition and mobility started to wane.

You got it.

He came one morning, unusually alone, for his driving licence check. I'd thought that his wife did the driving.

Putting it all together and dividing by the number I first thought of, I advised that he no longer had the physical or brain power to safely drive. I was presented with all the usual reasons to reconsider…. never had a crash, had been driving for 55 years (when do they rest?)…

Before the afternoon consulting, the front of house staff asked if I would see his wife.

Timorous with the belief that she was going to ask me to reconsider, I showed her in. She declined the offer to be seated.

"Thank you, doctor…. Our daughters and I have been waiting for three years for someone to do that!"

Unfortunately, Old Jack's chronic brain failure later led to a period in the Hospital's Nursing home type accommodation, where he might from time to time investigate crimes and even arrest and lock purported miscreants in a cupboard. He faded away in a local Nursing Home. The dementias are seriously horrible processes.

Lastly, we come to 'Old Reg" another of my regulars for

years.

Reg presented in his late 60s, short, very round, grumpy-as-all-get-out and quite disabled by rheumatoid disease, in those days when $120,000/year biological agents were not available to actually improve them.

He had a huge abdominal hernia that the surgeons agreed would be unethical to attack surgically.

I'd seen him struggle, getting into his car, but understood that many disabled people drive safely.

Eventually he came for.... you got it ... the driver licence check.

With some misgivings, I signed him off, given the sentiments above, but it was on the proviso that he also have a formal driving evaluation. This was accepted with his characteristic poor grace.

Some weeks later, he plodded in saying that he had a bone to pick with me.

"I passed the test... Just!" "And I have to do it again in 12 months!"

He ceased to see me professionally, but a year later, a partner cobbled me up, to relate how Reg came for his check; my colleague was not happy but insisted that the driving assessment was mandatory.

And showed me the report. Recall how I began these tales with a comment on some people should not get into cars, let alone drive them. I was given a vision of the assessor sitting white knuckled, peering from slitted eyes and praying to any deity who cared to listen.

Reg had driven with no regard for the task at hand, failed to stop where required, drove across roundabouts, unable to park in any way and mounted kerbs often.

Reg's plight worsened quite quickly thereafter, as his physical problems became overshadowed by his cognitive failure, resulting in Nursing home care and a relatively early passing.

I would be certain that all Rural GPs have similar stories.

Those who rail against the State in trying to maintain some standards on the roads just don't get it.

THE BARN

By Colin Gamble

In 2002 my partner Terri and I moved from the east coast of Australia to Port Lincoln in South Australia to escape from what had become an unpleasant way and place to live.

When we had settled into the very attractive and pleasant town we bought the 50-acre block where we still live and breed cattle for the local market.

The property was very run down and had very little fencing other than the boundary and no sheds or decent cattle yards. The effort to get this place up to scratch was exhausting and expensive but we managed to make slow but steady progress.

It has been my experience that I have always had friends who might be called "characters". Perhaps I attract these sorts of blokes as Terri has suggested a few times, well often actually.

Two such characters I met were good blokes we shall call Rod and Lou because they are not their names. They could best be described as knock about blokes. Both men were friendly, polite and adept at doing any and every thing they turned their hands to and they were absolute drunks.

They were always welcome at our farm because they were as entertaining as any two blokes I have met and even more important they assisted me with many jobs around the place and if the job was a big one they would be paid.

We decided to build a barn to keep hay, machinery and miscellaneous equipment out of the weather. The way we went about this was to buy a heap of wood and screws and so on with a set of instructions that showed how to put it together and turn it into a barn.

Rod and Lou were invited to help us under the standard conditions of a hundred bucks a day each in the hand and copious amounts of beer, lunch being optional and rarely eaten.

We live at a place called Duck Ponds that is 10km or so inland and is both colder in winter and hotter in summer than downtown Port Lincoln only metres from the sea.

Sadly the barn arrived at the farm at the height of summer with temperatures getting into the low 40s. Before we could assemble the barn we had to put in foundations and before we could do that we had to dig holes in sheet bloody limestone and that took a lot of time. Eventually the foundations were in place and the actual assembly began.

We did OK and put the sheet iron walls in place and finally the roof.

Both of these steps required me, as the gopher, to get the iron and hold it in place to be screwed in correctly. As previously stated the days were hot and the final day of assembly was a stinker of about 43 degrees and if you were on the roof even hotter.

As was the agreement the two roof workers called for beer and to my embarrassment all my beer had been drunk. I immediately told the roof boys that "I am on it," and headed off at high speed to Liquorland, the closest grog shop.

When I wheeled in there to my amazement all the products in the cold room were warm. I asked the attendant what was wrong and he told me the freezing plant had been broken for a few days. Needless to say I went elsewhere to get some cold beer and headed home to a rousing welcome.

We soon made a hole in the first carton as there were some very dry throats to moisten. While we were yarning, I told them about the problem with Liquorland having their cold room on the blink for a few days in such hot weather.

Rod pricked his ears and said that he had bought a carton there the night before.

I asked him what the beer was like. He thought for a while and said "Yair now ya say that I thought there was something different about the beer but I couldn't really put me finger on what it was."

Just about every time I go near the barn I think of those two blokes, they sure were an item.

HOW DID WE GET INTO THIS MESS?

By Steve Ballad and Peter Morton

INTRODUCTION

I was a partner and later associate general practitioner at The Investigator Clinic in Port Lincoln from 1980-1996 and then worked separately but cooperatively with that group of doctors until I left Port Lincoln in 2002. From then until 2017 when I retired from medical practice my wife Leonore and I were away from Port Lincoln while I had various jobs in half a dozen or so places for about half the time, but always regarded Port Lincoln as home.

Steve Ballard worked at The Investigator Clinic from 1983 to 1995. I owe him special thanks in the way he cared for my parents and indeed me before and at the time of their deaths. We were and still are friends. I don't think anyone else could have written this excellent story and compress so much wisdom and foresight in so few words. Steve is a special doctor and person.

Steve is 10 years younger than me and in many ways we are quite different but we had a similar approach to patients in that we would do anything to help people but did not suffer fools gladly.

Steve described leaving Pt Lincoln in 1995 when "The intense intrusiveness of remote town practice became too much". It is an interesting comment because I found it hard going also and from the mid 1980s I became more involved in medical administration and project management until my general practice withered to almost nil by the late 1990s.

I am not sure if it means anything at all but I can recall 20 members working at the clinic since 1980. Now there are only three remaining, two of whom are about to resign. Most left to be general practitioners elsewhere but five at least left general practice and two, Richard Watts and David Mills, maintained an interest in association with academic careers.

In recent years the term "Rural Generalist", "General Proceduralist" and maybe others have been used to describe general practitioners who have extra training and qualifications in such things as surgery, anaesthetics or obstetrics. Readers may be somewhat puzzled to know that doctors with a Fellowship in General Practice are registered as Specialists in General Practice. The term "recency" of training is used frequently, and it simply means being "up to date", or more precisely, practice in particular disciplines is current rather than distant. The expression comes from Aviation, from which a lot of current training and quality and incident reporting has been transplanted into Medical/ clinical templates.

Over to Steve Ballard:

A PATH TO RURAL GENERALISM

I served my internship in 1978 and then second year with terms in neonatal medicine (The Queen Elizabeth Hospital in Adelaide delivered babies then), pharmacology, respiratory medicine and my most enjoyable term...Intensive care in 1979.

Most of these rosters were unattractive to second years, so I was thought to be quite odd for enjoying them.

I then spent three years at the Lyell McEwin Hospital and

cultivated an interest in critical care, resuscitation and transport medicine and then fell into a six-month position in obstetrics leading to a Diploma in that field eighteen months later. It was a great place then to do Obstetrics, with chirpy mothers as midwives and no students or registrars.

A period as Divisional Surgeon in Saint Johns also helped in what was to come in my career.

Five years after graduation, having been rejected for specialist training by the Anaesthesia Faculty and at another time, Paediatricians, but with a wealth of bread-and-butter experience, the "Doctor-robber-barons" of Port Lincoln took me on immediately after the 1983 Ash Wednesday fires.

My then wife, baby daughter and I had driven to Lincoln in October 1982, to be interviewed. The lads found that I had no great skill in tennis or barbecue cooking, yet seemed to see promise in my skill mix.

My chief interrogator was the late Ian Fletcher, the local surgeon, who was entirely separate from the Investigator Clinic group. Ian became a great friend and support over the next 15 years and we still feel his passing *ditto Ed*.

Before starting, I was asked to do some anaesthesia training and Bill Fuller at TQEH helped, as he knew me from the ICU days.

A few months into my tour in Lincoln, the group decided that they had enough GP anaesthetists, so I was excused from that, until a year later when two partners abruptly left for greener pastures.

I returned to the QEH for three months of the next year, to formally learn the more physical skill-set required in anaesthesia, the boss again being Bill Fuller.

Much of the ancillary knowledge and skills were learned in the earlier terms that no-one liked to do! Bill agreed that those other skill sets were relevant to anaesthesia.

I never really enjoyed obstetrics and when all my Aboriginal girls finished having babies the obstetrics dried up.

Concurrent with the fall-off in obstetrics, the anaesthesia work blossomed and my colleagues seemed happy to look after my routine patients in return for my taking on the complex resuscitations. The Saint John Ambos would sometimes call me up to attend crash scenes. I was the "go to" for some of their training and larger Multi-agency disaster simulations. All good fun.

I developed an interest in Aboriginal Health, (something of an oxymoron) and I was invited to become Patron of the new Aboriginal Health Service.

I learned much in Pt Lincoln, upset a few people, and came close to the dreaded "burn-out".

It would be unlikely that my path was so unusual, in the seventies and eighties. More on that later.

PORT AUGUSTA – THE ROYAL FLYING DOCTOR SERVICE (RFDS) AND BEYOND

My Lincoln colleagues recognized in 1995 that I was battling and that it was time for change. A rather blissful six weeks off the emergency roster ensued, during which the RFDS offered me a position in Port Augusta. News of my being on the move spread quickly, and resulted in many unsolicited job offers, mostly to do what I was trying to leave behind!

My new family and I moved to Pt Augusta, at the end of

1995. I remained with the RFDS for almost 21 years. This was entirely separate from the hospital initially but my role there grew slowly, especially in anaesthesia, resuscitation and critical care.

The RFDS work was rewarding for a long time, but a combination of factors resulted in, again, near "burn-out" and we parted ways, in August 2016.

However, we love living in this true desert town, which, after a long decline, seems to have a very rosy future, but will need a lot of careful forward thinking and hard work.

We remain here, 22 years on and I provide anaesthesia, resuscitation and emergency services, mostly in Port Augusta, but also in Whyalla and avoid primary care where possible.

By way of a bridge, I offer a couple of clinical vignettes to link my clinical training path to some thoughts on the post graduate training matters that those late in their professional lives ponder.

Earlier this year, I was requested by an emergency doctor to do a Lumbar Puncture (LP) for a patient with suspected Meningitis. Antibiotics were administered, the LP done, and the diagnosis was subsequently proven, with a grateful patient and wife resulting.

Anaesthetists are very familiar with invading the central and peripheral nervous systems, so the request was spot on.

Stone the crows, a couple of weeks later, one of the senior GP Registrars made a similar request. Her problems were that she had not done a LP since her student days and the ED was frantic. The patient's story indicated a clear need to offer the diagnostic LP.

The ED was a circus, so we did the LP in the Post Anaesthesias Care unit, being roomy, quiet, and away from the hurley-burley of ED. The complexity of the patient's background required expedited transfer to his "home specialist unit" in a tertiary hospital. The Registrar's throwaway comment on procedural recency is germane to us all.

As a "Rural Procedural GP", as previously mentioned, we get to do fun things like put needles into spaces they don't normally go, or paralyse people, bringing them perilously close to disaster, for them to recover fully, none the wiser. *(This is called a general anaesthetic and is not only about putting people to sleep it is all about waking them up. Ed)*

Others deliver babies... good luck with that... and others do surgery in tents, using candles and ether, (a grim mix), or whisky poured over the wound. I jest...ether is highly flammable! The rest is true. I have colleagues who have done these things in Sub-Saharan Africa and this tome's editor sutured his son's facial wound, cleaned with whisky, in New Zealand.

Some play footy using a couple of gum trees as goal-posts, or golf with rabbit burrows as the holes, while employing the simple expedient of filling in most of the burrows with a tractor and plough.

Our Learned Colleges wrestle with determining the minimum numbers of exposures of those in training to core conditions. They also estimate the minimum workload notionally required to maintain skills and knowledge, so that the lotteries inherent in training and care provision are not so stark as they seem to be at times.

Educators believe that 5000-10,000hours of immersive training are necessary to develop basic competencies... be this surgery, football, golf or music.

Put another way, there are no over-night successes and from an economic standpoint, this largely unrecompensed training has to be considered in any discussion of pay scales.

On another hand, as the QLD Health discovered with Jayant Patel, bits of paper may mean nothing useful; we saw there, serious break-downs at many administrative levels.

SO WHERE ARE WE GOING AS A MEDICAL COMMUNITY?
This is harder to gauge than one may think.

I don't think the task(s) is/are at all well-defined.

Sadly, "Big Pharma" and huge corporations with advertising budgets larger than the GDP of many small countries, drive much of the debate. The Commonwealth is troubled by the notional "up front" costs of modern immunisations, but fund new biological agents for managing an increasingly large number of uncommon conditions, at $120,000 per patient per year.

In 1978, a new medical graduate had very few absolute requirements to be met in order to practice unsupervised. Graduate, do intern year and away you go. This is not to say that there were not training programs in just about any field, but the notions of delineating skills and formal accreditation to apply such skills were still nascent, let alone validation, or re-validation and providing proof of pudding.

The pathway to unsupervised GP work is now highly structured.

Since the early 1990s, to work in unsupervised medical

practice and allow patients to gain meaningful Medicare Benefits, one needed Vocational Registration. This now requires a College Fellowship and a clear maintenance process, with quite onerous documentation and proof of pudding requirements.

To practice GP Obstetrics requires a Dual-College Diploma, maintenance and recency.

Anaesthesia training remains very difficult for rural procedural GP aspirants to obtain and formal training is not well supported in a practical sense. We do however have individual specialist anaesthetists who rail at their College and Society over those august bodies' lack of real support for GP anaesthesia.

A reality is that very few specialists venture beyond the major cities and a large number of rural centres do not have a work-load that would support a specialist, who still would require recreational leave, meaningful nights off and maintenance of professional skills (MOPs).

Queensland has grasped this nettle to an extent, and other states have followed, though SA has dragged the chain, until very recently.

It is only very recently that training and recency have been tidied up somewhat in GP anaesthesia. *Our former Pt Lincoln GP Anaesthetist colleague, Richard Watts, had until recently, chaired the relevant joint college Committee.

South Australia, functioning as a city state with remote hangers-on, has developed a mature retrieval and transport system. For a multitude of reasons some of the 300,000 persons not living in Adelaide may need services that cannot be available near their homes.

Most of these people reside in towns with hospitals of some sort, admittedly with limited capabilities.

Another 120-150 persons per year require transport from their remote home, roadside, paddock or mine-site, to an appropriate care facility, using fixed wing, or if within 200km of the City, rotary-wing platforms.

Several conundra plague the nation. These are mirrored in Canada, South Africa, parts of the USA and I suspect, Russia.

What services can reasonably be deemed as essential, that is to say, "needs".

And by corollary which services are really "wants"?

If I may be allowed a conceit here, I suggest that an MRI facility in remote rural unit would be a want, but an excellent emergency medical service is a need.

This does not belittle the good-will, training or expertise of those who do provide emergency services. It does point to how it is relatively easy to provide physical facilities, (hospitals, clinics, machines), without meaningfully addressing the difficulty in attracting and retaining well trained professionals to work within those facilities.

Poor outcomes attributable to perceived deficiencies in timeliness of care, or inadequacies in training/ knowledge seem quite uncommon, but we cannot be seen to ignore the realities wilfully.

On another hand, picking "degree of crook-ness" is not always simple, nor is determining the hidden potential of the outwardly innocuous.

Many highly trained Doctors cannot detect manifestly lethal deterioration of a chronic disease. This results in the common occurrence of "changing a place of Death".

This is a critical aspect of emergency care, commonly ignored, and where management can only improve with repeated exposure to the issues and being embedded within a community.

A CULTURAL SHIFT

Over a few decades there has become a widespread belief within our communities that modern medical practice can prolong life indefinitely, against the attempts of patients' bodies to have it otherwise. Coupled with this is the belief that such expertise must always be applied in all cases. This is the "always resuscitate forever" default.

This has never been an ethical standpoint and certainly is not a legal one.

The ways that such scenarios are portrayed in the popular media do not help.

Another related problem is the application of American Medico-legal constructs to Australian situations. Television again. For example, we have here, at least in law, very different notions on the central role of patient autonomy and the limited role of relatives in decision-making.

Readers may ask why this seeming digression is relevant.

It turns on training, exposure, and being part of a community.

Doctors in this country have to work within the Law, and a number or specific Acts are relevant. I would invite readers to learn if their doctors are at all familiar with any of these.

Our over-reliance upon short-term GPs or even emergency physician locums and overseas trained doctors does little to engender robust long-term solutions. The loneliness of professional exposure to critical illness increases the likelihood of inappropriate referral or transfer. This is a national problem and is not a criticism of those who take on those roles.

For the non-medical readers, we need to be aware that some emergency conditions are very uncommon, or even rare, but our rural and remote doctors and nurses are expected to deal with them expertly.

By way of illustration, I have collected and needed to care for seven patients who contracted invasive meningococcal disease aka meningitis.

Invasive meningococcal disease affects about 25-40 persons each year, within a SA population of 1.6 million in a sub-context that that we kill 90-100 on our roads and drown about 20 other souls every year.

So, it is likely that a very large proportion of GPs will never see a case of this seriously bad disease that affects 1 in 40,000 South Australians each year.

At a community level, that is about 1 each ten years at Roxby Downs or Ceduna, one every three years in Pt Lincoln, Pt Augusta or Pt Pirie. The statistics of small numbers will clobber us regularly.

And, it is very hard to pick in the first few hours, when time counts.

We accept now that a hospital that has one or two babies delivered a year is way below a threshold (in Australia) for maintaining recency in care.

We recognise that there is no such thing as a low-risk obstetric patient.

Should this principle not be applied to other conditions?

AN ILLUSTRATIVE TALE FROM MY PORT LINCOLN DAYS.
A couple of 20y.o. students, on leave from a maritime college in Tasmania, had a disagreement of sorts with another chap, at a Football Club. Their tormentor left, only to confront them later outside the clubrooms. With a stream of profanity, the man, armed with a large knife, launched himself at them like Warner Brothers' "Tasmanian Devil".

(These lads were extremely lucky that the club was still open and that an intensive care trained nurse, Jane Mackereth, was inside picking up her husband. She ripped the long bar towel from the bar and controlled the bleeding from the throat injuries and used a Twisties packet to block the hole in the chest of one. She later received an award from the Premier of South Australia.

A couple of things follow from this that would be unlikely anywhere else than the country and are special. About 10 years later my son and I and one of these victims (a long-time friend) were driving home from fishing and Jane happened to call me. I handed the phone to the guy and the look on his face and joy in his voice was a sight to see and hear.

Fast forward to 27 March 2018, two days ago, when I parked next to the GP mentioned below who I had not spoken to for at least 10 years and mentioned this story. Her instant answer was that Jane's actions made it possible for what followed. Ed)

A very competent GP colleague, seeing the two injured when presented to the ED, quickly realized that her excellent Obstetric credentials were inadequate to the tasks at hand.

And, she only had two hands.

Both victims had deep neck wounds; one had upper

airway bleeding. The other a penetrating chest wound.

Both had other wounds of undeterminable depth or threat.

We dealt with the airway threat first, as the bubbles in the wound indicated tracheal injury, the other lad's chest wound second. The other wounds were triaged. Many hands and good processes made light work.

Within three hours of presentation, the lads were on their way to a major trauma centre.

I made the comment to the retrievalist that these events were major tests of our resources.

His comment was that a similar presentation to his major trauma centre would be a major stress to them!

Port Lincoln is a town of 13,000 with many doctors, nurses, laboratory, blood, and surgeon.

Coober Pedy, more remote, has one doctor and a nurse or two.

Ceduna not much more.

Those of us in the 12,000+ towns are spoiled!

A few weeks later, those lads bailed me up in a local eatery, well enough and pleased to return to college.

SO, WHAT IS MY THESIS?

There are several, inter-related.

Firstly, our lives rarely come to be what we might have hoped, but survivable adversity focuses learning, books ain't all and official bits of paper not necessarily protective.

From a doyen of Obstetric teaching, Alan Donald…"Life is our greatest teacher, but her dues are large"

An Emergency Colleague talks about the "carnage of

learning", meaning that we learn from stuff-ups and it is critical to have plans B and C. Get out of jail free cards as it were.

Secondly, just as the Community needs well trained and proficient doctors and nurses, it also needs education on the realities of what can, or cannot, or SHOULD NOT, be done.

We need to know what is real and is fantasy.

Thirdly, the remote and Rural Communities' Medical and Nursing professionals are mostly quite different from those who remain in Metropolitan areas. Their initial training and continuing adult learning requirements have been, until recently, poorly served. The establishment of the Australian College of Rural and Remote Medicine (ACRRM) in the late 1990s has helped to specifically address these matters.

With increasing certification requirements and increasingly onerous prescriptive training demands, it is disturbing that the "system", such as it is, is so arbitrary in its pronouncements.

The clear support of the Learned Colleges needs to be developed and take the lead shown by ACRRM in bringing erudition, clear thinking, transparency and professionalism to these vexed issues.

*FOOTNOTES

Richard Watts (mentioned above), was the first GP to address a National Specialist Anaesthetists meeting in Adelaide assisted by an electronic slide presentation.

He spoke to the topic of epidural anaesthetics for women in labour and presented some problems.

I believe that he mentioned an extremely difficult epidural where he was very much at sea but a successful delivery resulted eventually.

He then showed a picture he took of a whale with calf swimming in front of his house and bowed to the applauding audience.

It is noteworthy that Two Port Lincoln GPs moved into championing Rural Proceduralism, and remain heavily involved in undergraduate and post graduate education in these areas.

Prof David Mills is the other.

Part 6   Jobs I fancied

A WOULD-BE POLITICIAN

By Peter Morton

I had been interested in politics since my father Bo was a candidate for what is now the Liberal Party in the safe ALP seat of West Torrens in Adelaide, held by Fred Walsh in the early 1960s. I helped in his campaign.

He stood twice and lost but in the Dunstan deluge was the only LP candidate to improve his vote.

I met a lot of politicians and generally was impressed with them as people and how hard they worked.

At university about the same time I stood for and was elected to the Student Representative Council (SRC). This was near the height of the Vietnam protest and anti-conscription era. I was pro Australia being in Vietnam and conscription as seemingly most of my friends were at and outside of university.

I had been too young for National Service and too old for Conscription.

It was a waste of time being on the SRC because I was always the dissenter but I did have a lot of friends and acquaintances from school, football, medical school and university in general who agreed with me about Vietnam and conscription. Many members, of that SRC, such as David Combe, Chris Sumner and John Bannon became ALP luminaries in one sphere or another.

Medicine was too important so I lost interest but was

awoken in Woomera and Warrnambool in the beginning, middle and end of the Whitlam years. Malcolm Fraser was very visible as the local member in Warrnambool.

After a year or two in Port Lincoln I joined the local Liberal Party and had some kudos in that someone thought I was involved with Malcolm Fraser's campaign, so I was soon president of the local branch and a delegate to the State body that met in Adelaide.

After long deliberation and discussion with Leonore I decided to stand for the Federal seat of Grey that ran from the WA to NSW border and north of Port Augusta to the NT border. After Kalgoorlie it was the biggest electorate in Australia.

I had a lot of help from SA politicians Graham Gunn, Arthur Whyte, Peter Dunn and Senators Don Jessup, Robert Hill and Harold Young.

Of course, before I could stand for Grey I had to get the party's endorsement.

There were a number of branches in this huge electorate and each one had the right to appoint delegates to the Grey Electoral College that elects the candidate. It is interesting that at the time of writing the NSW Liberal Party was torn with debate about introducing that system of letting party members have a say in electing candidates.

I tackled this in two ways. One was to learn as much as I could about the economic and social drivers and concerns of the electorate and secondly to visit the local communities and to meet the delegates.

I had access to Senator Don Jessup's research assistant who provided all sorts of information, most of which made some sort of sense, but I soon gave up on education. I thought I would examine the wisdom of a flat or progressive tax rate. I must have had 10 expert opinions and they were 50:50. There were two acceptable economic models and it just depended on one's moral compass or social view as to the right one so I put that in the too hard box with education.

For months, I visited delegates from the length and breadth of the Grey electorate armed with Arthur Whyte's golden rules not to argue with farmers because they listen to parliament on the radio while driving their tractors and if in doubt talking to a farmer go right, politically speaking.

I found the delegates polite, interested and well informed but two were particularly memorable. The first was a gentleman who sat me down with a cup of tea and asked me what I thought about Aboriginal Land Rights. I remembered Arthur's second rule, went right and muttered something about too much too soon, poor management of projects etc. His comment was "I cannot agree with that. I have been involved with aboriginal people for years and they deserve much more care, land, money" and so on. He was in no way rude but firm, so I thought hmmmmmm maybe a tad left would be the way to go.

Next question was "What do you think about legalising marijuana"? This one is easy with plan 'left turn' now in place. "I think there is some merit in considering it as maybe it would break the connection between marijuana use and the more dangerous drugs that were the purvey of criminals. Perhaps the legalisation of marijuana use in some way would reduce the number of people dying from heroin"

His answer was "I cannot agree with that. All these drugs

are bad and should be banned"

Two strikes and not looking good. "Just one more question, what does your wife think of this"? Answer. "As you see, I am a family man (our little girls were with me being looked after by his daughter) and we have discussed it at length. I do not enjoy the idea of being away and it has only ever been 55% for to 45% against but my wife has agreed to support me." His answer "That is what I like to see, clear roles in the family". I was back in the game.

The other delegate was a woman aged 55 or so who ran a farm in the middle of Eyre Peninsula somewhere with the aid of a younger woman.

She was a nurse and asked why I was wasting my time doing this rubbish when I was a bloody doctor and should be doctoring.

I muttered something, enjoyed my cup of tea and disappeared.

Next step was the Electoral College at Whyalla to elect the candidate for the 1983 election. There were two other guys as candidates and a late entrant, Joy Baluch, the very colourful, unsmooth, call a spade a bloody shovel, ex ALP member and Mayor of Port Augusta.

I had spent hours on my speech and was well informed about the content but knew nothing about politics. Later someone said I was too clever or knew too much to be in politics. I do not think it was meant to be disparaging. The other guys said the right things.

Joy got to the microphone looked around and addressed the crowd.

Her comments were along the lines of 'These nice

gentlemen will not get the bloody votes. I will. They are not tough enough" I suppose she said more but that was the take home message. She was elected the candidate and got a belting in the election.

My disappointment did not even last until we were out of Whyalla. I looked at Leonore and said "I am satisfied I did my best and I am pleased I tried but gee I am glad I did not win."

THE END.

BY APPOINTMENT TO HRH PRINCE CHARLES

By Peter Morton

In 1978 I was Medical Superintendent of the Warrnambool Base Hospital in Wannon, the electorate of Malcolm Fraser, the Prime Minister of Australia at the time.

Prince Charles, who had attended Timbertop School, an annexe of Geelong Grammar, was in Australia and scheduled to visit Warrnambool and Malcolm Fraser.

I received a telephone call from someone in Canberra the morning of the Prince's visit advising that Prince Charles, who was flying himself, was expected to land at 1500 hours and they required a surgeon and physician to be standing by.

Of course, with that short notice, we did not have such august people waiting for something to happen. I mumbled something like "Ok you have got him" and wandered around to my mate, Deputy Matron Kate Taylor's office. I asked her to come with me to usher in Prince Charles and she said "OK let's go".

There are low hills near the airport and I was told there were snipers about the place. There was a staffed ambulance standing by.

While we were waiting, I adjourned to the boys' room and shared the white porcelain wall with Malcolm Fraser. I am 190cm and he dwarfed me; he had a big head, nose and even bigger ears - at which point my scrutiny ceased.

The plane duly arrived with His Highness in the left-hand seat. He opened the window and took out a little flag and put it in a holder outside the cockpit. Kate and I were quite near the plane and could see that the flag was faded and patched.

The Prince walked past within touching distance. I was utterly gob smacked when he stopped, shook hands and said "Good afternoon Dr Morton and Deputy Matron Taylor, it is good of you to come". Boy those folks do their home-work.

No, that was a figment of my imagination, but I was surprised that he was shorter that I imagined, very slim and with fine features.

Kate and I returned to the hospital and there was a bunch of people having afternoon tea including the head of the Victorian ambulance organization, whom I had met many times.

I mentioned Prince Charles' stature and I was told that he is 5'7". I asked the ambulance boss how he knew that and he said "Mate we know EVERYTHING about him".

It was an interesting day but I was upset that our future monarch did not have a smarter flag on his plane. Somehow, I found out who was the head of protocol or the relevant bureaucrat in charge of flags and sent a nice note and $10 so they could buy a new flag.

I must have forgotten to put my address on the letter or maybe they had no sense of humour but either way I received no acknowledgement. It is nice though to write *By Appt HRH* after my name but no one ever seems to notice.

Part 7 Ken Martin

KEN MARTIN - SCULPTOR

By Ken Martin and Peter Morton

INTRODUCTION
It is often the unexpected that shapes a life

I was born March 1952 in south eastern South Australia to Ailsa and Des Martin. My early childhood was spent immersed in the daily happenings on the family farm. These were the remnants of pioneering days in the upper South East with virgin scrub and indigenous wildlife in relative abundance. My first savoured memories are of the sounds of kookaburras laughing, the pet kangaroo and feeding chooks with Mum.

I was six years of age when my father lost his financial interest in the prosperous family property and what ensued was a near nomadic life, for my younger sister Jeanette and me, moving from one small rural community to another with our parents.

My father returned to his craft of blade shearing sheep. I spent many pleasant days in shearing sheds watching blade shearing of stud merino rams. I feel blessed that as a young lad from nine to twelve years old I experienced the atmosphere of a craft from another time in history.

An intelligent man, my father was also a troubled soul. Disinherited by his parents and disappointed with his lot, he embellished life with fantastic stories that became his personal reality. Nonetheless he was a wonderful storyteller with a great sense of humour. Dad had a very strong work ethic and his socialising took on a comparable vigour. One lasting impact he had on my view of the world was his empathy and respect for animals, qualities that made him a good stockman. He could read animals' behaviour and wellbeing with remarkable skill and affection.

My mother led a difficult and lonely life raising two children, often stranded on farms where my father worked, isolated with little or no money. She was a strong disciplinarian who rewarded honesty with kindness and encouraged creativity. A skilled crochet worker and accomplished pianist, her creativity was reserved for the domestic environment with the exception of occasional piano performances at school concerts.

Mum saw in me a natural aptitude for drawing and would tell stories of previous family members who could paint or draw and encouraged me to copy drawings as a means of self-education. Like many in previous generations in rural Australia, almost without exception, creative pursuits were put aside and all energy and abilities ploughed into the development of farmland and infrastructure to support it. My drawing efforts regarded only as a pastime would later prove a creative asset. The family moved to the city of Adelaide when I was 13 and Dad pursued a career as a land salesman.

At 14 years of age I left home to work on my uncle's farm and at 16 moved onto a sheep station 40 kilometres from the small town of Tintinara. It was not uncommon to work 10-hour days on the station and in the evenings with no radio or television in my hut, I would often entertain myself by drawing.

I experimented a little with oils and watercolours but it was the light and shade of pencil that held my fascination. Living on this and other properties and being close to nature I revelled in the daily challenges of working with animals. My reward was to learn a multitude of skills. One such skill I learnt from a farmer whose former vocation was as a master butcher was the precise art of butchering animals and birds. I was fascinated by the workings and beauty of anatomy. This experience unbeknownst to me at the time would prove invaluable in the years ahead.

At 19 I learnt to shear sheep and this was my primary occupation up to the age of 25. Shearing is hard physical work and when I graduated from learner shearer by shearing 100 sheep per day I had developed an appreciation of what it takes to achieve a professional level of manual dexterity. My shearing partner and I shore 45,000 sheep a year collectively, providing a respectable income and some free time for other pursuits. There are many stories to be told of characters I met and experiences I had over this decade of working life, some best reserved for dinner parties, others best told around a campfire.

The explanation of a seemingly sudden change in career choice when retiring from shearing to embark on a creative journey is best told simply. A series of events in 1975 at the age of 23 set the stage for altering the course of my life. Within a space of six months the demise of my first marriage and the failure of a small farming venture were followed by serious illness. The culmination of these events led to a nervous breakdown.

After some months and improving health I came to appreciate that while it seemed I had lost everything, the flip side to this situation was that I had nothing left to lose, leaving me free to consider what I would truly enjoy doing in life. As part of this search for answers I created my first sculptures in Mount Gambier stone and wood, crude but interesting interpretations of human form.

Simultaneously life took an exciting turn. I fell in love with Elisa Giannini who had recently returned to Australia from a four-month stay in Tuscany, her father's birthplace in Italy. Elisa was passionate in her encouragement and promptly bought me my first set of wood carving chisels. A shared enthusiasm for the creation of art and craft added fuel to the fire. Later that year Elisa and I rented a farmhouse and we established a small workshop in one room where I worked with wood as often as possible when not shearing. By early 1976 Elisa was pregnant with our first son Cain and our focus revolved around establishing a home base.

Later in 1976 lengthy philosophical discussions were entered into with two friends who harboured notions of pursuing careers in hand crafted furniture – Malcolm Averill, an aspiring wood finisher, and Bernhard Koker, who was making some furniture on his farm. They had recently begun working together and proposed that with my developing woodcarving skills we could forge a creative union that had the potential to support itself professionally. I knew both men well. I met Malcolm when he emigrated from England to his uncle's farm where I once worked and Bernie shortly after, when he emigrated from South Africa in the early 1970s, buying a farm nearby. Bernie and I had also worked on some wood projects together in 1975.

Elisa and I were enjoying our independent creative lifestyle and we now had a baby boy and stability in our lives, making any commitment to such an entrepreneurial venture very onerous. On the one hand, I could maintain a reasonably secure lifestyle as a shearer with aspirations of further developing wood sculpting skills as time permitted. Alternatively, I could pool resources with two partners in a venture that provided me with the potential to be woodcarving full time. The final decision was made with the support of our wives, in the knowledge that any such commitment, however conducive to forging an artistic career, would require enormous dedication. This is a case of saying, "Yes I can do it", then finding ways of achieving the desired result. Discussions went on into the early morning hours and revolved around ideologies of the handmade object and lifestyle with agreement reached in early 1977.

All three men and respective families committed every financial and emotional resource to moving 980kms from Naracoorte S.E. South Australia to Port Lincoln on the West Coast of South Australia for a new beginning. Arriving in a caravan of vehicles, Constantia Furniture Workshop and Gallery was established in August 1978. A fourth member of the initial team, Herman Pruis, arrived in Port Lincoln with his family a few weeks later. Herman was the eldest member of the quartet and a great mentor to all of us. He later went on to pursue a solo woodworking career in Port Lincoln.

A mixture of camaraderie and stress of having a functional facility with no work was welded by a fierce desire to succeed. We did whatever woodwork presented in order to survive financially while embarking on an intense learning curve. Each partner focused on their speciality with the highest ideals of craftsmanship in mind.

As the woodcarver my journey through the history of furniture focused on carving in the style of past English masters such as Chippendale, Hepplewhite, Sheraton and others as well as Americans such as Duncan Fife and many other global influences.

These studies took on marathon proportions frequently requiring 80-hour weeks. I'd often spend hundreds of hours executing the carving on pieces produced in collaboration with the maker and finisher. Being invited to participate in the first national craft exhibition in Sydney NSW in 1981 "Craft Expo 81" was an exciting acknowledgement of the quality of work produced at that time. A philosophy based on the premise of sound understanding of classical works being a prerequisite to developing new styles was now ready to be tested. Acknowledgement of remarkable craftsmanship was tempered by calls for original ideas.

A fascination with organic form so beautifully expressed in Art Nouveau, the fleshy acanthus leaves of Thomas Chippendale, voluptuous scallops of Philadelphian carvers and sensuous knees of Massachusetts Queen Anne cabriole legs, armed me with technical skills to express impressions of indigenous Australian bush within the confines of furniture ergonomics. Drawing inspiration from eucalypt bark and eucalypt leaf forms, organic form was carved into pieces of furniture whose proportions were also drawn from the Australian bush. Applying those observations to furniture through proportions and form was in my view a most significant breakthrough for the original partnership.

Grinling Gibbons the great sixteenth century woodcarver was inspiring in his ability to capture the softness in bird feathers, a fold in paper or lace on cloth. Sculpturally these insights were invaluable. At this point in time these and other sculptural observations were achieved through literature and photographs; it was not until 1992 that I saw first-hand any volume of European sculpture by past masters. I was pleasantly surprised on viewing Grinling Gibbons' work in the UK by how well the photographs I had pored over conveyed the essence of his work.

My first commissioned sculpture in 1979 was a Huon pine female figure standing 900mm high. There were numerous humans, birds, animals and sea creatures sculpted in the duration of the partnership, some adorning furniture, others as free-standing sculptural compositions.

The intensity of creativity during the period 1978 to 1987 was remarkable but not without a price. With the encouragement of the Australian Craft Council and Australian Design Council we participated in national exhibitions and enjoyed substantial media support. There are often many sides to one story and it would suffice to say that this remarkable creative journey had run its course. The partnership disbanded in late 1986 with Malcolm Averill and I pursuing new directions and Bernhard Koker taking over as sole proprietor of Constantia Designer Craftsmen.

Malcolm and I spent the first five months of 1987 in Melbourne installing architectural wood panels and cornices in a corporate office building. This paid the bills and afforded time to contemplate our futures. Malcolm remained in

Melbourne and I returned to Port Lincoln determined to continue with my love of sculpture in the medium of wood. Establishing a small home studio in Port Lincoln in May 1987, I had 150 woodcarving chisels, a vice, clamps, bench, electric engraving tool and a small quantity of wood. I look back on this time now and think Elisa must be the bravest person I know, supporting my decision, particularly given the financial hardship of that time. I was under no illusion and knew this was going to be a challenging road ahead. Technical skills in woodcarving and wood sculpture gained in the previous nine years and substantial knowledge of exotic woods armed me with the confidence to press on.

My wife Leonore and I have known Ken and Elisa since 1980 when our paths crossed in Port Lincoln. We had little furniture and some savings and the Constantia Designer Craftsmen made furniture so it was a good arrangement. We were fortunate to be in the right place at the right time.

We knew the other partners of course but Ken was the person who we dealt with. I am sitting in a dining chair and writing on a table they made for us in 1982. I was reminded of this when I read about the search for things in nature that were unique to Australia. Our chairs have gum leaves of a type that is native to Port Lincoln carved into them. Maybe they were the first Ken did.

We had many discussions about his work in theory and very much about practice and the business in those days.

In first year medicine my group was the last to take a subject called "Medicine and the Humanities" and included the Renaissance. In 1974 we visited Florence in Italy so I had a smidgeon of knowledge about different columns, proportions and the golden mean so I really hung on Ken's words.

When they made our dining room suite the carver was designed for me ten years later and the back is an open frame with two vertical supports made in the shape of Ghost gums.

Ken mentions tradition and technology. The shape of the backs of our chairs is modelled on astronauts' seats. They were designed using data from prisoners in the USA who allowed their intra spinal pressure to be measured in different positions-read needles in the spinal column. I hope they got some time off.

The three Constantia blokes and two wives shared with us the first meal served on this table and I think that we were still talking at 0200 so the chairs were very comfortable indeed. *Please note it was 0400 from Leonore the proof reader AND Ken!*

As Ken said in the introduction to his book, the partnership broke up but Ken has gone from strength to strength supported all the way by Elisa. She has modelled for him, learnt how to finish and polish wood and goodness knows what else.

We saw a lot of Ken and Elisa in the 1980s but much less in recent times but, whenever we do meet, we seem to take up where we left off. At our last meeting we planned to have dinner together on March 3 2018 at that very same dining room table but that did not happen due to a lack of, or poor, communication between two certain male people!

I saw the word "ursine" somewhere and had no idea what it meant other than it might be related to canine, bovine and so on and indeed it is. It means "bear like" and it suits Ken. He is big, kind, patient, listens intently, very courteous and has amassed a vast store of knowledge in his life and career but is a modest man. He actually likes the description as "it could be a lot worse."

He is famous in Australia and internationally recognised. He has travelled widely in Australia getting inspiration and works from the unique characteristics of our fauna and flora. He also camps in the desert to gain an empathy with the land, sky and aboriginal people.

Not surprisingly Ken has visited Rome and his descriptions of the effects on him by Leonardo Da Vinci's "St Jerome" and the works of others is exciting to read. He writes at the end of one museum visit. *"Leaving the Vatican Museum through the Sistine Chapel at day's end I felt transported to another plane. Not only had I experienced a dream of seeing work by Michelangelo, I experienced a sculpture which had inspired him"*

In his book he describes 100 pieces of his work. There are animals, fish, real people (some I know), nudes, birds, draft horses and organic forms in wood and bronze and of course the "big ones".

The works he is best known for publicly are the bronze statues of the triple Melbourne Cup winner Makybe Diva, the cricketers Darren Lehman and Jason Gillespie, footballer Barrie Robran and recently Ken Farmer, who played for North Adelaide and kicked 100 goals a year from 1930 to 1940, 62 goals in 1929 and 86 in 1941. I met him once and remember his big strong hands.

Ken is extremely articulate in describing his work. I

opened his book at the chapter headed "ORGANIC FORM AND SYMBIOSIS" and some lines "jumped" off the page. *'Initially, I found this work akin to a dream where you find yourself standing naked in a public place. An overwhelming passion for expressing humanity's intrinsic connection with nature and the excitement of entering a new personal creative frontier conquered any fears of laying bare my inner thoughts."*

I find the above most enlightening and it seems to me that a person has to think in that way to visualise what the final result will be.

I discussed this and the question of people's perception of his work with him in relation to a piece "*A Desire For Personal Space*" and he replied, "*That it related to oceanic form and social interaction*" and he added. "*I find it important to be able to articulate the concept in my mind during the creative process.*

This work is about a sea lion trying to escape from his school and I can now see it to the extent that I asked Ken if it could be Jonathon Livingstone Sea Lion and to my great pleasure he said, "It could well be".

I have seen many of his organic form sculptures in real life and of course all of them in his book. Recently I saw one and said it reminded me of a human vulva or maybe labia. Ken laughed and reminded me that is what I always said about those pieces.

I was going to exclude that comment but it really is what he portrays in those pieces. Life, lips, swelling, openings, gaps, secretions, pods swelling, emission of seeds, structures entwining each other and so on. Ken uses words such as abundance, nurturing, life force, responsibility, hinges, open doors and so on describing these pieces.

He also has a series of female pieces that ran the full gamut from virginal innocence, to budding and then rampant sexuality. The bodies are superb, wonderfully done images of people with beautiful, slim, muscular bodies. Breasts are beautifully done and genitalia skilfully blurred. Clothed models also reveal musculature, beauty and sexuality.

Ken has also done a well- muscled, naked, seated man with only curling pubic hair visible in the genital area.

Female parts of humans, animals, plants and even likenesses in nature's stones and wood are used to celebrate birth, creation, the human spirit and fertility but what about the male contributor to fertility, reproduction and life.

A penis, erect for a small time, squirting seeds. Maybe it is just a tool to serve the procreative needs of females and named well by small boys of my generation. An interesting thought on St Valentine's Day 2018

Ken used to tell me that sculpture was fairly easy and that you just need to cut away the bits that didn't belong. I always thought he was being flippant but maybe that is the secret.

It just takes a master thinker to clearly articulate the bits that do not belong and to have the skill with chisels to ensure that the right bits are removed. It is important to be strong, agile and coordinated to be a sculptor and I was most interested that Ken attributes his years of shearing to his professional level of manual dexterity. So there you have it.

Ken has met and worked with many celebrities in the world of art, politics, racing, fishing, business and goodness knows how many fields but as Kipling wrote is his poem "If". Ken has "Walked with Kings but never lost the common touch".

Ken is quite a man and has been immensely fortunate to find his life's partner Elisa and I have been immensely fortunate to count him as a friend and to be allowed to use his words in my book.

Part 8   Crazy things we have done

JERKER AND THE DOCTOR MAN

By Jerker and the Doctor man

JERKER'S STORY
I was born, raised and educated in Gawler and joined the Savings Bank of South Australia (SBSA) when I was 18 after leaving school.

In 1982 I was transferred to the Port Lincoln branch of the bank at my request so I could play football with the Marble Range team

I enjoyed living in Port Lincoln and it soon got even better. In September Marble Range won the premiership, the only A grade premiership I ever played in, and the night of the grand final celebration I met Leanne Dennis the sister of Rosie Dennis a Marble Range Stalwart.

Leanne and I became very close and were married in 1984 when I still worked at the bank and Leanne at Demasius, a local department store.

We loved the lifestyle and the people in Port Lincoln. It was a friendly place with a pleasant climate that was great for the outside activities we enjoyed such as fishing, boating and water skiing.

But this dream was threatened when the State Bank of SA asked me to return to Adelaide after it had been formed from a merger of the State Bank and the SBSA.

My luck was still heading in the right direction as the local hospital had a position available for a finance manager. I was the successful applicant and worked there from 1985 -1988. This proved to be a pivotal time for us and had a major effect on our lives.

It was a very different job to the bank

There were many more staff than I had worked with before and more diverse positions, roles, professions and ages.

The doctor I had most to do with was Peter Morton a local general practitioner, who was the part time Medical Superintendent at the hospital. He had specialist qualifications in both fields and was influential in my appointment.

We worked well together and had common interests in football and outdoor activities and with our wives became good friends.

After I had been at the hospital for a year or so we decided that the hospital needed a social gathering place so we tidied up and old on-site Nissan hut and made it into a recreation room.

With the help and gifts of equipment from our surgeon the late Ian Fletcher, GP Steve Ballard, Jenny McAuliffe, Ian Matthews the CEO who I admired greatly, Peter, me and many others, we managed to turn it into a nice place.

Brett Ralph, an orderly, drew a wonderful mural with caricatures of staff and with some slate that Steve Ballard donated it really set off the place.

We were able to cook, make tea and coffee, keep drinks cold and play music all with donated equipment.

We often met Friday night for drinks. Although it was accepted that Friday nights at the pub were a good thing for work mates but when they involve the opposite sex the "other halves" may get upset. Our little hut dealt with that. A chat, a drink and a snack and then home worked well.

One day Peter was talking about some "chopper drivers" he had met at a pub. He told me he knew that they were helicopter pilots because they had knives strapped to their lower legs or stuck in their flying boots.

The world of people who flew aeroplanes or helicopters and doctors who had worked around Broome and Port Hedland was not big. Peter had been in that world and met someone at the pub whose cousin knew the brother-in-law of the wife of one of these blokes that Peter knew - or something.

That was good enough for these new best friends to drink up and make plans for Peter to get a seat on a trip out to an oil drilling rig south of Port Lincoln on a day to be arranged.

I was green with envy. My brother was in the Army and whilst on officer exchange with the US army he flew in helicopters and I have always wanted to do that. Perhaps I grizzled in the right tone of voice and Peter said that he would fix it for me to go with him and he did.

There was however one huge slip between cup and lip as they say. We were allocated a routine flight one Saturday morning at 0700. As most people would know Saturday morning follows Friday night and THAT Friday night was the greatest blast ever in the Nissan Hut. Peter and I got home very late indeed but the good troopers that we were got to the airport at the right time.

It was a full flight and we had a roll call and when Dr Jenke was called. I stood with my mouth open trying to say BBBBUUUUT when I copped an elbow in the ribs from Peter.

I think I said "Yerrrkkk" and got a tick and was zipped into a space suit. I got my nickname from when Peter called me "Yerrrkkka" after that incident and from then on and soon turned into "Jerker"

Off we went and it was a great flight over land and sea. Fortunately, Peter had told me that after lift-off when the helicopter moves forward it appears to be flying into the ground for a second or two so that saved me some heartburn or worse under the circumstances.

We landed on the rig and a medic ran in under the main rotor and we were let off first that I thought was pretty cool but the medic told us that a crewman had fallen downstairs and hurt his back.

I thought Peter said "duck" which was very nice of him to think of my safety with this fan whirring around.

We went to the sick berth and there was this guy looking and sounding very anxious and in pain. Peter checked him quickly but thoroughly and told the Sick Berth Attendant (SBA) to give him some Pethidine which he did and then Peter said "Stay there Greg the SBA has to get on the chopper but his replacement will be here soon" and off he went.

That was OK as far as it went but the guy was still very anxious and vomited, fortunately into the bowl I was holding and after that he really panicked and pleaded with me for answers. "What is the matter with me doc, what is wrong?" I probably should not have said "How the f---- do I know I am not a f---ing doctor". At that he fainted but only for a little while.

I waited until the new SBA arrived and found Peter having breakfast with the Captain who was telling him about his house and boat in Florida from where he commuted every four weeks.

Peter was oblivious to the terrible experience he had put me through-perhaps.

I like to think I am a kind and forgiving person and about 18 months after that incident I let Peter buy me a beer. One thing led to another and I told him about a night I was showing Rod Marsh and Dennis Lillee around Adelaide after a function at my football club. It was late and the three of us were outstaying our welcome at a night club.

The barman said "Dennis, you and Rod are OK but this other bloke must leave". One of my new friends said "No mate he can't go. He is Ken Hunter, number nine for Carlton" (only a middle level player but I looked a bit like him). "OK welcome Ken sorry mate I recognise you now".

Fast forward to 1988 when Peter and I met in Melbourne. He and his mate Dave Simpson used to go to the Melbourne Grand Final. They were able to get tickets, from the Sturt Football Club where Peter's Dad was a leading light that admitted them to the Carlton pre and post- game drinks and a bus to and from the grand final and special seats. They would then play at the Victoria Golf Club for a week and then go to the Adelaide Grand Final.

Peter visited my brother's place and asked me would I like to go to Football Park for the Adelaide Grand final if he could get me a ticket. I said yes and as he was going to Adelaide on Friday night. he would meet me at the Adelaide Airport on Saturday, the day of the Grand Final and duly did.

He told me that it was hard for even his dad to get a ticked but the Sturt Secretary Ross Tuohy had managed and we picked it up on the way to Football Park.

The Carlton team, who I barracked for, were guests at the Grand Final. As we were walking in Peter with impeccable timing told me the ticket I had was from a Carlton player who was unwell. We were climbing the stairs and he said "You will have to sit with the Carlton team" which sounded like fun but I was a bit anxious and then Peter with a real poker face said "Relax Jerker I told them that you are Ken Hunter". I thought my life was over, the decision to laugh or cry was beyond me and I think I said "They would know I wasn't etc" Then the bloody masterstroke Peter reached towards his bag and said "It'll be OK. I have a number nine Carlton Jumper, put that on and you will be fine"

We were just a few metres from entering the area where I was supposed to go and I was like jelly. Peter grabbed my arm and dragged me along the concourse and went into the box that his father shared with some other Sturt people.

I was made very welcome and had a great day. I never did find out whether he really did have a Carlton jumper in his bag.

Last but not least Peter and Leonore invited Leanne and me to stay at Coffin Bay one Saturday night. After a very pleasant meal we started talking about the world and our various futures.

Peter asked me what my plans were and commented that Port Lincoln was a great place but there was a limited career progression for me at the hospital because Ian Matthews the CEO would be there for years, as indeed he was.

He also suggested that I needed some sort of hospital management qualification as that was becoming the way of the world and time was moving. Peter had recently finished a Bachelor of Health Administration degree and I think he just wanted me to suffer as well. We had a long discussion about this course of action when around midnight there was crash and we rushed outside to see that a car had run of the road and partly into his front yard.

We both knew the couple and goodness gracious me they must have left her husband and his wife somewhere else.

Peter found a rope and asked me to bring my shiny new Nissan Patrol out onto the road and back up to the car. He tied the rope to the two cars and went up the road because it was a sharp bend with a light to warn others. Anyway, I pulled the car to safety and it was left over night. I was a bit annoyed that he made me use my car when he had a perfectly good old Land Rover that was made for that stuff. I was even more annoyed next morning when old mate appeared with a thank you carton and gave it to Peter who graciously accepted it.

Back to what led to a life changing decision. I must have been looking for the justification to do something and Peter pushed all the right buttons and my career would not have happened the way it did without Peter's encouragement—maybe later but who knows. Thanks mate.

Almost immediately I applied for and was successful in getting the position of Chief Executive Officer of the Clare and Blyth District Hospitals and we moved to Clare and lived there from 1988-1992.

I had a funny feeling when all this happened in that it reminded me of some words in a play we did at school written by Shakespeare.

"There is a tide in the affairs of men

Which taken at the flood leads on to fortune".

I forget the rest but it was an omen and I never forgot it.

Clare was a lovely place to live although a bit too cold in the winter. We met a lot of fellow wine lovers and I played golf with gusto if not skill and enjoyed my work but the real highlight was the birth of our son Sam in 1989.

I had taken Peter's advice and enrolled in a Bachelor of Health Science Degree at Charles Sturt University in Bathurst while still in Port Lincoln and I continued in Clare.

While in Clare I had the most amazing opportunity when I was awarded a study scholarship by Rotary International. This meant that two doctors and I visited hospitals in five East African countries and doctors from those countries would do the same in Australia.

The trip had a profound and lifelong impact on me and soon after the trip in 1992 we moved to Mildura to manage a private hospital and were there for three years. Our second son Bryn was born in Mildura in 1992.

In 1995 I joined Ramsay Health Care and moved to manage the Coffs Harbour hospital with long stints in Tamworth and Port Macquarie.

I had completed my degree in 1994 and started a Master of Business Administration in 1995 through Deakin University and finished while in Coffs Harbour in 1999.

We lived at Coffs Harbour for 13 years. I loved my job and I liked to think I did it well and never got sick of the complex tasks of people and financial management particular when they the two things can be on a collision course.

Last but certainly not least I was transferred as Chief Executive Officer (CEO) to a new hospital, John Flynn Private

Hospital, a large private tertiary hospital just over in Tweed Heads in 2009 and anticipate spending the rest of my career here.

Life is still good. Leanne pursues a successful real estate career she commenced in Coffs Harbour, Sam is a financial accountant in Melbourne, and Bryn pursues his dream of one day singing in a Broadway musical. He is currently singing on a ship somewhere in the Mediterranean.

I am nearing the end of my career having managed my current hospital for nine years and taken it through a major growth phase.

My career could have been so very different had it not been for Peter and that one night in Coffin Bay.

THE DOCTOR MAN'S STORY

I liked Greg when I first met him. He was straight forward and pleasant to everyone he met and I don't think I ever saw him lose his temper. We had a common interest in football but the fact that neither of us achieved what we might have done was perhaps an unspoken thing we shared. The shenanigans described by Greg are true and we did become good friends.

I graduated in 1968 with the degrees of Bachelor of Medicine, Bachelor of Surgery. By the mid- 1970s it was obvious that further qualifications would be needed and eventually I became a Fellow of the Royal Australian Colleges of Medical Administrators and of General Practitioners with the degree in Health Administration that Greg mentioned.

In parallel with these changes in medicine, physiotherapists, nurses and others now did degrees rather than diploma courses and Hospital Administrators were also in the act and needed degrees.

I really did see something in Greg and although he could have lived the life of La Dolce Vita in Port Lincoln, if he did not get some serious qualifications that was where he would stay. And bugger it I had done one of those degrees part time, so why shouldn't he?

The rest as they say is history.

He is a senior manager in a big private hospital and that is not easy. Managing doctors is said to be like herding cats and there is a lot of truth in that saying.

We had the pleasure of visiting Greg and Leanne in 2007 when they lived in Coffs Harbour. Greg had organised a thank you cruise for some of the doctors who worked at the hospital which I joined and watched their interaction. They seemed to have respect for each other and also friendship and trust. I don't think that can be acted.

The other attribute Greg has is physical courage like most guys who are "Kinda broad in the shoulders and narrow in the hip". That actually came from a song we wrote in Port Lincoln for a review called "Big Jerker" but it didn't go anywhere.

He played football, surfed, swam and tried a lot of other sports and recently rode a bike with "Limpet" Leanne hanging on from Cape Town to Victoria Falls.

We have obviously communicated about this story and at the time of writing he told me 'I am 63 but feel like I am 50" and that is as much a mental as a physical thing.

The words Greg wrote about that night in Coffin Bay have meant an enormous amount to me.

Last but not least Greg quoted some words of Brutus in the

play Julius Caesar by Shakespeare about how he approached life from Port Lincoln on and what prophetic words they were

The following lines if the tide is not taken are:

"Omitted, all the voyage of their life

Is bound in shallows and in miseries"

You know I don't think Greg forgot that line. I doubt he ever read it he just acted on the first two. That was and still is the measure of his life.

THE SAGA OF THE STAINS AND US

By Phillip and Chris Stain, and
Leonore and Peter Morton

I met my wife Leonore in May 1968 at the National Medical Students Convention 'meet and greet' evening held at Norwood Football Club in Adelaide just down the road from my old school. We were final year medical and nursing students respectively. We had a great time that night and, during the rest of the week, we really clicked and were married in June 1969, but I get ahead of myself.

Leonore was studying and working at Calvary Hospital and living in part of a faded mansion in North Adelaide with a Christine Cooper, who belonged to the family that made the famous Adelaide beer.

I collected pine cones, did the dishes, gave Leonore tutorials and even brought some fire wood back from a trip to the south east, all to ingratiate myself into their world.

Unfortunately, the Cooper challenge failed, as Chris was a cousin too far from the centre of gravity of the operation for free samples and had to purchase her beer, of which she was quite fond, from a pub.

Leonore and Chris were great mates who had travelled on the same school bus to their Catholic and Church of England schools, Cabra and Woodlands respectively, in Adelaide.

At that time there was still a lot of friction, rivalry and prejudice between Catholics and Protestants. It was waning but we were all discouraged from marrying outside our religions.

Chris was from the country and a great deal more worldly wise than Leonore and organised two extensive bus camping trips for them in the remote parts of Australia. Leonore's mother was born in the kitchen of a cattle station and Chris had a big influence on fostering Leonore's inborn love of the Australian bush.

It took little time for Leonore and me to realise that something very special was happening between us. About six months after we met, I graduated and decided to continue with my plans to work in Broken Hill in 1969.

The feeling that perhaps things were moving too fast between us had influenced my move to Broken Hill and also Leonore decided to go to Perth and do a course in intensive care nursing. This was a great idea, as Chris Cooper had preceded her to the Royal Perth Hospital to study operating theatre nursing.

Leonore's course, however, was interrupted. On the night of my graduation ceremony in February, Mum and Dad took me out to dinner and after seven martinis I rang Leonore in Perth from a restaurant reservation desk and proposed to her. We were married four months later in June 1969.

What happened, you might ask, to Chris? She finished her course and went to England to further her theatre nursing career. She married in the early 1970s and returned to Australia in 1975 and soon after visited Warrnambool, where I was Medical Superintendent of the local hospital.

It was a short but memorable visit. Chris accepted an invitation to be in charge of the operating theatres and the three of us were laughing and joking while getting tea.

Then high drama; Chris threw a slice of raw bean in the air

and caught it in her mouth and choked. I grabbed her and put my finger down her throat as she instantly collapsed, biting me half way between my knuckles and wrist.

Maybe I panicked, maybe I thought Heimlich manoeuvre, but I grabbed her from behind with my hands locked just below her sternum and lifted her. To my great joy the bean popped out and she was fine. I doubt it took more than five seconds.

Chris, her husband and baby James moved to Warrnambool and stayed there for about three years. We had a few adventures in the Grampians and other places but sadly her husband was a lesser man than she deserved and they split up. She returned to Adelaide where her life took a turn very much for the best.

Through the JAYCEES she met Phillip Stain, also on the wrong side of a divorce, and they hit it off because of their shared interests in footy, fornication and fine beer. Chris had to convince Phil that he liked fishing and camping but this was not hard as there were concomitant attractions.

Phil soon realised that I was the bloke he went to school with and, like himself, had been successful in football and athletics. I was in an older age group than Phil but I remember him running like the wind with his fair hair flying. He was the premier sprinter of his generation at our school and even perhaps Adelaide. We respected each other a lot so it really was fertile ground for a great friendship.

About a year later they both visited us at Coffin Bay and Phil describes that visit in another tale "Snakes." It was the first of many bizarre, weird and funny things that happened to us in almost 40 years of an exciting friendship.

Phil was very much a city boy and Chris a country girl. With endless patience Chris and, to a lesser extent me, managed to introduce Phillip to the things we loved and he certainly was a good student -sometimes.

He was and is bloody frustrating. He would eat whiting but nothing else in the seafood line as it was too "fishy".

He loved red wine but had appalling taste. I remember a conversation at Coffin Bay when he told Christine that "I have some nice wine Love" and Chris replied "It's like bloody mouthwash Phil". I am not a mean person but confess I have used the odd bit of sleight of hand to give him different wine to other guests.

I could go on and on but Phillip and Chris are two of the bravest, most generous, loyal and kind people I have ever met. They both have had huge battles with their health, Phillip with his knee that he injured playing football when he was 17 that was very deformed and quite stiff. He has played tennis all his life and still does. Modern surgery in recent times has restored a lot of function and reduced the deformity so now he looks much more like the athlete he was instead of a bandied legged cowboy.

Chris has very significant multiple medical problems that started at or perhaps before they were married but she worked until retiring age and has enjoyed camping, caravanning, golf that she started late in life, fishing anywhere anytime, boating particularly in houseboats, volunteer work and keeping up with her legion of friends and son James.

She has been a great support to James and has stuck with

him through thick and thin. They have done a lot of fishing together. He is a typical Cooper male, big and strong and definitely a mite handier in a boat than Phil.

She is a very special and brave person and the things she has done physically are beyond belief.

There is no doubt that living in the country can be out of sight out of mind to city friends and relatives who typically say, "Don't forget you are always welcome to stay with us when you visit Adelaide" and yet an invitation to Port Lincoln is too far, interferes with golf, kids sport etc. Sometimes I think that there is an ill-defined law of physics to explain why Adelaide is 635 km from Port Lincoln and yet Port Lincoln is 4357 km from Adelaide.

Chris and Phillip have always been there for us on birthdays, weddings, fishing trips, olive picking, camping trips and so on, whether in Port Lincoln or further afield.

They have visited us everywhere we have been in the past 16 years on our various excursions away from Port Lincoln, except maybe Portland. They have been to all the important celebrations of our family and we are always welcome at their home.

When we lived in Gladstone in Queensland Phillip drove to Port Lincoln, picked up our boat and towed it back to Adelaide and then to Gladstone-that is friendship.

That is enough Mr Nice Guy. I have some notes in front of me from Phillip about things we have done and I quote:

Camping experiences
We purchased a small portable toilet, effectively a folding seat, for our second camping trip.

I was keen to try it in the MacDonnell ranges near Alice Springs and being a private person placed it some distance from the camp during the day. After two hours at night the urge came upon me so I headed for the toilet with a feeling of pleasant expectation but I took an hour to find it -and just in time. It was a great feeling of peace and relief on a beautiful starlit night.

My solitude was shattered by a herd of camels galloping past on all sides that frightened the devil out of me.

I jumped up and pulled up my trousers, delayed as usual by my bad knee, and tripped over and fell in front of a camel that fortunately hurdled me.

The second incident was 10 years later and relates to the same toilet. Chris had warned me that it had a crack in the seat but I ignored that negative attitude of hers that she shows at times. Once more in remote country near Innamincka in South Australia, with Chris, Peter and Leonore, I was in trouble. No bowel action for two days, which was a major catastrophe for me.

Again at night, the build-up reached a crisis point so I disappeared into the night to our toilet. The sad part to this tale is that having finished my business the toilet instantly reached its use by date and collapsed, as did I, into what I believe is called a large lump of ordure. Peter jumped at the opportunity to try his new camp shower and hosed me down. Chris reminded me of course that she had told me many times I should replace the toilet seat.

This story of ordure reminds me of the time I was babysitting James when he was about three or four and he had diarrhoea that overflowed his double nappies. I tried tucking the cot sheet in but he still cried. Just kidding, I was courage incarnate and did what a man had to do.

I was not good at this and had only changed one dirty nappy before but this demanded action. I woke my daughter Kirstin, who was long out of nappies and didn't know where they were so I undressed James, chucked him in the bath and double folded the cot sheet and used it as a nappy- job done.

Fast forward 10 years to the Port Lincoln prison, where I worked part time and had to do a medical examination on a new prisoner who was the son of good friends of ours. He was in prison because he drove a car while his licence was suspended. His girlfriend had gone to the pub and left her baby with him and he had run out of nappies so drove down the street to get some and was picked up by the police.

I was almost hopping mad and dressed him down in no uncertain manner. He said "What do you think I should have done, used the cot sheet as a nappy". Then I did become literally hopping mad. I yelled something like "Yes that's exactly what you should have done". He did look at me in a very strange way! I must send a copy of this to his parents as I doubt that they know what experience foreshadowed my comments.

Phillip is quite illogical at times, driving me mad repeating his personal political mantra, the same bloody stories about tennis and his knee, and showing everyone his hernia (the whole bloody lot I might add, from knee to navel) and for such a polite man his rudeness prying into the affairs ("but I am interested mate") of others.

Chris and I have told and told him that it is impolite to ask farmers how many acres, cows or sheep that they have because it is like asking someone how much they earn.

I did teach him a lesson of sorts at Tennant Creek when he visited us in 2012 when I was working there. I briefed a lovely young English female Social Worker I worked with about Phil. I introduced them and Phil started asking what she did. She let it be drawn out that the she ran an escort agency. Naturally Phil kept on prying and going on and on and eventually she said that she also acted as a prostitute if the occasion warranted. He was gobsmacked and went very quiet.

Phil writes in the notes he gave me for this yarn. *"I could not believe that Gillian was a prostitute and when Peter told me the truth, I was pleased but I did not really understand his motivation because I was just interested, that is why I ask questions. I was with my mate BJ and we enjoyed the run up to Tennant Creek to see Peter and Leonore in my Maxima that really performs well at high speed on the Northern Territory roads.*

Telling this story reminds me that the next day BJ, Peter, Leonore and I drove to a high spot and who should turn up but Gillian and a girlfriend on their push bikes. The occasion was an electrical storm that was setting the grasslands on fire a most spectacular scene that is engraved in my mind. Poor BJ doesn't remember it he was so infatuated with Gillian. I was very polite but reserved as Peter had not told me the truth at the time and her pretty and buxom friend did have a strategic button of her white shirt undone."

In 1988 we went to "Opera in the Outback" with Phillip and Chris and I ran into the late John Bannon who was Premier of

South Australia at the time. John was wearing a brand-new head to foot RM Williams outfit his wife, Judge Robyn Layton, had bought him for the occasion. I was rather pleased that he thought enough of me to ask how he looked in this unfamiliar clothing. I told him that he looked the part.

I gestured to Phillip to come and meet him and he turned his back and walked away.

I later asked him why and he said something like, "You think I am a gentle person but I am not and I hate to think what I might do to a Labor man like him. Rather a strange comment about a fellow traveller who hates multinationals, state governments, foreign ownership, banks etc and is indeed a very gentle person.

Phillip must have forgotten his next exploit that would have been a great sequel to the broken chair and ordure story. Sort of dog bites man and then man bites dog to follow. We were billeted with residents of Leigh Creek for the show and the first night when we returned to our or billet a caged Tom cat piddled on Phillip as he walked past the cage - and boy that stank.

The next night after the magnificent "Opera in the Outback" Phillip prepared a product for the passage past the piddling pussy. He had kept the fluid from the beer in his own intra pelvic fluid storage container. He casually crept to the cat's cage and discharged the fluid through a handy tool he had brought with him and directed an s shaped stream back and forth over the cat until the dispenser was empty. This was accompanied by maniacal laughter.

The cat did not enjoy this and failed to pat away Pip's piddle with his paws.

Oh, and there was the time Chris bogged the Navara in the Gawler Ranges and Phil finally realised how much better a 4WD drive was in the bush than a 2WD. Phil was seriously annoyed about this as he did not like guns and Chris had taken James and his girlfriend shooting and had been away several hours. *"With my dear friend Peter, a superb bushman, tracker and navigator, we went looking and eventually found them walking along a track a long way from home. My relief took over from my barely suppressed anger which quickly returned when I saw my beautiful maroon and silver Navarra dual cab ute bogged up to the doors 100m or so off the road. Chris told Peter to follow a particular route but he didn't and got his Nissan Patrol bogged. Two hours later with James and Chris doing a sterling job the Nissan Patrol was out of the bog and I must admit pulled the Navarra out like a cork from a bottle. In due course we bought 4WD instead of two- wheel drive dual cabs."* I let Phillip get away with the outrageous exaggeration that I did not follow Chris's directions on the condition he put the nice bits in the first sentence. It was a smoke screen to hide the fact that I actually forgot to engage 4WD. This sin, particularly in public, can result in wayward drivers having their RM Williams boots and Akubra hats confiscated for six months.

Filthy dirty we headed for our accommodation where another couple were staying as well. After showers and a beer or two we sorted, cleaned and removed the stones of native peaches known as quandongs and put them on the wood stove to slowly cook. Next morning ever alert Leonore yelled out "Chris have you taken the quandongs off from last night?" to be greeted with sniggers from the other guests. Might need to read that out aloud.

Then there was the time Phil opened a gate for a car and shut the gate with himself on the other side. I have done that and was silly enough to climb over the gate instead of opening it.

Phil's also described another typical bizarre thing.

"One day I went into a drive-in bottle shop near home, bought some wine and joined friends I had seen walk into the bar for a couple of beers. An hour or so later my attention was drawn to a message on the loudspeaker. I had ignored it mainly because I had left my hearing aids in a restaurant a week before. I got a hell of a fright when it was repeated. "Would the person who left a Navarra dual cab ute number xxxxx in the bottle shop driveway please remove it as it is blocking the driveway, the engine is running and the exhaust is not helping one of our staff who gets asthma and we do not want the car to be stolen"

I must admit I added that last bit about asthma for balance. There was no one who suffered from asthma that I knew about. When we discussed this yarn only yesterday he said that when he went to the car someone was leaning against the counter blowing a whistle and he didn't hear because he had lost his hearing aids.

I just thought of this while writing. I reckon that was my subconscious acting. Exhaust fumes, bad for chests, silent whistle, maybe an inhaler for asthma. Hell's bells maybe it was an example of "Many true words are spoken in jest."Mmmmm-I wonder.

They both have had difficulty in their immediate families

that perhaps should not be mentioned in detail but Chris was treated extremely shabbily by her sister but kept smiling and doing her best to enjoy life.

She has also been unfailingly kind and caring for her own relatives and friends and this continues.

Phillip separation from his children and grandchildren for so long must have been hard to bear but that has been sorted out now and he is a doting grandfather. When I see them and their mother, I can see Phillip at the same age running like the wind. His son Tim is now a Captain working for Cathay Pacific airlines and lives in Canada. They have an excellent relationship and the difficulties of distance are smoothed out somewhat by Phil being able to get el cheapo tickets at pilots' rates.

His love and care for his late father, Jack, who I knew well, as did my mother, can only be admired as can Christine's devotion to Jack and Phillip's children and grandchildren. A special mention to Phil for what he has done for James and Chris.

I have been privileged to know Phil and Chris in good and bad times. They are generous, kind, loving and courageous people and they cope with whatever life tosses at them. They truly meet the ideal criteria for a long, happy marriage that I read more than 50 years ago. He is her father, lover, brother and friend but I have never have seen or heard the female equivalent. Surely it can only be mother, lover, sister and friend.

This yarn was meant to be fun, to tease Phil and me and to be a record of some of the things we have done together over the last 40 years.

There have been some very sad and tough times in those years for all of us.

We have all done what we could for each other in the past and will do in the future in the dark times that are inevitably ahead. I expect all of us will "Rage against the dying of the light and not go quietly into the endless night" that Dylan Thomas pleaded with his dying father to do.

There is how ever one thing that does worry me about the likelihood of this saga continuing and I explain as follows.

Chris you are the bravest and toughest person I have known and a true friend to Leonore – I thank and salute you.

Phillip you have met the criteria of a great husband from where I sit mate and you are a wonderful friend to me.

BUT

We got a double swag – you got a double swag.

You got a dual cab – we got a dual cab

You got a Heaslip camper – we got a Heaslip camper

You got a caravan – so looks like it is all over because I don't want a BLOODY caravan.

God be with you both and us. I bet there will be a future that we can share for a while longer.

Peter and Leonore Feb 2018

Part 9 Outback stories

RMW – THE SALE OF HIS FIRST BOOTS

By Peter Morton

Reginald Murray Williams, known to millions of Australians for the pack saddles and boots that he introduced in the 1930s, the work he did on the Stockman's Hall of Fame, organising equestrian events and the business that bears his name and famous gear for male and female rural workers, horse lovers and the multitude of others in Australia and internationally who simply like, use and wear the long-lasting goods with the RM Williams brand.

He was a remarkable man born in 1908 near Jamestown in the mid north of South Australia and died peacefully at his property in Queensland in 2003 aged 95.

No one could describe his life better than Paul Myers in a story "Bush Craftsman" where he writes. "But there has always been much more to RM than bush clobber. This remarkable Australian was also an explorer, pastoralist, horseman, stockman, stonemason, leather craftsman, goldminer, well sinker, author, businessman and historian-excelling at all and more". The details of those last five words can be found in his autobiography, "Beneath Whose Hand" and other books he has penned.

His father was a blacksmith and made RM "want to make things" and he certainly did. When he was 10 the family moved to Adelaide for the children's education. At 13 he rolled his swag and headed off in 1921. In the next few years he worked at incredibly hard jobs well sinking, tank building and even camel driving. Somehow he wound up in Oodnadatta and met a William Wade who, in RMW's words, was "Born in London, a Cockney, spent his early life as a sailor, was converted by the Salvation Army and spent the rest of his life as a missionary to the Aborigines". Says a lot in one sentence doesn't it?

Wade needed someone to look after the camels he needed for his first expedition. They seemed a bit like big horses to RMW so, with a few lessons from an Afghan Cameleer, off they roamed unarmed, in the Victorian, Gibson and Great Sandy Desert for three years from 1926-1929. To put this into perspective the area of these three deserts they roamed were more than 300,000 square miles and that is a third the size of India. The last white men to venture there were Forrest in the 1860s and Giles in the 1870s and the next was Len Beadell in the 1950s, when he surveyed the Woomera Rocket Range and built the famous Gun Barrel highway, many other roads and the odd atomic bomb testing site.

RM returned to Adelaide and was married in 1929, but the Depression took its toll and with his wife and child he moved to the Gammon Ranges and camped in Italowie Gorge for what became two years. He did odd jobs and one day a most unlikely harbinger of fame and fortune drove into his camp in a one mule powered buggy. This was one Michael George Smith, aka Dollar Mick. He taught RMW to make boots from one piece of leather and the rest we know. I believe that the last for those boots was made at Wertaloona Station near Lake Frome in SA and I have a photograph of Dollar Mick taken at that property.

In the early 1930s, he returned to Adelaide because his child and he had 'Sandy Blight" a very painful and potentially severe eye disease we now call Trachoma.

He settled in Adelaide and in 1932 sold his first pair of boots.

In 1979 my wife and I moved to Port Lincoln to work and live. In 1982 with Brian and Pam Murray, who managed Parakylia, a 1000 square mile sheep and cattle property in the Woomera prohibited area. We formed a partnership and bought a grazing property 60-70 km from Port Lincoln.

The land agent was Frank Lillecrapp, a name well known in South Australian rural circles. He and Brian got on well as Frank had been a boundary rider on the Dog Fence that was the northern boundary of Parakylia in the 1930s. This is a 5600 km long fence from west of Brisbane in a most circuitous way to west of Fowlers Bay in South Australia that protects sheep from the depredations of wild dogs.

Frank joined the RAAF and was a bomber pilot in World War II. Brian flew a small plane on the station, which was something else that they had in common.

Somewhere in this discussion Frank mentioned that when he was 14 he camped for the night with a mob of sheep near Orroroo east of Port Augusta on the other side of the Flinders Ranges. Frank was just settling down when a man rode into his camp on a push bike and it was none other than RM heading to Adelaide to make boots.

Frank was a well-respected and lovely man and I have no

doubt he was telling the truth.

Frank said he promised to and did buy RM's first pair of boots.

About 10 years after this conversation there was an advertisement in "Outback" magazine and other publications with a picture of RM and a caption. "I wish I knew the name of that bloke from Hiltaba Station who bought my first boots."

Our daughter's rusted on best friend worked as a designer for RMW and when I told her about this she flicked it to the boss. His comment was "Couldn't he be on a horse when he rode into that camp?"

To digress: horses were expensive and need cleaning, feeding and shoes and so on and travellers such as shearers, labourers and battlers often rode bikes. Horses in the early 1800s cost 18 months of a labourer's wages and that is the price of a second- hand Land Cruiser today—well they were four -wheel drive transport animals.

The boss did not know about the Hiltaba advertisement, Frank, his wife and one daughter were dead and I did not know the name of his other daughter. RMW wrote in a personal letter to me that he could not remember but knew the Lillecrapps. So it all faded away.

There is no reason that Frank may not have worked at Hiltaba. In the book mentioned previously, written in 1986, RMW mentioned how, near bankruptcy, he put an advertisement in the Adelaide *Chronicle,* "Elastic side boots made to measure, 5 Percy Street Prospect. Twenty Shillings. Cash with order."

He goes on to write "Within days came a letter with a

pound note enclosed" and that set him on the road to success. He did not remember the man's name but "Hiltaba Station ever after was a romantic name".

I can still remember Frank telling that story and I cannot credit that he was not telling the truth.

Hiltaba Station is 280 km west of Port Augusta as the crow flies and 340km as the train would have gone to Kingoonya and then 160 km to Hiltaba by motor vehicle so it was not tenable that a newspaper would travel there and a return letter would get to Adelaide "within days".

Most likely the writer was in Adelaide, maybe for the Adelaide Show and saw the advertisement but gave his address as Hiltaba because he worked there.

I like to think that it was Frank who was expecting an advertisement of some kind after the meeting near Ororoo

But wait there is more. Another 10 years or so went by and a man doing the RMW history contacted me and he elected to believe Frank's story and that is why there is a sign R M WILLIAMS WAY in the main street of Ororoo.

TROOPY

By Gillian Harris

I was apprehensive when I boarded the aircraft to Australia. There had always been unrest within me, a curiosity which I knew could only be satisfied somewhere on my own. For this and other sorts of reasons I decided to visit Australia.

I should not have worried because, as soon as we were airborne I felt alone but right, with a strange but pleasant openness to the future. I had not felt this before and I was curious and interested in those sharing this airtight cylinder with me for the next 24 hours.

My heart and eyes were open together for the first time and as I relaxed, I became more intrigued about my fellow travellers. By chance I was seated next to a fellow 'Northerner' for one leg of the flight and we chatted and laughed our way through the skies before I fell into a gentle sleep weaving fantasies about those around me and my imminent future.

I arrived in Perth happy and as they say in Australia was "rarin' to go".

Some hitch hiking in the south of Western Australia gave me a good feeling for the place and people. I had tested my resolve and I had passed the test so I head for my number one destination: Broome - a place I had dreamed about since I was a little girl. I stood in a hostel in Broome almost pinching myself to confirm it was real.

I checked out a travellers' board and later rendezvoused with others at Cable Beach feeling very fortunate to be alive at that very moment. The anticipation of new company, new friendships and shared adventures, but mostly the unknown filled me with a vitality I had not felt before.

I was with a pal who really was a "diamond" girl who had shown me more fun in the three weeks we were hitch hiking than I had ever experienced in my life. My fellow adventurers strolled towards us. Sitting there with my sun hat shielding my soul I leapt up with my exuberant, chatty, best self, shining through - what a great feeling!

The next day we departed in two Toyota Land Cruiser Troop Carriers, universally known as "Troopies", in convoy for a 2,790 km trip.

Our first trip was to Cape Leveque, a dusty 200km on a dirt road to the northernmost tip of the Dampier Peninsula in the Kimberley region of Western Australia. The sea here is a unique blue-green colour and the tides are amongst the highest on earth. It is very beautiful, dangerous and exciting with sparkling rip-roaring water contrasting with the white sand.

This was our first campsite and my first experience of getting bogged and of the significance of PSIs and tyres. These became of some importance when we headed for the Gibb River Road through some first gear low range crawling in places. There were moments I would sit at night and really wonder if this was happening.

"The Gibb" is 660 km though the Kimberley from Derby to Kununurra. It is dirt and only 4WD vehicles are allowed. It was September so it was dry and passable but the going was slow, tough and rough, it being so late in the dry season that thousands of vehicles had already traversed it. The Gibb is on "everybody's" bucket list. I had read that it was built as a "beef road" in the 1960s to move cattle to the port of Derby and sometimes inland to the Northern Territory and elsewhere. I also read that it hastened the end of the legendary stockmen droving their cattle hundreds of miles to or from markets in Australia.

Whatever else this road did it was unpaved, dusty and gravelly and there were days when I felt as if I was one of the cattle: hot, dusty, cramped and sweaty and jangling over the corrugations in the road. But regardless, these moments were not painful. I had found joy and I was happy to be there.

The next stage took us 300km north off "The Gibb" to Mitchell Falls. The drive there was exhausting, the road is exhausting... shuddering over corrugations hour after hour in unrelenting heat is hard going, but I loved it and we were consistently rewarded with impressive waterfalls, free spots for camping and incredible nature. Harsh, unwelcoming terrain surrounded by a blue like no other and a red dust that warmed me. I knew that I was somewhere special, somewhere rugged and spiritual, mystical and breathtaking. We continued to drive forward into endless horizons and other worldly landscapes. At night those "Aussie" stars hung in the sky like grapes just as 'Wilco' describes in his song "California Stars". Those stars felt so close and yet so far out of reach and they followed us on our journey night after night and provided certainty.

I had been 100% ignorant of the significance of the Gibb River Road amongst travellers, even with my door stopper of a Lonely Planet guide book adorned with rainbow coloured post-it stickers in its pages. I had enthusiastically carried the book around the world despite it weighing me down. But this road had not registered.

The adventure had an intensity. Five strangers, two Troopies, working through each day together. Adrin and I shared his Troopy. I paid a bit more money to travel with him for the luxuries of air con and a roof top tent which I loved. Each day we put it up together. Adrin was often kind enough to allow me behind the wheel, driving through terrain I had never dreamed of and feeling the freedom with the windows down letting the hot therapeutic air seep in.

Getting to know each other was fun. One to one is intense,, but for days on end we were effectively two strangers. We slept side by side in that roof top tent and chatted our way into our sleepy dreams. Secretly I'd imagine holding him in my arms. I just missed being held, the humanity, kindness and connection that human touch can bring. Wonderful days passed by and we swam in so many remote and beautiful water holes and waterfalls, we camped in wild and free spots, lit campfire after campfire, made dampers and watched so many night skies together.

However weaving its way through the days there was also a tension, that I suppose, looking back, inevitably infiltrates the good stuff in a situation like ours. We arrived in Kununurra, hot, sticky and ready to let our hair down in what was going to be our first time in weeks in a pub. Wearing our cleanest dirty clothes and subtly sneaking on some makeup, we awkwardly separated into guys and girls and off we went into the depths of the dance floor, a new sense of freedom away from our adopted brothers.

We were parked on a dark and deserted road, but by now

I was still not used to having no facilities. I always remember David laughing at my insistence on walking until I could no longer be seen with binoculars before I would have a pee in the bush.

We went to bed. However that night and delicately put, I soon found myself interrupting this peaceful, pitch black but starry night as I hurriedly climbed down from the tent and onto the unknown ground. Spinifex was everywhere-hellish stuff that could not be avoided as I had failed to find the bloody torch. I think this annoyed Adrin about me. I often lost important things like the time we had a flatty and I lost one of the wheel nuts. This time it was the torch for about the fifth night in a row. Not wanting to draw any more attention to my situation I crept in and out of the roof top tent as quietly as I could. I left the zipper open. Up and down I moved, no doubt reaching my quota of 10,000 steps for the day during those few miserable lonely hours. Throughout my "Jack in the box" antics, I wished it to all stop please. I have lived with these people for weeks but please not this!

Adrin said nothing. In hindsight I should have taken my sleeping bag out there into the Spinifex but for the first time I felt vulnerable. Morning came to my blessed relief. I felt awful. The girls joined me as I sat in the glaring sunshine wiping my face with rough wet wipes while simultaneously trying to brush my expanding lion's mane of hair. Adrin fastened away the tent without my help that morning. Everyone else seemed oblivious to my night shift marathon or maybe they were being polite. We were subdued.

Hungover...we crawled into our seats and fired up the Troopies once again.

We were silent driving along. That day there was a conversation stalemate. I remember the radio playing, the straight open road and the bush on either side of us. In my shame from the night before, I shuffled into my seat for comfort. The road was smooth now that was a welcome relief and there was a tranquil air and with this and my nocturnal adventures I immediately dropped off into a deep sleep. Maybe 30 minutes later I was woken by a strange noise the tyres made as the Troopy meandered out of control. I woke to see Adrin asleep while the car climbed the bank of dirt the graders had left and ran down a bank towards trees, through thick, tall grass that whipped against the windscreen.

Glass Bundaberg stubbies flew around and hit me on the head as I felt the Troopy lift off the ground and then we stopped. In slow motion we looked at each other. We didn't speak. Windows were broken and it was eerily quiet. For milliseconds I did not know if we were alive or injured.

Adrin moved and I asked what happened. "I think I fell asleep," he cried and crawled out of the car and was gone. My imagination went into overdrive as I envisaged the Troopy bursting into flames with me inside. The door was stuck. My window was stuck. In that instant my vulnerable Child inside wanted someone to come and get me, to scoop me out and keep me safe. It didn't happen. I was to get myself out. I untangled the seat belt and crawled out through Adrin's door. He had gone and was in the distance waving his arms to get the attention of our friends back on the road.

We had so much luck that no one was seriously injured but the car's impact was fierce. The bull bar was bent, both axles were broken and the body was damaged. Adrin's sadness and fury at himself and perhaps me and the whole situation which was a tragedy for him came out in torrents as he tried to salvage some of his self-respect - but he couldn't. This in itself was traumatic. He sat quietly with his Troopy while we stayed near the road to get the attention of someone passing by. At this I realised for the first time the significance of his Troopy in his life: the energy, time, money and emotion he had invested in this machine. It was his totem, his badge, his colours and in short his raison d'etre. The disbelief and regret were tangible.

An Aboriginal family eventually took us to a roadhouse in silence as we tried to digest what had happened and what we were going to do. Adrin phoned for help. "Ran off the road dodging a kangaroo," he proclaimed.

Back at Kununurra with his belongings spread around the campsite ground we huddled, trying to remain sensitive to his situation and how we were going to get to Darwin. That is another story for each of us. We all got there, but not as a team.

It is now 2018 and I sit here in England with a short time to go before I finish my training and become a registered nurse and begin my ultimate adventure. Wherever I live and work, I am sure that there will be elements synonymous with that Australian Road Trip.

FITZROY CROSSING:
AN EXTRAORDINARY LONG WEEKEND

By Peter Morton

In 1970 I worked in Broome for six months immediately after finishing my intern year in Broken Hill. We had been married for less than a year and the whole experience of that place was extraordinary and unforgettable. We have many wonderful memories but none more exceptional than an extended long weekend ostensibly playing tennis in Fitzroy Crossing a little town 400 km east of Broome.

I had heard that a Vic Jones, the manager of Go Go, a cattle station, near Fitzroy Crossing had a cat he loved dearly and the cat loved fish just as dearly so I loaded up with fish for said cat and off we went.

In the dark and no doubt driving too fast I hit the rear end of a bullock and damaged the radiator but successfully limped into Fitzroy and next morning contacted my Broome policeman mate "Thirsty" Carlton to see if he could help. Of course he could, my mum always told me to ask a policeman if I was in trouble but this was on a grander scale than mum ever dreamed of.

The police plane was coming from Perth the next day so "Thirsty" got them to chuck in a Falcon radiator and he and the boys replaced mine when I was playing tennis. There was nothing crook about this as it was a government car.

I picked up the car and asked him about fishing for Cherubim that are yabby like critters. He took me to a bough shed at the back of the police station, opened the door and invited me to borrow as many traps for these delicacies as I wanted to fish in the beautiful Geikie Gorge.

Next Vic Jones turned up with a nice clean sugar bag of meat, full cuts of porterhouse, rump and fillet of beef. I was told by an impeccable source that he provided the pub with a beast a week for a carton of beer and a bottle of scotch. The same source told me that it was most unlikely to have been animals from his property.

Next was the tennis and I cannot remember much except there were several nurses playing from the local Australian Inland Mission (AIM).

After the tennis understandably there was beer and a barbecue. I had seen my share of bush barbecues before and certainly since but have never seen anything remotely like this.

A long and a short wheel base Land Rover turned up at Geikie Gorge where we were camped. The bigger vehicle had a generator, lighting plant and lights, a huge barbecue, an 18-gallon keg and a temprite unit to cool the beer and a gun to serve it. The "Shorty" Land Rover was carrying a forequarter of beef and that filled the back- the stray cattle they find are always big in the Kimberley. There were 30 people there at the most and the keg was gone by 11 o'clock, quite a performance really and yet there was no drunk and disorderly conduct just a wonderful time on a glorious night with the Fitzroy River burbling by.

We did have a game of two up the ring being a rug chucked over the front of a vehicle. I reckon that they even had a proper kip, the piece of wood used for tossing coins and it belonged to the sergeant of police who wanted to ensure there was no bad behaviour. His name was Tom Carlson known through the Kimberly as "TC" but a different bloke altogether to my mate who was obviously too junior to adopt such a responsible position.

We were travelling with Len and Liz German from Broome and they introduced us to some friends in the pub the next day. One thing led to another and we met two fencers Kevin Blinko and Robbie Wyatt. Kevin had something stuck under his eyelid that was very uncomfortable and I was able to remove it and made him much happier.

Later I was asked to play darts in the country versus town darts tournament. Anyone can play darts but how well was another matter and I had only ever played socially years before but nothing surprised me this weekend. I do not even know the numbers but they were at two and four o'clock on the dart board and I had to throw a treble and a double and did so winning the game. Errands of mercy, man of the match –how good was that.

We won't even dwell on 'Thirsty" falling in the drink, running over a rubbish tin in his yellow VW and then facing an irate tourist complaining about the racket next day at the police station but the good officer that he was, the incriminating vehicle had been put to bed and remained undiscovered.

But wait there is more to this story. I was interested in getting a movie camera and projector and one of the nurses said she or someone had them for sale. She duly turned up in Broome with said items and left them with me.

We were transferred to Port Hedland soon after. I was not sure who owned them as I had been unable to contact her so

I sent her another note and took them with me.

Fast forward a few months. We had met and become good friends (and still are) with Ian and Lyn Phippard in Port Hedland. One Sunday afternoon we were having a few beers with them and another two or three couples at their house and someone said that they had a pornographic movie from Singapore. But no one had a projector so I went home and picked up "mine' and returned.

Now let us pause for a while. This was 1970 or 71, porn movies were unknown or about as alluring as a mannequin in a shop window, no probably not. My wife of a little over a year was a modest person and quite frankly I was embarrassed so much to Lyn's disgust I asked Leonore to stay in the kitchen and of course Lyn stayed with her.

To set the scene some more. It was in the middle of a tropic summer; people had been drinking and were sweating and there was certainly an air of sexual tension developing as I assembled the projector and film.

I flicked the switch and away it went for all of three seconds and the film melted as did any sexual tension. I suppose that was bound to happen when I ran it at 240 volts with the switch on 12 volts. I have no idea what happened to the camera.

But you thought that is the end –no, no no.

My mate "Thirsty" told me that he and "TC" the sarge went looking for a lion that had allegedly escaped from a well-known circus en route to Fitzroy Crossing. They asked Vic Jones if he had seen it and his comment was "No and if I do, I'll shoot the bastard-it is vermin".

Sadly "Thirsty" also confirmed that Vic Jones, who had

always said he would die in the Kimberley, did so at his own hand when he was made redundant by the station owners.

LA GRANGE MISSION, THE WATTS AND US - 1970 PLUS

By Chris and Ann Watts and Peter Morton

Leonore and I lived in Broome in 1970, having married the year before. It was a beautiful and exciting place with a population of a few thousand people. We met many people with interesting jobs and lives. Two were Ann and Chris Watts, who taught at La Grange Mission where I visited once a month as medical officer.

We have been fortunate to keep in touch and saw them as recently as December 2017 when cruising in a ship that berthed in Port Lincoln.

La Grange was a pastoral property operated by the Pallottine Order under the auspices of the Catholic Diocese in Broome. The Mission, in collaboration with the Education Department of Western Australia, offered schooling to the 70 aboriginal children. The only school staff were the two teachers employed by the Education Department - in 1970 that was Ann and Chris.

Chris wrote that he and Ann also were married in1969. Ann had completed her first teaching appointment as a Physical Education teacher at Bunbury Senior High. While teaching at North Innaloo Primary in 1969 Chris was approached by a District Superintendent with a view to applying for the position of Headmaster at La Grange. Ann was offered the position of Junior Primary teacher, while Chris would teach Years 4-7. Negotiations were completed for a one-year appointment to La Grange followed by a year of leave without pay.

We arrived in Broome at 0400 from Perth on an MMA flight

in February 1970. The temperature and humidity were stifling. Fr Michael McMahon, Acting Superintendent of La Grange Mission, in the temporary absence of Fr Kevin McKelson , met us at the airport and took us to the Broome Catholic Church where we waited while he completed some church and mission business.

As the sun rose, the heat and humidity became more oppressive and we sought shelter under a mango tree in the grounds of the church. After what seemed like an eternity we set off for La Grange, 200km south of Broome where we arrived mid-afternoon. The road to La Grange was unsealed except for the first 35km.

Chris and Ann were not enthralled by the very limited accommodation of a small hut with one bedroom with only a desk fan for cooling, and that only between 0700-0930 and 1600-2130, when the mission power was on.

There was only a basic shower and toilet and Chris reported that *'On entry it was a good idea to check the toilet seat for large green frogs'* And *"After settling into our accommodation we were invited to join the mission staff of about 16 people gathered around a long table. While the menu can't be recalled we remember that as we ate, perspiration dripped from our foreheads into our dinner plates.*

Limited non-perishable goods were ordered twice a term and perishable goods every two weeks from Perth and delivered by Gascoyne Trading trucks. The mission provided fresh bread, beef and vegetables from a large garden.

Chris wrote about Jimmy the gardener. *"He was a significant figure in the tribal structure of the mission community and often brought us fish on Friday evenings after* he had the afternoon away from work.

Jimmy was a tremendous asset to the school. As well as keeping the school grounds and gardens in good condition, he would arrive at school each morning well before staff and students. His first duty each day was to survey the school site for any reptiles that may have entered the ground during the night. Death adders were prolific in the area and Jimmy took great pride in draping his 'kill' on the school fence.

The mission had established a reticulated and productive market garden that yielded crops of tomatoes, capsicums, watermelons, rockmelons, pumpkins and paw paws. As well as supplying the local community some produce was sold in Broome and beyond to amongst others, our friends Leonore and Peter.

We soon learnt the costly, inconvenient and sometimes downright dangerous reality of rough, rocky, sandy roads, long journeys and sharing these roads with animals.

After several incidents we soon learnt to carry two spare wheels and to have a protective "roo bar" on our 1969 Toyota Corona.

A good example was the Anzac Day weekend in 1970 when we and Peter and Leonore Morton from Broome went to Fitzroy Crossing to play in a tennis tournament. We hit two kangaroos and they hit a bullock that wrecked their radiator. A local policeman organised a replacement radiator for them and the mission staff did an admirable job repairing the damage to our car when we returned to La Grange.

The housing conditions at the mission made life very uncomfortable. From very early in our stay at La Grange we lobbied for improved housing through appropriate agencies without success.

I met Western Australia's longest serving Premier Sir David Brand in Broome and took the opportunity to make him aware of this. My efforts were successful and by October a three-bedroom house had been built, trucked to La Grange on two low loaders and erected ... AND THERE WAS MORE. An independent diesel generator was included BUT THERE WAS NO MORE-The house was NOT air conditioned.

As I mentioned, Chris and Ann recently visited us and we spent a very pleasant day reminiscing about Broome. Chris had already started writing this story and Ann added more after our meeting.

Chris had lived and worked with Aboriginal people in Fitzroy Crossing in the Kimberley area but I had no such experience so it was a challenge, particularly with the appalling accommodation, but overall I loved it. I particularly noticed how bright, clean and healthy the children were due to the care of their parents, a good diet and the ceaseless vigilance of our nurse Margot Toohey, finding and treating skin diseases, bacterial and parasitic diseases. She was also able to keep the dreadful ear infections clean so the consequences of perforated ear drums could be surgically repaired. In other words, deaf children could then hear.

Daily rituals at the mission were fascinating. The residents would attend the mission 'shops' at dusk every day in family groups to pick up meat, locally baked bread and firewood. The gender divide was apparent. The indigenous women would carry the meat, bread, firewood and children, while the men would walk ahead empty handed. I was not a rabid feminist but--------------!

Our tasks at the mission were many and varied. The Education Department supplied evaporated milk for our students. The students were more "contented" (just like the cows in the old advertisement) with the Carnation brand milk rather than others that sometimes turned up. Each morning before recess I made enough milk for the 70+ students. The milk was mixed in a bucket with water. The first few days the water was obtained from the school's new and modern water cooler. As they became more confident with us, the students let us know they preferred unchilled water.

We conducted classes in Adult Aboriginal Education that included literacy and numeracy and coached basketball. The standard of basketball was quite high and the young adults played with skills that were highlighted by a lack of physical contact.

We had the privilege of attending a corroboree. There were parts of the ceremony I wasn't allowed to attend but I was taken to another location with the women and I found it a privilege and most interesting.

Chris said that the boys were dressed in ceremonial clothes and were painted for the occasion. The women were very much spectators and the male only part of the corroboree wasn't particularly noteworthy on this occasion.

Away from the sporting field we often screened 16mm films, hired from Perth, for the community. These shows were was always well attended

Things were not always straight forward. Famous author Mary-Durack Miller visited the mission seeking some school children to participate in a stage production of the book she had written, "Way of the Whirlwind" and was co- producing with ballet and dance teacher Diana Waldron.

She asked Chris to see if he would intervene with Father McKelson, who was reluctant to allow the children to participate.

Chris smoothed the waters after some discussion with the children's families and Father McKelson and four students were selected to perform at the Octagon theatre in December.

We were fortunate to attend a performance on the very evening we arrived back in Perth from La Grange. Afterwards we joined the cast and I must admit I had trouble making conversation. I was so tired I felt like I was asleep standing up.

Pieces of a conversation behind me kept breaking into my consciousness along the lines of "They were having trouble getting the priest to let the kids do the show and now that he is retired Mary asked David if he could help and he told her to speak to a Chris someone at La Grange". It seemed to take forever for me to understand "Mary" was Mary Durack-Miller and "David" the recently retired premier Sir David Brand.

I turned around but the group had broken up. Chris was chatting and did not hear the conversation. Maybe in my exhausted state I dreamt the conversation but I do not think so.

Not long before they left Margo asked Chris and Ann to help with a nasty injury from a boomerang in a fight between a young lover and an older man to whom a girl had been promised. Chris notes. "This man had severe cut to his eye that needed cleaning and the area shaved. As we shaved the eyebrow Margo took care to remove pieces of the hair. It became apparent that what we thought was hair was in fact splinters from a boomerang. The patient was transferred to Broome hospital for further treatment where it proved *necessary to remove the injured eye to preserve vision in the other eye".*

In a lighter vein Chris describes the magnificent fishing in these lonely creeks. *"Fishing was one of our leisure activities. In the winter months Tom Fitzgerald, the gardener, took us to the tidal creeks in his 4-wheel drive vehicle. Mugs like us could even catch fish! Ann didn't like the "Long Toms" with their sword mouths. She'd pull them up on the beach and let Tom or one of the other men stun them before retrieving the hook. Sand flies were also a problem for Ann, often looking like a measles case on return home. Fish was a welcome change in a predominantly beef diet and they were great outings."*

Some people in the La Grange community had been in contact with western civilisation for a relatively short period. They came from the desert area to the east and their features were different to the coastal aboriginal people in that their skin tones were much lighter. There has been recent, twenty-first century speculation that the ancestors of these people may have had contact with the sixteenth and seventeenth century European explorers.

No tales of the Kimberley would be complete without a cyclone story but Ann and Chris let us down. When they were about to depart La Grange, a cyclone was imminent and threatened to delay their farewell. The Education Department assisted them with a charter flight to the all-weather airport at Broome to board their flight to Perth and so they missed the cyclone. Their year of adventure in the Kimberley ended, not with a bang fortunately, but with a whimper.

Just to steal their thunder, Leonore and I had moved to

Port Hedland in late 1970 and were actually in the cyclone that they missed.

THE MOUNT LEONARD SAGA OF SADNESS AND COURAGE

By Peter and Leonore Morton

My wife Leonore and I have spent our married life in outback and rural Australia and on reflection it was not a surprising path for either of us.

My forebears were miners, my father lived and worked in Adelaide for a company and later in his own business processing and selling fruit, nuts, ham, bacon, rice and so on.

My uncles were all involved in rural activities and I had positive experiences working on farms and socialising with country people at school and university.

Leonore, however, is part of a much greater and a tragic saga.

In 1908 her great grandfather Elliot Scott, of Kersbrook in the Adelaide Hills, his son John James and partners Allan and Stanley Sinclair bought Mount Leonard, a cattle station at Beetoota,165km east of Birdsville, in south west Queensland.

John James was appointed manager and on the second of March 1913 he married Alberta Jasmine Tucker at Currawilla Station, a relative "stone's throw" of 50km east of Mount Leonard.

Alberta's parents had owned a pub in Birdsville. Her father died young after being "poorly" for years when her mother was pregnant with her. Sadly this was a harbinger of the cards life would deal her as the years passed. Her mother continued in this profession for many years

Scott was a Methodist and Tucker a Catholic, a situation

that Leonore and I experienced and sorted out amicably 55 years later.

Their wedding must have been a day of great joy and soon children arrived. Leonard and Mary were born in Adelaide, Jean, Leonore's mother on the station with an aboriginal woman to help, and Clare and Fred in Longreach.

When pregnant with Leonard and Mary she had to travel, in horse drawn coaches, 165km to Birdsville, 517 km to Marree and in the train called "The Ghan" 650km to Adelaide.

Horse drawn coaches driven for 10 hours a day with fresh horses every 30 km could travel 200km in three days. Maybe Mount Leonard to Marree would have taken 10 days in perfect conditions but much longer if conditions were bad as they often would have been and still can be. Board and lodgings were included.

John James wrote about owning a car but it was unlikely he had it for the first two babies. It was likely to be a T model Ford and in theory could travel the same distance in an hour as a coach in a day.

She decided to have Leonore's mother, her third baby, at Mount Leonard to avoid the trip to Adelaide but the mid wife did not attend and she had the baby, helped by the Aboriginal house girls, while her husband was frantically riding for a neighbour.

I cannot help counting fingers. Her first baby probably was in January 1914 and her fifth was born in late December 1920.

But tragedy soon struck. In 1918 Frederick Tucker, Alberta's brother, wrote a letter from the Western Front full of optimism about his plans to buy the adjoining Arrabury cattle station, but he was killed in the last few weeks of World War One. A cruel irony is that this station is now part of Mount Leonard.

Worse was to come for the Scotts. After Fred was born in December 1920 Alberta was recovering in the Longreach hospital when her husband John James Scott was drowned swimming his horse across the flooded Diamantina River on the 28 December, 1920.

Scott's waterhole on Monkira Station about 100km from Mount Leonard marks the spot.

She probably found out from the police. How she got home God only knows.

To complete the picture, her sister May had attended a boarding school in Adelaide and never went home as she entered a convent immediately on leaving school.

Realistically in those days she lost her sister as well as her father, brother, husband and then later her son Leonard.

Fate would not let these good people be. About 20 years later, in another wretched war, the older son Leonard and three other pilots were captured by the Japanese, alleged to be spies and executed. A film *Blood Oath* was made about the war crimes trial of the Japanese who did this, with Bryan Brown as the prosecuting officer.

Alberta left Mount Leonard with her five children and settled in Alexander Avenue, Rose Park a leafy suburb of Adelaide opposite what used to be the Victoria Park racecourse. She was supported by dividends from Mount Leonard and later was cared for by her daughters Mary and Clare, who never married thanks to World War Two, when they served with Leonore's mother driving trucks and things.

Fate was also cruel to two of Alberta's grandchildren, Leonore's siblings. They died as adults but all too soon.

We have pictures of Alberta and her husband "Jack" aged about 30 in our dining room. He is a man of strength, determination and character. She is pretty, small but strong and I often gaze in wonder at her shiny hair piled medium high and try and imagine the heartache she experienced. I am looking at her picture now with tears in my eyes. She was what made Australia.

I have only seen one other picture of her aged about 60, soon to die. She was a sad, broken, sick figure physically and mentally.

At last a light side to this story. When Alberta and her children moved to Adelaide they lived next to the Jolly family. The late Mark Jolly was a friend and contemporary of mine at school and university.

We became very good at driving Holden cars in the lane behind their house. The main game was changing into first gear by double declutching that involved a lot of revving and grinding of gears (aka "cog swapping") and making a lot of noise that bounced off the iron fences of the lane.

I have always felt a bit guilty about this but now there is a sneaky thought that maybe Alberta Jasmine had a little smile when we did these silly things.

Her husband's letters were sometimes addressed to "My Dear Wife" or "Jessie". Her name was "Jasmine". Some where I have seen her name "Jess O' Mine".

I had a glass of red handy and drank a silent toast to Jessie outside looking into the dark and rain. As Shakespeare might have written:

"She and her ilk were women,
Take them all for all in all
We shall not look upon their like again"

Cheers Jessie

Leonore and I have visited Mount Leonard twice, both times with our friends Phillip and Chris Stain.

The first trip was short, sharp and shiny on the way back from my godson's wedding in Brisbane. The bride was the cousin of the manager of Mount Leonard. A small world!

Later we were talking to the "babbler," an attractive 35-year-old South African lady. She told us she was leaving the next day as there was too much drinking at the station. Well it is bloody hot there so I can understand this.

She also told us that the boss was flying in from Sydney later that day and would we like to join them for dinner.

Being a very sensitive man in touch with my feminine side, I thought that her departure, complaints about excess drinking and the boss visiting may be connected by some chance.

We thought discretion was the better part of valour and camped on a nearby flat.

Phillip arose early and scarcely clad wandered outside to have a wee. While so occupied he said later that he thought he heard giggling and a horse neighing.

Leonore gets cross with me teasing Phil, so this is the first time I have told the story. He had an audience of three mounted jillaroos who are trainee female station hands. They had reined in and were giggling and pointing at Phil.

One girl held up her hand with her thumb and forefinger about an inch apart in a pinching movement. Must have been asking for a cigarette I suppose.

It was a horse that Phil had heard and it was neighing quietly with his head down and shaking it from side to side looking rather sadly at Phil, I thought.

Anyway I quietly suggested that next time he embarked on his morning ablutions he wear his pants, glasses and hearing aids.

The next day we headed home via the Strzelecki Track.

The second trip was about ten years later and we travelled via the famous Birdsville Track and apart from wrecking a tyre all was good; but boy did that change.

We left Birdsville with a suspicion of rain but the coppers and the manager's wife at Mount Leonard thought we would be ok. But it did rain- and heavily. It is 165km from Birdsville to Mt Leonard and for a quarter of that distance I towed Phil and Chris's dual cab and 20-foot caravan because they could not get traction in the deepening mud in the increasingly heavy rain.

We were pulling a Heaslip Camper with a chain hooked onto the back joined to the front of Phillip's ute. Phil and I both knew Rob Heaslip from schooldays and he certainly built strong gear.

The station, of course, was also water logged and we had to stay put for a few days, well looked after by the manager and his wife, "Chook" and Lorraine Kath.

Near the Mount Leonard homestead is a headstone inscribed "In Loving Memory of John James Scott" and "Dearly beloved husband of Alberta J Scott" and 'Died 28 December 1920 aged 37 years. So sadly missed"

The stone is at the southern end of what seems to be a grave. There is a little decorative wrought iron fence 20-25 cm high enclosing an area consistent with the size of a grave.

Surrounding this structure is a metre-high steel pipe fence protecting it from cattle, horses and vehicles. The stone had been made in Adelaide, date unknown and was in excellent condition. The wrought iron was rusty and some of the concrete supports and the headstone had sunk into the ground.

We levelled the supports and the head stone and sanded and painted the grave surrounds.

It looked like a grave. Why would a memorial stone have grave surrounds? He was found and buried on Monkira Station. This was confirmed by the coroner's report.

Did his wife or other relatives arrange to exhume and re inter him? Tradition was important to the family. For example, my wife's name Leonore, is the female version of Leonard, who was killed by the Japanese.

Was it a grave or not? We had a front-end loader and that would give us the answer.

Further comment would defy iron outback lore and that is "What happens on a cattle station stays on the station" and perhaps other laws as well. For further information refer to the last sentence.

By the way, if the name Monkira rings a bell there is a picture of the Monkira Ox in the Birdsville pub. The animal was so big I could not get a decent picture even with a wide-angle lens.

He was killed in Adelaide in 1884 and it took 40 years for a bigger animal to be killed in Australia. Another source says he was the biggest grass -fed animal in the world at 3000 pounds alive and 2000 pounds dressed.

The ground dried in a few days and, very relieved with the hospitality and satisfied with our work to maintain the grave structures, we headed south and home.

It has been quite moving to write this and Leonore's sister Jacqueline and her brother Michael have shared that journey and we will do it for real in July 2018.

Part 10   A pot pourri of other tales

QUIZ NIGHTS

By Peter Morton

These can be a lot of fun and usually are made up of kindred spirits, such as the staff of a hospital, school or a progress association. My wife and I have been to perhaps a dozen with a degree of success, including two successive Coffin Bay International challenges and a big one in Melbourne to support two girls who were running a marathon for a charity.

It is always a good idea to have mothers in a team because they know about nursery rhymes, stories for and about children and Sesame Street. If they can be captured, a teenager or two are handy because they know about songs and television and teachers are gold. The Coffin Bay victories were directly attributable to mums and kids.

The Quiz Night in Melbourne was between teams of 10 and the master of ceremonies, in his introduction, gave a variation of the old standard "There are two rules. Rule one is that the judge's decision is final. Rule two is to refer to rule one".

His rule two thundered from the podium. "RULE TWO: THE TEAM OF ANYONE USING AN ELECTRONIC DEVICE WILL BE FINED $250". In a flash it was like a western movie backwards with phones being tucked into pockets all over the place. Not our table as we were ethical and I probably couldn't find the interwhatsit on a mobile phone anyway.

Our team was amazing and our division of labour was

brilliant. Most of us were reasonable but two girls were sensational. There were two papers on the table for completion over the night. One was a puzzle with hidden words such as "X1 p i a CT". The answer to that is there are "11 players in a cricket team" but they were much harder clues than that. A lawyer lady beavered away all night and got them all correct.

The second one was an A4 sheet of paper with 150 flags of the world and the young lady charged with that got some insane number like 90% correct. I asked her had she travelled and she said 'Sort of. When I was little, I wanted to travel but was too young so collected the flags of everywhere I wanted to go". What a memory.

Most people get cross if they find it all too hard but one of our team had not answered any questions, sitting there quite happily enjoying the atmosphere. The very last question was "What fuel does a jet plane use"? He immediately said "Av (as in Aviation) gas" to our scribe. I waited for someone to correct him because that fuel is for planes with piston engines, jets use kerosene. Strangely perhaps but apparently no one else knew that.

I crossed my fingers and said nothing and we had enough in reserve to win.

I have run several Quiz Nights for the Port Lincoln Hospital when the late surgeon Ian Fletcher and I would dress up as Heckle and Jeckle in our dinner suits. The late Ian Matthews the hospital CEO, and Helen Dalby a senior nurse would mark the quiz sheets.

When I ran quiz nights, I usually made up the questions as well and that can be quite hard to do because contestants do not like to feel belittled. Alternatively, if it is too easy everyone scores highly and the challenge disappears.

On one occasion our Hospital Board Chairman, who had been on television quiz shows, made them up. I could see people getting irritated so I changed a few questions as I went along but forgot to tell the markers. This was very confusing for a time and it was sorted out, but Ian never let me forget it.

Something we did that was meant to be funny and a good prize was to award a 25kgm bag of cow manure to each member of the team that ran last. A lot of people would run dead for that but others were most insulted.

Another trap is to assume that you know the answer to a question. Once I asked "Who did Cazaly play for". Cazaly was an Australian Football legend in his own time and "Up there Cazaly" is a haunting and exciting song that sends shivers down my spine. It refers to Cazaly's custom of jumping high into the air to mark a football, often high enough to kneel on his opponent's shoulders.

The answer was Saint Kilda. After that round was marked I visited the boys' room as did a lovely man and a neighbour Jasper Smith who said that the famous man played for South Melbourne, the forerunner of the Sydney Swans.

I demurred and Jasper told me that he went into the South Melbourne club rooms with his dad and Cazaly's photograph was on the wall. I happened to know that Cazaly had played in Tasmania. As quick as a flash I told Jasper that the picture was taken after he returned from Tasmania. Jasper thanked me and off he went. It was an absolute guess.

Fast forward 12 or 13 years. We were entertaining Ian Matthews in Darwin, the man who marked the answer papers when I had changed the questions. We were reminiscing about that very night and I told him about Jasper Smith and Cazaly.

As I was finishing the story the telephone rang. It was our son Peter, who was working in Tasmania at the time. I said "G'day what are you up to" and he answered "I am helping behind the bar at the footy club quiz night" and then "Hey Dad what was the story about who Cazaly played for?"

Talk about reacting like a stunned mullet. I was speechless as were the others when I gained the power of speech and told them what Peter had said.

I checked and Cazaly played 99 games for South Melbourne and St Kilda, captained both teams and played 378 senior games altogether from 1909 to 1941 - an unbelievable career and I am sure followers of AFL would enjoy and be amazed at his exploits.

Not the least was that he coached, the then lowly ranked, Hawthorn who did not win a premiership until 1961 but he planted the seed that grew into the team that has been a power house in the football world for more than half a century.

He did that by simply giving Hawthorn their nick name the 'Hawks" as he thought that "Mayblooms" was not tough enough---- hard to argue that!

FROM MINNIECROW TO THE ROYAL ENCLOSURE AT ASCOT

By James Paltridge

I am flattered that Peter Morton has asked me to write a few words about my time on earth for his book of tales, having first met Peter as a shy young bush kid and then again, many years later, when tragedy brought us back together.

My family, originally from Devon, were tanners at Mount Barker in the Adelaide Hills in the late 1800s before my Great-grandfather Bill Paltridge eloped to Mount Gambier and bought grazing land in the locality.

In 1904 he bought Minniecrow, a relatively undeveloped property near Lucindale, 160 km north of the fertile and reliable Mt Gambier country. My grandfather Lou and his brothers Phil and Romie moved to Minniecrow while their father and other brothers remained at Mount Gambier.

Lou, Phil and Romie all married exceptional ladies and by the time I came along in 1960 they and their families had settled on Minniecrow. This expanding and tightly knit family of Paltridges made my childhood wonderfully vibrant, with plenty of cousins nearby to play and grow up with.

As a child, my brother and I would watch Dad and his mates play in the local cricket team Coorong –Keilira and lived in hope of getting a bat or a field if the team was short, as it often was. This is when we got to know Peter Morton, or Mort, as he was known affectionately. He regularly came to stay locally and worked on farms including ours while at university.

He soon established himself as a cricketing legend. The son a of a top-class footy player, in our eyes Mort could to do no wrong. He was fun and irreverent and paid all the kids plenty of attention by telling stories and jokes. But most importantly, when Mort played in our local cricket team he was able to hit six after six, often after drinking a few beers! My job at the cricket was mainly as scorer and it gave me tremendous pleasure when Mort strode in to bat, tall with a casual menacing swagger. I knew it was time to pay attention as my scoresheet was all but guaranteed from then on to be littered with runs instead of dots and we tooted the car horn madly every time he hit a boundary!

Mort then disappeared from our lives to become a doctor and start his own family, while we went off to boarding school and life beyond. That was until he reappeared into my life soon after Dad died, when he kindly agreed to read an emotional and accurate Adam Lindsay Gordon tongue twister, 'The Sick Stockrider" over Dad's grave at his funeral. He didn't miss a beat. Then Mort's son Peter, who is a very capable young farmer, provided terrific support to me and Dad's brothers on Minniecrow for a couple of years after Dad died.

My childhood was spent trapping rabbits, doing stock work and riding in shows and pony clubs. Mum worked as a teacher throughout my life and in the evenings often played hockey or attended choral society, putting on highly professional drama performances. Dad worked long hours on the farm, attended horse club meetings and working bees, along with taking us to horse shows, hunts and pony club in our old farm truck.

Other than occasional trips to Adelaide with Mum in the school holidays, my influences were limited to the local rural school, bush yarns and the ABC radio country hour. TV and mains power came later. Christmas lunch was always a huge family affair held in my Granny's house on Minniecrow with loads of fun, chaos and noise, while the roast turkey and trimmings were cooked by Granny in a wood burning stove in sweltering heat.

My brother and I boarded at St Peters College and I spent my final year at Westminster, having been expelled from Saints when caught smoking. I loved the mateship of school, but was a lazy and unsuccessful academic. The only things of interest to me were horses and farming.

However, my uncle Chris, a leading stud stock auctioneer at Elders, took a risk and found me a job at Elders Building supplies in Port Adelaide. After a year, it was clear that selling bricks and mortar was not for me.

Mum then made an inspired decision to send me to Marcus Oldham Agricultural College in Geelong to study Horse Management.

This was to be a turning point in my life. I met and worked alongside a young British lad at racehorse trainer George Hanlon's stable during my work experience and this short meeting gave me the incentive to seek out wider challenges overseas.

A trip soon after to Newmarket in England began a lifetime spent outside of Australia for which I have few regrets, except that I miss Aussies more and more the longer I am away. We really are a wonderful race of people, if I say so myself! Early days in Newmarket were spent mucking out stables and riding some track work for top young trainer Willie Hastings-Bass (now Lord Huntingdon) who had a string of horses for the Queen.

Being a farmer's son, one thing I could do was work hard. Soon I was rewarded with more managerial work and Willie and I got on famously. He is a terrific bloke and we are still very good friends today. Back then he would arrange for me to escape the British winters by working in California and so I would fly over to Los Angeles with horses and work at Santa Anita racetrack for champion trainer John Gosden.

Soon after, on one trip home to Australia in 1983 with horses, I met my current business partner who was based in Melbourne and who had started his horse flying company, International Racing Transport (IRT) in 1972. He was ambitious and wanted someone to go to Los Angeles to set up a new office for IRT there.

I was offered the job and as farming in Australia was still in the doldrums, I jumped at the chance. Being only 23, I thought it would be terrific fun for a few years. As it was, I stayed until 1989, opening up IRT offices in New York and Kentucky, before meeting my British wife Mary in the Turf Club bar at Santa Anita Racetrack in Los Angeles. That changed things a bit...In 1990, when the Managing director of IRT's UK office took early retirement I bought his shares and moved back to the UK to live and marry Mary.

I have been here in the UK ever since, living first in London and then in Newmarket with my wife Mary and our three children Amelia (20), Zara (18) and Jamie (15) and play host to plenty of visiting Aussies, including I am pleased to say, the editor of this tale.

A LONG WAY TO WANILLA

By Shaun Kurovec

My father came from Lhotka, a small village on the Becva River in Moravia in the Czech Republic. The nearest major city is Ostrava which is near the Polish Slovak border in the northeast of the Czech Republic. He had six sisters and one brother. His brother was murdered in a concentration camp towards the end of World War II. He was married and had a daughter who he never saw.

When the Germans invaded in 1939 Dad managed to escape through Yugoslavia and Italy to southern France where he enlisted with the Czechoslovakian Army in exile at Agda. They had formed an Infantry Brigade and fought the Germans until the French capitulated. The Czech Brigade managed to retreat to Marseille in southern France from where, after pleading with the British Government, they boarded a ship for England. In England they remained as the Czechoslovakian Independent Brigade Group and they trained to protect England and eventually for D- day.

They became the Czech Army in exile and existed alongside a Czech Government also in exile also based in the UK. Many joined the RAF and were amongst the English and Polish pilots involved in the Battle of Britain.

In September 1943 Dad's group converted to an armoured group and became known as the CIABG Czechoslovak Independent Armoured Brigade Group.

At one point a contingent of these soldiers trained for Operation Anthropoid, with two selected to parachute into

Czechoslovakia, where they eventually were successful in the assassination of Reinhardt Heydrich who was assigned by Hitler as the chief Protector of Czech and Moravia. He was known as the 'Butcher of Prague' and his assassination brought on terrible repercussions for the Czechoslovaks, including the razing of the village of Lidice and murder of its residents and anyone connected with the families and assistants involved.

CABG consisted of three armoured regiments issued with mostly Cromwell tanks. My father was a tank driver in 1 Squadron, Second Armoured regiment.

About 6 weeks after D-Day they landed in France with the Canadian Army and were assigned the task of fighting the 45,000 Germans garrisoned at the besieged city of Dunkirk. They were a force of 4000 and isolated the Germans there until the end of the war when 11,500 surrendered.

This action has received little fame but it may have had a major effect on the outcome of the Normandy landing or even the war.

Soon after the landing Allied forces were held up at Arnhem in Holland and suffered significant losses eloquently described in the film and book that echoed the prophetic words of General Browning, "A Bridge too Far." Dunkirk was only 300 km away and the thought of 45,000 angry Germans attacking the rear of the trapped Allies is very scary indeed. Perhaps more should be made of this action in the historical record.

My father managed to pick up a couple of military medals for valour. One was for rescuing a stricken tank under enemy fire and one for capturing a small group of Germans.

Apparently, he went to a house looking for food when a group of German soldiers threw up their arms and surrendered to him.

When the war finished, he returned to Czechoslovakia and it was not long after that the communists took control and made life unbearable for returned soldiers. One of his sisters spent time in prison because anti-communist propaganda was deemed to have come from her typewriter.

Again, he left home, not telling his family and made his way to Italy as a displaced person. He found his way to the Australian mission and was accepted to immigrate to Australia.

Once in Australia he was required to work for a government service for two years, after which, he was free go his own way. He managed to find his way to Port Lincoln where he worked for the Highways and Engineering and Water Supply departments.

Upon completion of this tenure he worked at the Wanilla State Forest where he was accidentally struck by a saw and lost a leg below the knee.

While recovering in the Port Lincoln Hospital he met my mother who was nursing there. He was fitted with a prosthetic leg which allowed him to continue working.

He and Mum set up residence at 'The Fountain' in the district of Wanilla next to the forest and had three sons. Eventually he set up his own mobile sawmill where he moved around the district cutting fence posts, shearing shed dunnage and railway sleepers. At home they ran some dairy cows, pigs and poultry and did a bit of share farming.

He was an active member of the Wanilla RSL and on a

couple of occasions we hosted holidays for Legacy wards from Adelaide.

He died in 1968 from a massive heart attack in the Port Lincoln Hospital and is buried in the Port Lincoln RSL Garden of Remembrance cemetery.

PETER HARVEY PhD

By Peters Morton et Harvey

INTRODUCTION

We are all many things but few people have as many attributes as Peter. Right brain-left brain balance, Renaissance man, scientist, teacher, scholar, author, humanist, leftist intellectual, musician, singer, businessman, grape grower, wine maker and drinker, international traveller, motor bike rider, runner, bon vivant, cook, gentleman, father, husband, generous, affable and loyal friend readily come to mind.

In 1993 I was appointed the General Practice Director of the Eyre Peninsula Division of General Practice (EPDGP). The Divisions of General Practice were an initiative of the Federal Government and the Royal Australian College of General Practice with a number of goals. Some of these were to act as an organisation that would provide continuing medical education for general practitioners, act as points of contact with other players in the health field, provide administrative support for projects and to help general practitioners have input and contacts with other health providers.

With the help of Kris Bascomb, who later became a doctor, an active management committee and with willing help from officers and the Boards of Management of other hospitals on Eyre Peninsula this became a very successful organisation.

I have mentioned administrative support and this soon became defined as providing a building with high quality clerical staff, offices, appropriate, equipment, cars, networks on Eyre Peninsula and with the South Australian and Federal Health Departments and their Ministers, Universities, Divisions of General Practice, consumer groups, politicians and more. It was a "can do" organisation.

In parallel with this it was recognised that chronic diseases were becoming a major problem in South Australia's ageing community and an organisation had been set up in the South Australian Health Commission as an initiative of the Council of Australian Governments. This was known as SA Health Plus and was to run a Coordinated Care Trial under the direction of Professor Peter MacDonald from Flinders University.

Peter was a well-known clinician but also a visionary and change manager of national and international repute. He had recently managed to somehow find his way through the Federal and State Government bureaucracies to access a package of resources for the management of people with AIDS.

Housing, pensions, drugs, doctors, hospitals and other resources were bundled together making the lives of these unfortunate people much better than they had been with the fragmented care previously available.

The management of chronic illness was to be trialled using this model. Peter Macdonald visited me one day in my office and laid it all out for me and asked me if the EPDGP would be interested. Peter and I are about the same age and he is the brother-in-law of Chris Kennedy, my ex-university colleague and partner at The Investigator Clinic. I said yes and of course followed it up with the management committee and got their go ahead.

We employed 10-15 people including doctors, nurses, project managers, IT people and office staff and of course Peter Harvey was embedded in the EPDGP in a symbiotic relationship after I recruited and employed him as the Trial Director.

He was undeniably the choice for the position and we worked closely together on this project for some years and, together with our wives, became very good friends and have kept in contact (read making wine) during the last 15 years as our paths have widely diverged.

Many times we discussed our love of rural Australia and I was aware of his disappointment that he was unable to continue on the land of his family, but when I knew him in Port Lincoln he grew plants as a hobby and business, planted many trees on his block of several acres and even made a few bottles of wine from the grapes he grew.

His work in Port Lincoln led to a PhD and he is now a Professor of Rural Health so he has followed his roots so to speak and if nothing else that is an interesting image.

I am deeply appreciative that he agreed to contribute to this book, which he has done with "Sisters." Peter has also given me a copy of Chapter One in the book he has written recently, "Across the Great Divide" published by Cambridge University Press. This is about his life from very early until the time I met him in his early forties.

PETER'S STORY

Peter describes a time in his life as "a personal nexus"- when and how his family lost the ability to maintain an idyllic rural life due to the changes in Australia after World War 2. There have been thousands of people that have experienced the pain of leaving their family farm then and at various times of crisis ever since. Yes, the big have got bigger and in one sense rural industry is doing very well at present but most 'family' farms now are run by 60-year-old men and their 58-year-old wives or vice versa and sometimes a widow alone. Suicide is common.

Peter refers to being *"ejected from the family farm like the sun expels its own progeny in solar flares cast to the universe as it runs down its fusion fuel"* and the sad realisation that *"small family farms could no longer be improved or expanded enough to provide for and include the next generation adequately"*. The practical reality was that Peter and a sibling out of the four children had to make their own way in the world. Perhaps fortunately they managed to go to University.

I am 10 years older than Peter and when he failed year 12. in 1970, I was working in my first job as a doctor in Broome. I had nothing similar to Peter in my life but I had a reasonable knowledge of the rural crisis and the inability of all children to stay on farms.

I remember a road in the South East of South Australia 100-150 km as the crow flies from where Peter was brought up that had a school bus carrying 10 kids or more every day in the 1960s. Now, with only a quarter of the previous farm families on the land, there is no bus.

Peter lived an exciting life in many respects studying and teaching maths, physics and chemistry and later became embroiled in music, literature, poetry and politics, travelled to far lands and met "crazy girls singing these new songs". He joined the Police force in 1972 and *"upset by the growing injustice on the beat returned to tertiary study in 1975 and this time determined to succeed and make a difference in the lives of the people I encountered as a police officer".*

I had always wanted to help people hence my choice of medicine as a career, but I was quite uninterested in the left-wing politics of the early 1970s. Getting jobs and having babies will do that to you.

Peter clearly cared for people from the experiences he had personally and in the police force and I wonder whether he saw this as symbolic and compensating for the pain he had suffered, indeed the nexus in his life. He writes of the adventures and challenges he had in the 1970s but there are frequent examples of his distress and even tortured soul such as *"Flying around the world in jet planes rather than going around paddocks in a tractor"* and being *"The first member of my family to lose touch with the land and to be forced by circumstances to make a new and very different life in a foreign land".*

He graduated as a teacher in 1978 and moved into counselling. This included extra-curricular activities such as helping Aboriginal children with food and in other ways not mentioned in the book.

There is a very poignant line in his discussion about this role that reminded me of the truism, "People teach best what they need to learn". Peter refers to his *"personal journey out of affliction was still very much at its raw and innocent beginning."*

It took him 20 years to emerge from the chrysalis of the classroom and to become more involved with the community when he became a consultant to the local health service in Port Lincoln and then to Health Plus as discussed and where he gained a PhD and later after a stellar career became a Director of a University Department of Rural Health.

As the evocative title to his book infers he has spent the last twenty years working to describe and remedy the health disadvantages that add to the social and economic problems of his "flock" in Australia.

Pete, I have learned many things from you but the most important one is to eat oysters I have opened myself, with added lemon juice left in the freezer for two minutes accompanied with a red wine by the fire in the winter.

I believe you have laid your ghosts to rest but would not be the least surprised to see you settle on a few acres in Tasmania and retire in harmony with good food, a bit of meat, glass of red wine and frequent fireside chats with your ancestors about the essence of your beloved rural life and in particular what determines the size of a man's chainsaw.

RETURN JOURNEY

By Rory Barnes

In 1967 I should have been completing my degree at Monash University but for various reasons I decided to take a year off. I worked for a while building taxiways at the Canberra airport, and then driving a biscuit delivery truck in Melbourne. Then I flew to London. The plane left from Sydney; neither Canberra nor Melbourne did international flights in those days. I found my seat and discovered that by pure happenstance I was sitting next to a girl I vaguely knew from Monash, I'll call her Z. I greeted her and asked her where she was going.

"My bloody parents are shipping me off to some relatives in Brussels." I said something fairly inadequate, probably: "That'll be nice."

"This whole damn plane can go down in the sea for all I care."

I knew enough about Z to understand her sentiments. She and her boyfriend had wanted to get married but her parents wouldn't give their permission. Z had forced the issue in the time-honoured way by getting pregnant. Her parents had smartly signed on the dotted. Then Z and her new husband were in a horrendous car crash. Z survived but her husband and unborn child did not.

The plane leapfrogged its way across the globe, stopping in Jakarta, Singapore, Bangkok and Tehran before taking off for Cairo. I spoke to Z occasionally, trying to be a friendly presence while not intruding on her grief. We reached Cairo an hour or two before dawn on the second of June 1967. The date is important. Things were tense in the transit lounge with machine-gun toting soldiers keeping a cautious eye on the milling passengers.

But in the grey early light the plane took off for Brussels without incident. As we left the ground it was possible to see the Egyptian air force's collection of MIGs lined up - wingtip to wingtip - at the other end of the runway from the civilian terminal. I mentioned to Z that to me the MIGs looked like sitting ducks - "You'd think they'd spread them out a bit," I said. Z remained gloomily unimpressed by my observation. I sensed that she'd be quite happy to have the Israelis bomb us as well as the MIGs.

Exactly seventy-two hours later the Israelis did indeed bomb Cairo airport as part of the series of pre-emptive strikes that started the Six Day War. The neatly parked MIGs didn't stand a chance. I was in London by then and took little comfort from the fact that - as far as the MIGs went - I'd shown more prescience than the entire Egyptian High Command.

I had a great six months in England and Wales, and then it was time to go home.

One other result of the Six Day War was the blocking of the Suez Canal by bombed shipping. I had been planning to return to Australia by boat (it was still cheaper than air flight in the high season) and I still did – but the boat had to go via Cape Town.

I'd been to Cape Town before. When I was a baby in 1946 my mother and I had passed through on our way to Chengela in Northern Rhodesia where my father was already working as an anthropologist. Two years later as a toddler, I'd passed through Cape Town again, in the opposite direction. I remembered neither of these events.

But in 1967 my father had told me that he had written to one of his anthropologist colleagues and that she might meet me when my ship stopped in Cape Town. Beauty, I thought, I'll get the lowdown on bloody South Africa from an expert.

The ship arrived at Cape Town. I waited for a while but the anthropologist didn't turn up. I decided to go exploring by myself. I made my way to the gangplank that had been set up between the ship and the shore. There were a lot of passengers jostling for position, officials checking passports etc. Getting ashore would take some time.

Earlier, hanging over the side of the ship, I had noticed another gangplank leading from the dock to the crew's quarters. I decided to use that gangplank instead. I made my way through the bowels of the ship, passing through a door into the section of the ship, normally out-of-bounds for passengers. I started to descend the gangplank. This gangplank was very narrow, wide enough for only one person. Half way down I was met by a man coming up. He was carrying a crate of something on his head, as Africans do.

We should note the following:

I was 21 years old; the other guy was probably in his forties.

I wasn't meant to be there, he was.

I wasn't carrying anything; he had a heavy crate on his head.

I was going down; he was coming up.

I was white, he was black.

I stood aside, as much as this was possible on the narrow gangplank to allow the bloke to pass. He stood aside to allow me to pass. This involved bracing his whole body against the flimsy rail and leaning backwards over the void, with nothing between the crate and the drop to the dock but his own head. For a few seconds nothing happened. It hit me that this was how things were in this country: black people stood aside for white people, regardless of circumstance. I edged my way past the other guy mumbling something like, "Sorry mate." He said nothing, there was no eye contact. I arrived on the dock feeling a bit sick.

As I started to walk down the dock the ship's loud speaker system announced, "Would Rory Barnes please report to the Embarkation Point." I returned to the ship via the official gangplank and met the anthropologist who had just arrived. She took me for a tour of Cape Town. It was a Sunday afternoon – things were pretty quiet, Cape Town was very pleasant.

At one point we were at a lookout half way up Table Mountain: the bay was spread out before us, including Robben Island. I knew what went on on Robben Island, I could even have named at least two of the island's most famous inhabitants: Nelson Mandela and Walter Sisulu. But I decided that my best chance of getting a real conversation going was to play the naïf.

"That's a nice Island," I said brightly. "Do people live out there?"

The anthropologist was quiet for a few seconds and then she said, "It's a prison. The real hard cases are out there...Oh, them and a few politicals of course." There was a certain finality to this information.

I wasn't stupid and neither was she. I knew she was refusing my offer of a proper conversation. I was just a passing foreigner still wet behind his ears – some things were too hard for casual chat. I said nothing more and we drove back to her flat where she made me a very tasty asparagus omelette. Then she drove me back to the ship, which left a few hours later for Fremantle.

The trip across the Indian Ocean was largely uneventful; a pod of whales off the starboard bow being the high point. In those days passengers on ocean going ships were effectively cut off from the world of international affairs: no newspapers, no radio, no television and certainly no internet. But the ship could still receive brief telegrams and a crude one-page roneoed newsletter was available every day.

It mainly contained football results - Tottenham Hotspurs defeated the Wolverhampton Wanderers two nil etc etc. One day, sandwiched amongst the British footy results was a single sentence "Harold Holt, the Australian Prime Minister, has disappeared." Disappeared? The PM? Gone missing? Gone walkabout? Done a bunk? Kidnapped by enemy aliens? Shot through with a stripper? What the...?

But then I realised there was really nothing very odd about the sentence. I was simply coming home. Welcome back, the roneoed bit of paper said, to the only country on Earth where such an event might actually happen. Doubtless the next day's newsletter contained a bit more information, but that first bulletin was quite surreal. And yet it inadvertently made the point that Australia in those days was still a place where the top bloke could wander around on his own and not come back.

Even in those days one couldn't imagine an American reading the same sentence about LBJ or a Pom reading it about Harold Wilson. And nowadays we'd be unlikely to read it about the present guy. Maybe the prime minister of the day can thank his or her lucky stars that an army of minders and security folk, encrypted mobiles, drones even, know his or her whereabouts 24/7. But it is a different country to the one I knew when I was twenty-one.

THE DAY I NEARLY MET PETER MORTON

By Robin Dutton

During my final year at Sir Roger Manwoods Grammar School, in March 1964, I sat for the entrance exam for the Royal Military Academy Sandhurst, as I had decided to join the Army, following in the footsteps of my father and two older brothers. A few weeks later I learnt that I had been successful, which may, or may not, have influenced my later commitment to my studies.

It is at this juncture that the course of my life abruptly changed direction. Dad told me that he had the opportunity to become the ELDO Representative in Australia, but that he and Mum thought that at 18, I was too young to leave on my own in England. My instant response was that I was more than happy to go to Australia.

Occasionally, I have wondered about the course my life might have taken if I had not come to Australia. I imagine that I would have been in the Army for 5 to 10 years. In the early 1970s the owners of the extended Byrom family plastic moulding factory called the Byson (of which my mother was one) were looking to the future and I am fairly sure that I would have been asked if I wanted to manage the factory. I would have probably accepted and would now probably be living in the north of England and speaking with a Lancastrian accent.

I finished school in July 1964. Mum had returned from Paris and was living back in Otford. Dad was commuting to and from Paris. Mum and I did most of the packing for the move to Australia. Dad was a hoarder, unlike Mum and Me. What we torched and threw out, we would never have got away with had Dad been with us. In Australia Dad would often enquire about the whereabouts of things, Mum would look at me and say "I haven't seen that since Otford"

We sailed from Tilbury Dock on the P &O Liner SS Oronsay in the middle of August 1964. Ports of call were Gibraltar, Naples, Port Said, Aden, Columbo, Fremantle and Adelaide. We arrived at Outer Harbour on the Tuesday before the SA Grand Final. I remember this so well because I was left at Outer Harbour to ensure that all our luggage came off the ship, I then caught a taxi to Fulham Gardens and the first thing the driver asked me was who would win the Grand Final, I didn't have a clue what he was talking about. As it turned out Neil Kerley led South Adelaide to victory after South Adelaide took out the wooden spoon the previous year.

An enquiry to the University resulted in me having to pass leaving Honours Maths 1 and 2 in order to matriculate. I attended Pulteney Grammar for nine weeks, and in that time learnt how to learn from a book, rather than being spoon fed. I passed both exams and enrolled at the University of Adelaide to do Civil Engineering. It was just before Orientation Week 1965, that I met Judy. Four years later, we were married, with final year engineering still ahead. The Engineering Faculty had a dinner at the Morphett Arms Hotel to give us our final year results. Bearing in mind that I was not one of the more brilliant students, I was pleasantly surprised to find that I had achieved 3 C's thinking that a D might be a fail, when I saw the slip of paper belonging to my mate, who had 2 Cs and a P. I asked what the P was, and was told that it was a pass. It was at this point, having just realized that I had achieved 3 credits, that our Senior Lecturer, George Sved tapped me on the shoulder and asked me what I thought of my results. I told him that I was amazed, George smiled and said "you are not as amazed as I am!!

I won a cadetship with the Commonwealth Dept of Works covering the last two years of Engineering studies. When I think that at a graduate engineer commenced on a salary of $4,400 per annum, I realised that $3,400 as a student was quite generous and it was certainly sufficient to allow Judy and me to get married.

Upon graduating, for a while it appeared that I would be posted to Perth, as it was unusual to be posted in your home city, however a late breaking cancellation meant that I remained in Adelaide. My first year after graduation was spent in the Roads and Aerodromes design section of the Department of Works, the second year in the Construction section. At the end of 1972 an opportunity arose to be seconded to the Dept of Defence as a Class 2 Engineer in Woomera. I successfully applied and with Judy and our first son Nick moved to Woomera at the beginning of January 1973.

It was here that I first met Peter Morton. Judy had met Peter many years earlier when she lived in Naracoorte, but I still had that pleasure ahead. Soon after arrival in Woomera I was informed that I needed to have a medical check-up as part of the induction formalities, so I presented myself to the Hospital, and was told that Dr Morton shouldn't be too long. WRONG!! Dr Morton appeared, looked around and called someone else, who had just walked in. This happened a couple of times, and after 50 minutes I thought bugger this, and walked out. I never did have that medical. Luckily Judy convinced me that Dr Peter Morton was really a good guy, and when we later met socially, I found it hard to disagree with her. Many a time Peter and I found ourselves singing the song RED RED WINE!

I had been to Woomera in 1967 or 1968 for one of the successful firings of the ELDO Europa rocket. I think it was F4 or F5. We stayed in the ELDO Mess and went down range to the viewing site for two consecutive mornings. It was a major disappointment when the launch was cancelled the first morning, but what a fantastic sight the successful launch was the following morning. I can always remember the two responses my father had for the press after a launch. If the launch was successful his response would be "I'm delighted" and if unsuccessful it would be "We learn more from a failure, than from a success" Spin was alive and well back then!!

Five weeks after we arrived in Woomera in 1973, the rain came down, 5 inches in one weekend. The damage to the infrastructure was huge, roads were washed out, the dams at the sewerage treatment works were washed out, there was damage to the water supply pipeline from Port Augusta. As a young Engineer, a day labour force of 100 men, experience was gained very rapidly.

Our second son Geoff was born in Woomera, being ushered into this world by Dr Peter Morton. Peter was playing cricket at the Arboretum Oval that Sunday, when he was called away. I was watching the cricket and having been present at the birth of Nick I saw no reason to go through that experience again. Just after lunch, Peter returned and with the words "It's got a spout" I knew that Judy had had a boy and that visiting time had commenced. On the way home after visiting Judy, I met one of the head nurses who lived nearby. She asked me what I thought of the new baby, I replied, pretty good, but not as good looking as Nick had been when he was born. I learnt a valuable lesson there and then – that it does not always pay to tell the truth, especially when it comes to new born babies!

I remember being invited by Peter to go out shooting with him south of Pimba. He shot a couple of rabbits, and finally gave me the gun, and invited me to take a shot at a pigeon at about 25 metres. He said make it a head shot, or it won't be worth eating. I took careful aim along the open sight, squeezed the trigger, and lo and behold – head shot. I have never shot a gun again in Peter's presence for fear of spoiling my perfect record. I should probably admit that I had achieved a marksman rating on the rifle range back at school, but don't tell Peter!

Life after Woomera is a story for another day, but we have maintained our friendship with Peter and Leonore over the years, having stayed with them in Warrnambool and Port Lincoln a few times and for some reason the song Red Red Wine seemed to rear its ugly head on every one of them!

THE DAY MY BROTHER SHOT ME

By Robin Dutton

In November 2017, my eldest brother John applied for, and was accepted as a contestant on the quiz programme 'Who wants to be a Millionaire' on Channel 9. It seems to me that to be selected, apart from having broad general knowledge, one needs a good story. Well, John had one and it was about the time that he shot me.

John, somewhat reluctantly, volunteered to be first cab off the rank. He then strategically elected to pass one of the simple questions early on, in the hope of getting back into the hot seat later. That didn't work out, and to his chagrin, he knew the answers to all subsequent questions!! One million dollars slipped through his fingers. Life is full of regrets.

Before getting onto the questions, Eddie McGuire asked John about the time he shot his brother, and John told the story as follows:

"About five years after the end of WW2, aged about 9 or 10 I found a bullet. I think it was from a Sten gun. There was a group of about half a dozen of my friends and my younger brother Robin. I tried to detonate the bullet by hitting it with a brick, but nothing happened, so I told Robin to run home and get a hammer out of Dad's workshop. Off he went and about 10 minutes later back he came with the hammer. I struck the bullet, and the second time it went bang, and Robin's leg was bleeding"

"What did your Father say", asked Eddie

"He never found out, well, not until twenty years later" said John

"What" said Eddie "He's wandering around with a lump of lead in his leg, and your father didn't find out"

"That's right" said John "but he does set off all of the metal detectors in airports"

John is known for his ability not to let the truth interfere with a good story, so in the interest of setting the record straight, this is my version of the story.

As background, my father was a Major in REME in the British Army. We had recently returned from Germany where he had been posted for a couple of years. He was second In Charge of the Lydd army base where we were living. Our house looked directly down a rifle/artillery range, and as children we had an amazing degree of freedom to do what we liked. We used to ride about three miles down the range and play in tanks and on anti-aircraft guns abandoned on the shingle beach after the war. Another time John and I went down the range looking for bird eggs very early one morning (about 5.30 am). What we did not see was the red flag being raised at 7.30 am warning that artillery was about to be fired down the range. Luckily for us, an observant sergeant saw us wandering around about 2km down the range. We were picked up, and dumped unceremoniously in the back of a Land Rover, and later deposited in our *father's office.*

But I digress.

John found a bullet, I think it was a .22 bullet, not a Sten gun bullet, I don't remember him hitting it with a brick, but he could have done. He certainly sent me home to get the hammer. When I got back, John was standing in the middle of a large concrete slab with the bullet on the ground in front of him. All his mates were standing on one side of the slab about 10 yards away. I retired in the opposite direction from them and was also about 10 yards away. John hit the bullet, nothing; he hit it again, there was a popping sound, and my leg was bleeding. This is where his story and mine diverge.

We went home, and told our German maid Sigrid that I had been shot. She promptly phoned Mum and Dad, who were having Sunday afternoon cocktails at the Colonel's house. Needless to say they were home remarkably quickly, and my Mum whisked me off to the Medical Officer. He probed and prodded around, presumably removing the offending fragment of the .22 bullet, dressed the wound and sent us on our way. So not only do I not set off all airport metal detectors, but I do not even have a scar to show for it. What I do have, however, is a scar on my knee on the other leg, because as I left the MO's surgery, I fell over in the gravel outside and opened my knee up!! The MO cleaned that up as best he could and told me to be more careful in future.

As a footnote to this story, my brother Peter, having completed his Army Officer training, was posted to Sarawak in 1965, and on the way had to fill in a couple of weeks in the Army Stores in Singapore. The Quarter Master, upon learning that Peter's surname was Dutton, went quiet and thoughtful, and then asked if Peter used to live on the Army camp at Lydd, and did he have a red headed brother? (That being my ratbag eldest brother John) Peter answered in the affirmative, and the Quarter Master was heard to say – that little bugger, he ran me ragged!!

THE HESSIAN BAG REVOLUTION

By Peter Morton

Like most people who enjoy camping and driving FWDs, I have read a great deal in magazines about the Holy Grail of ACCESSORIES for a vehicle. Never mind that Len Beadell drove through the trackless bush making the Woomera Rocket Range and north, south, east and west roads in a stock standard SWB Land Rover with a four-cylinder petrol engine. He did, however, have a bull bar with a vice bolted on to it. Anyone reading this article should know what FWD and SWB mean. If not put it down and read a Cleo or something.

Nowadays people spend $10,000 to $100,000 or even more on a vehicle and then to make it a really good off road, they need to spend more – lots more.

Time to introduce the HESSIAN BAG aka HB to our world.

These bags made from jute can be hard to find but are simple, strong, cheap, versatile and practical. I have scrounged these bags from people who have chooks and get their feed that way. Another source is bait shops for the smaller lighter bags from which they decant their cockles. If these sources fail, Port Lincoln Rural Supplies stock them at less than four dollars and sell lots because they have so many and varied uses and are so environmentally friendly. I assume other stock firms would do the same.

USES OF A HB

1. They are perfect for carrying barbecue plates and they can be used to protect cans of beer from wearing holes in each

other on a rough trip. They are also the perfect rubbish holder to hang on a tree or vehicle when camping and can be emptied on the way home and reused instead of adding more plastic bags to the world's rubbish

2. They have long been a standby in the bush for beating out small fires with their good mates, long handled shovels. Wet is best but dry will do at a pinch.

3. When beach fishing they can carry beer on the way in and fish on the way out and can be put in the water or buried in wet sand to keep the beer and fish cool and clean.

They also prevent bogging by carrying things that would normally occupy one or more 50 litre ice boxes; these are heavy and have to be carried to the beach in a vehicle, which may get bogged.

When rock fishing they are truly in their element because vehicle access is not usually a consideration.

4. The HB is useful for hunting and "scrounging". A nice HB will carry rabbits, ducks, kangaroos (all dressed of course). If the reader does not know what "dressed" means stop reading. The old HB will also handle seaweed, cockles, fish, bait, sheep and cattle manure, mushrooms, shells, quandongs, worms, kindling and crabs but do not carry a bag of live crabs over your shoulder as they can bite through the jute, particular "muddies". They can protect floors, seats and roof racks directly or carry things like stretchers and chairs.

5. A little known use of the HB is in the collection, transport and production of "olive dates". These are dried salted olives and are made by picking black olives and taking them home in the HB. We like to wash the olives and pick out the bits and pieces of rubbish and then dry them. An old

pillow slip can be used for the salting and drying if a small HB is not available.

Equal volumes of olives and coarse salt are put in the pillow slip, shaken about and hung under a verandah or in a shed for three weeks with a spare HB underneath them to catch the drips and prevent a mess. Taste at this time and if still bitter leave for another week.

Shake and or wash off salt depending on taste and store dry in a jar or in olive oil.

6. A HB is a great accessory for the dog that goes everywhere with you and gets wet, smelly and sandy. HB is a good cleaning towel, seat protector and bed. If your mate is a Labrador about a dozen HBs will do the trick. They are handy to put on the camp chair or car seat to soak up beer, blood and bait bits that get on blokes' bums.

7. If sleeping in a swag they make a nice mat to step on in the morning for comfort, protection and warmth. It is worth checking, particularly in the dark, that a snake hasn't found the value of a HB and has taken up residence.

It is more likely that the Labrador has taken it over so he won't mess up his nice clean HB bed with the lovely mature sheep's head he found. Another benefit is that you can chuck a HB away but if it is your $500 down sleeping bag where the dog has stored his sheep's head that is a different story.

8. A HB or two can save $250. If bogged in sand it is likely that the vehicle will need to be jacked up on the BBQ plate of course and something put under the wheels. A lot of people carry some coloured plank like things for this purpose and I am sure they are fantastic, but some HBs with a shovel full of sand in them are perfect for placing under the wheels.

You did chuck in the long-handled shovel with a foot sawn off the handle, didn't you? Oh, you left them home in its HB. Damn.

9. With imagination they can be used as a "raincoat". Push one of the corners in until you can sort of hang it on the back of your head and over your shoulders. If you have a hat, cut a hole in the bottom for your head and arms and wear it like a poncho.

10. If you have still managed to get bogged in sand and can't get out remove your snatch strap from its HB and hook up two vehicles. Get rid of the mob and check that everything is OK. Then drape or tie some towels, a shop bought thing that looks like saddle bags with lead in them or the HB about the mid-point of the snatch strap. The HB should have a shovel full of sand in it and be tied at the top so it can hang over both sides of the strap.

The point of all this is if the strap breaks when it is under tension it can slingshot a tow ball or piece of the other car or boat or camper trailer at or into another vehicle or a person. The HB or other things dampen this reaction by absorbing the energy of the strap. A simple, cheap and effective way to prevent what could be a catastrophic injury to you or your loved ones or serious damage to a vehicle.

11. Finally when the worn, torn and forlorn HB is laid to rest it will still contribute to your world by acting as mulch or a weed mat in the garden, not only preventing weeds but also gently delivering its organic matter into the soil and continuing the cycle of life. Quite possibly some worms will eat it and you can use them for bait. A final salute.

A farewell salute
To the old bag of jute
It will always suit
The back of a ute!

Part 11 The sad reality of life sometimes

A STRANGE AND EVEN SCARY TALE

By Peter Morton

When I worked in Woomera, my wife Leonore and I became very friendly with the USAF Commander Colonel Burley Vandergriff, his wife Loretta and children Cindy, Kerry and Nancy.

This was partly personal, partly administration and mostly social. Among other things Burley and I were foundation members of the Thursday Night Garden and Social Club that met weekly in a lined shed at our home.

If there was nothing interesting on the agenda, we filled in the time playing stud poker.

In 1977 Burley and Major Frank Nance, also a Garden Club member in Woomera, visited Australia and stayed with us in Warrnambool where I was working as the Medical Superintendent after leaving Woomera.

It was football finals time and they managed to get three seats for the North Melbourne V Hawthorn preliminary final game. I met them at Waverley Stadium and saw a game that North Melbourne won easily.

They had been staying at the Sheraton in Melbourne, so we called there on the way home and had a beer or two.

Burley and a guy from Sydney had a friendly argument about who would win the Grand Final, the next week. Burley thought North Melbourne and the other guy liked Collingwood and challenged Burley to a bet. The Sydney guy gave Burley odds of two to one and two goals in. This meant that Collingwood had to win by two or more goals or Burley would win the bet.

Out came the money; Burley put down $20 and it was covered by $40, which was a bit of money 40 years ago. I couldn't believe all this and stupidly asked who was going to hold the money and they both turned around and said "You".

It was a draw so Burley collected and that was fortunate because I had forgotten the Sydney guy's details.

Funny the things one remembers. We bought hamburgers on the way home and they had beetroot on them. Frank just could not understand why we would have "Beets on a hamburger".

The next day we went to the Grampians and relaxed with a fire, barbecue and beers in a bushy place. While enjoying this idyllic afternoon. I told Burley and Frank I had been offered a position to do an MBA at Harvard through the Victorian Hospital and Charities Commission, which must have had some pretty good connections.

I was reluctant to accept this because it was for 30-year-old "wunderkinds" from General Motors and the like. Secondly, I felt quite bad and unsure of myself leaving Leonore for that time and I would have had to stay in the same sort of job for two years in the Victorian Health System. That was probably not enforceable but it was a matter of honour and I did not want to commit myself for that length of time. Burley said he would give anything to get an offer like that.

We went on to discuss at some length the planned reduction of USA forces in the Pacific as the British had done after Burley left Woomera in early 1975.

At least 10 years later I had a dream about 0600-0700.

Burley and I were sitting on a log with Australian bush in the background and I had no doubt at the time it was the Grampians. We were talking about USA forces in the Pacific or very similar. Behind us there was the figure of a person, a wraith perhaps, moving and outlined in the bush. It was silent and appeared to be trying to find a way through the bush to join us.

The telephone rang and it was Burley saying Frank Nance had a massive heart attack and was on life support waiting for his family before they turned it off.

I am not at all into spooky stuff but that had to mean something surely.

AN UNFORGETABLE NIGHT AND PERSON

By Peter Morton

On July 8, 1963 Victoria and South Australia were the adversaries for an interstate game of Australian Rules football at the Adelaide Oval.

Victoria was virtually unbeatable. I probably watched every game played in Adelaide from the Carnival in 1953, when I saw the great John Coleman play in his long-sleeved jumper with the sleeves pushed up, until the late 1960s and I do not recall seeing South Australia win a game. Actually, much to my surprise when I checked, they won in 1965 which I missed when playing football for Adelaide University.

The Victorians did not even play their best team. The Victorian public insisted on their local competition being played, whereas Adelaide people were keen to see the champions. There were 12 VFL teams in 1963. They may have picked two from the top nine teams and one from the rest or something similar.

I was playing with the Sturt Football Club at the time and an extra shine on the day was that the Club ball was to be held that Saturday night and the Victorian team had been invited.

But back to the game, which I assume was going according to the usual script when there was much, albeit short lived, drama. Brian Sawley hit, or pulled the jockstrap of, or did nothing to Victorian John Peck who was on the ground. As Peck got up, in one flowing movement, his fist went from the ground to Sawley's jaw and knocked him out.

It was quite close to the boundary and maybe 15 metres

south of the members' enclosure. While the umpires were sorting things out, directly opposite the unconscious Sawley, a man in a leather jacket jumped the fence and charged towards Peck and straight into the arms of Neil Kerley, the South Australian iron man, and Alex Epis from Essendon. They literally grabbed one arm each and carried/dragged him off the oval and threw him back over the fence.

I thought at the time that if the incident happened in the middle of the oval or Epis and Kerley did not grab him others may have followed him over the fence and who knows what might have happened.

It was really quite strange. "Sawley" was a proud and feared name at the Norwood football club with several related people having played for that team over the years. The victim was a tough player and certainly not liked much by other than Norwood supporters. That day, instead of that "Bloody bastard Sawley" he was "Our mate good old Brian Sawley".

Later at Centennial Hall where the Sturt Ball was underway the beer was starting to talk. What we were going to do to these bloody Victorians was nobody's business. About nine o'clock they entered in a wedge formation formed up on captain John Nicholls, one of the toughest and strongest footballers ever, with Peck in the middle. They all wore light grey slacks and dark blue blazers and were power incarnate.

We turned from avenging demons into fawning puppies instantly. "Hey guys want a beer", "Want a smoke, I'll light it", "Didn't bring a girl here take mine". Just kidding about the last one but physically they were so intimidating.

Nicholls, particularly, had massive legs and it was a

noticeable feature generally that Victorians had bigger legs than South Australians perhaps because they played and trained on muddy grounds.

My partner at the ball was a Tina Lawton. She was a friend who happened to be a girl, not the other way around and we saw a lot of each other at university and around the place. She was a folk singer of renown and I must say that in the days of Joan Baez, Peter, Paul and Mary, Bob Dylan, Peter Seeger and so on it was pretty cool driving around on a summer night with her singing "Kumbaya," "Banks of the Ohio" etc. or to see and listen to her at the "Catacombs" coffee lounge, the "in-place" in the 1960s

She was a nice person and like many of her profession keen to see the world. Fuddy-duddy that I was I tried to talk her into finishing her Arts course but she was set on performing for the troops in Vietnam that she did twice.

Amazingly Burley Vandergriff, a USAF Colonel in Woomera I have mentioned elsewhere, who became a great friend of mine, took her out to dinner in Vietnam.

She had a stellar career in Australia touring, recording, performing on "Bandstand" and other TV shows and live with people like Don Burrows and in 1967 she went to live in Edinburgh. I don't suppose I saw her after 1964 as she was in a different world, literally, from mine.

In 1968 I received a nice letter from her in which she wrote that she wished she had finished her Arts degree as I suggested. It gave me a strange feeling to know that I had such an influence and in no way did I feel any sense of "I told you so". She went on to write that she was going to Kenya soon on a holiday and on her return would study fine art at the

University of Edinburgh.

Soon after I was driving down the Anzac Highway in Adelaide and heard on the radio that Tina and the pilot of a light aircraft were killed when it crashed in a volcano crater in Kenya. They were found three days later and buried at the site.

GERRY ALLEN FISHER, GATHERER, WARRIOR AND FRIEND

By Peter Morton and Peter Buttery

My schoolmate and lifelong friend Peter Buttery left school in 1959 to work for Coopers and Lybrand and to study accountancy at night school as was the training custom in those days. He progressed very well at work and with his studies. Gerry also worked in that office and had taken out a fellow worker, Jill Woods, who Peter eventually married.

Gerry was a year older than Peter and had an advantage when partnerships became available so this had some relevance to Peter leaving Coopers and becoming a partner in another firm.

Gerry was a schoolmate, football player and friend of my cousin Bevan Roberts and Tony Fuller, a friend who later became my lawyer, the name Gerry Allen was well known to me but not the person.

The warrior bit of Gerry made him a tough, uncompromising centre half back. He held the record for the most games for decades for Scotch Old Collegians until this was broken by a Michael Vadasz, another guy I knew in Adelaide, but that is another story altogether.

I have written another story about Noel and Ruth Linsell who in 1962 moved to the West Coast in South Australia and naturally had to borrow money to do so. Somehow this debt wound up in the hands of Coopers in the mid-late 1960s and Gerry, who I suspect may have been the newest partner, looked after their business.

Gerry loved fishing and foraging so now with wife Sally

and three boys he was like a kid in a lolly shop exploring the area north of Coffin Bay where the Linsells lived. They all enjoyed rock fishing especially for sweep. I should add that Sweep MUST be caught using pickled Goolwa cockles, a recipe passed to Gerry by his dad. Before and after cooking they must be covered in lemon juice.

Gerry proudly claimed he had never bought or grown lemons but gathered them around the Fullarton, Myrtle Bank or, heaven forbid, Springfield streets in Adelaide. He obtained firewood the same way, maybe extending into the Adelaide Hills a little further.

Business trips to the West Coast resulted in a few pieces of signed paper and a trailer load of wood, sweep and other fish, legs of hogget, fresh steaks, maybe rabbits and kangaroo and the fruits of his frenetic, fungicidal missions that took him far and wide.

I am getting a head of myself. We first met Noel and Ruth in 1980-81 when we bought some land near them and we became quite friendly and it was not long before Gerry's name came up. I have mentioned in another story how Noel and Ruth fell on hard times and of course Gerry was front and centre in helping them professionally and as a friend. Somewhere around this time we met and with Sally and Leonore the four of us hit it off really well.

There were three things that really stood out when we first met.

The first was a fishing trip to Frenchman's north of Coffin Bay where we fished from the rocks for sweep and Gerry and the family demonstrated how to do it.

Gerry and the three boys caught the fish and Sally sat in a rock pool and cleaned the fish being very fussy in getting rid of the black membrane lining the abdominal cavity. We caught 60 and later with our four kids and a couple of visitors ate the lot at our Coffin Bay shack and that really tightened the bonds of friendship.

The second story is about Noel's accident with a pig. Gerry, at the time was the President of the National Association of Chartered Accountants and the Practice Manager of Coopers in Adelaide and quite a mover and shaker. Noel found his way into the big shiny building in Adelaide and Coopers' office and asked the very efficient, well-groomed and attractive receptionist if he could see Gerry.

Noel took a seat as directed and Gerry duly arrived and walked towards Noel with hand outstretched. Noel had a limp from an old injury but took longer than usual to struggle to his feet and he held onto the counter. Gerry asked if had hurt himself. Noel replied in what may be described as a slow, loud, high pitched, gravelly drawl, "Yair I have hurt me self, a pig bit me in the bloody balls". Gerry couldn't stop laughing, the elegant receptionist choked on her Perrier water and the rest I do not know as Gerry was too blinded with tears from laughter to notice.

The third story is that Gerry, Sally, Leonore and I bought some of Noel's land and later sold it and bought an adjoining farm. That was in 1995 the year my mother, Glenys, died and we named the property Glenvale and successfully ran some cattle there.

For Christmas we decided to buy two Belted Galloway heifers that we named Sally and Leonore after the human people involved. Galloways are very similar to Aberdeen Angus (which now just seemed be called Angus) cattle being black, hardy and from Scotland. But they are not as pretty as the Galloways which have a belt of white fur 15-40 cm wide around their midriff. I had seen them at a show and thought they were cute and would stand out amongst our red shorthorn cattle.

Later I found out that the owner of Clifton Hills, one of the huge cattle stations in the north of South Australia, runs red cattle in red dirt and buys 20-30 Belted Galloway bulls and puts one in each mob of red cattle. When they are mustering, with aeroplanes, they can pick up the black and white cattle more easily than their mates. *(I saw their progeny in 2018 and was thrilled to do so)*

I rang a cattle buyer and asked him if he had access to Galloways. He replied. "Yair they're them bloody things that doctors and accountants give their wives for Christmas presents," with his voice dripping with scorn.

I informed him of our occupations and that we wanted two. The phone went very quiet and in the silence, I played a master stroke. It was probably only a few seconds but I let the silence stretch out and said, "Get us a coupla decks of shorthorn stores to go with 'em mate". This means "Please would you purchase and arranged the freight of sufficient shorthorn cattle, that are skinny, for us to fatten, that would fill the space available on the two decks of a semi-trailer that carries cattle." Clearly that impressed him much more and he said that he would attend to the request. Well that's what he meant when he mumbled "No wucken furries mate". One of those cows only died in 2016 aged 21 the other died a few years before.

Sadly, there is a fourth story.

In 1997 I was rung at work by Scott Linsell to be told that Gerry had been fishing from some rocks south of Port Lincoln and had been swept off by a wave and drowned. He, Sally and some friends were staying at our place at Coffin Bay at the time.

I later identified his body for the police, a task that was not onerous, but certainly sad.

"LAD HAD A HOBBY"

By Steve Ballard

Just before Christmas in our third year in Port Lincoln my wife Leonore and I moved into a new house we had built on a high spot above Port Lincoln on the edge of the scrub, yet a mere 2500m from our work places.

One morning, on leaving, I leaned down to pick up my doctors' bag from the floor by the front door. "Odd", I thought. I checked the other rooms, study, back door...most peculiar. Must be in the car-. No. Must be in my clinic office-. No.

I dismantled our Clinic rooms, treatment room and then the hospital, knowing that it was not in either, then made a formal report to the Police.

The officers duly cased the property thoroughly, finding no evidence of forced entry.

A security system was on order, but we crossed fingers.

Two days later, my distraught wife called, never a good sign, to report that the house had been burgled while she was shopping. Cancel consulting, call police, inspect property.

Missing: state of the art sound system, electric guitar, 12 string guitar, SLR camera, hundreds of slides...remember them, photos, wine, CDs....very new then.

No mess, no damage.

No news for three weeks, until a detective, now a very senior officer in SAPOL, called to ask me to come to the station. There was a lot of our stuff with some superficial damage.

A rather laconic story was spun.

A lad not long finished school had a hobby.

He collected keys from doors at pre-lockup building sites. And watched. Patience is a virtue, we should think.

He would enter unoccupied premises unhindered, take something minor, and later return.

Not having a car, he needed help for a big job. A mate had a car, and in return for the use of the friend's car, the friend received our turn-table.

The mate's policeman father had just been transferred to the South-East and the mate was to drive down to be with Dad. Recognizing that the property was "hot" and would be hard to explain to Dad, he toddled off to the Cop-Shop, plonked the device on the counter and said, "It's hot, and I don't want nuffink to do with it".

"Yippee" said the Police. They had a lovely night dragging teenagers and parents out of bed, searching houses and solving several mysterious thefts in one night. Archery bows from a school, several cartons of potato crisps... true.., and several fire-arms, some owners did not know were missing.

Most of our stuff was hidden under a tarp in the "bugger bush", not far from our house.

They got lucky, as, two days after its discovery, a dozer levelled the lot for subdividing.

I'd replaced the sound system and CDs. The camera was OK. And the wine. "What wine?"

Come on.

"Oh, we smashed 'em".

'76 Grange.

Patient, but ill-educated.

A very few years later, a regular patient came in and hesitantly asked if I would care for her grandson.

I recognized the name as being one of our gang of burglars, though not the prime mover noted earlier.

He had been rendered ventilator dependent quadriplegic in a car crash many months prior.

A salutatory tale from the family; lads out on the town in the grandson's utility. It was a defected vehicle declared by police not to be driven. The least intoxicated mate drove it anyway, but into a fixed object.

My patient's grandson, in the tray of the ute, propelled by the inevitability of Newton's First Law, struck his head on the back of the cabin, breaking his neck at a site which is usually lethal.

After he spent many months in Adelaide at Hampstead Centre, his mother became desperate to look after him at home and was preparing to kit out a van, and home, to this purpose.

He had a small child living in Lincoln with an ex-girlfriend.

The family were aware of my knowledge of the past.

Although we all agreed that this would be very difficult, in a practical sense, I agreed to the request. If his plight was a punishment, it did not fit the crime.

The care he received at home was first rate, but he ultimately succumbed to late complications of his injury.

His mother's chief complaint was about the ploddiness of the legal system in determining damages.

When I was 8yo, I appeared on Channel Seven's "Funfair", where Angela Stacey was a compere.

She became the grandson's solicitor. That is fate; that is life.

Part 12 It is not always a wonderful emerging world for girls

LITTLE GIRLS' SHOES

By Peter Morton

Like many people I am interested in genetics and the origin of mankind which is widely believed to have happened in Africa before the glacial period. An article in a Scientific American magazine describes the climate as mild, food was plentiful and life was good but this was to change. About 195,000 to 123,000 years ago the world entered a prolonged glacial era.

Homo Erectus lived mainly in Europe and became extinct in that period but had interbred with our mob *Homo Sapiens* to the extent that about 4% of our genes are from them.

Something that has absolutely stunned me is that the population of mankind plummeted from 10,000 breeding individuals to just hundreds. The details are unclear but genetic studies have indicated that everyone alive today is descended from a small population that lived in one part of Africa and some say that there was a single male and female from who we are all descended.

Curtis W. Maren a leading researcher in the field has indicated that this was likely to have been at Pinnacle Point in Mussel Bay in the Cape Floral Region. This area has the highest diversity of flora for its size in the world, particularly tubers that are fleshier than most and children could eat them. The diet was rich in calories, energy from tuber carbohydrates and nutrients from seafood. It is also thought that shellfish with their high protein and fat content, their availability and the ease of metabolising them makes them a prime food for the development of the brain and other parts of the human nervous system. Not a bad place to be in tough times.

Maren makes the point that these people were highly intelligent as judged by the tools they made and their probable knowledge of tides as the seafood by and large could only be harvested at low tide. I have often pondered why we love looking at the stars as it almost seems intrinsic to our very being. Perhaps the intelligence to understand the relationship of the moon to the tides and therefore their food supply emerged then.

It also is hard to believe that the later exodus from Africa could have occurred without knowledge or an instinct for navigation. Maybe there is a gene for navigation. If there is our older daughter, Kirstin, my wife and I have it. Kirstin's husband and sister do not.

These people also learnt how to heat a particular stone to harden it so it could be flaked for making tools. They also developed a sequential process for making weapons, a distinct advantage when they entered Europe and came in contact with the Neanderthals. Maren refers to the complex pyro-technology to make these weapons and opines that language would have been necessary to pass it to further generations.

Elsewhere I have read that there may have been other similar enclaves on the western coast about the same latitude. Wherever and how groups formed and whether they were nomadic or not they must have had a mental map of where and when food would be found. Probably they found their way by reference to the heavens and seasons.

The group at Mussel Bay was probably about 200 mating pairs. There is a branch of science that examines the minimum number of people needed to maintain a population and that is about the number. Inbreeding would eventually occur but statistically a population that size would continue to survive. I was also stunned to read that NASA had calculated that 150 pairs would be enough. The reason for them to turn their attention to this was the fear that a nuclear war would end life on earth and maybe they could send people to another world and maintain our race.

There would have been a clear division of labour with women staying in the camp looking after the children and certainly when they were heavily pregnant, they would have been significantly disadvantaged in fleeing from danger in any form. It is highly likely that many societies were polygamous as many women would have died in or after childbirth and of course men died from sickness and injury perhaps literally chasing women from another tribe or defending their own, all in the name of genetic diversity of course.

It was highly likely that females spent most of their waking hours with other women looking after young children, collecting and preparing food, supervising and teaching older children various tasks and tribal lore, about having babies and ceremonies. The men likely spent time away hunting and gathering food, fighting and searching for materials for and making weapons.

There was another more serious side to this way of living.

Women needed to be part of a group for security. If a woman did not belong to the group eagerly and agreeably, she might be shunned. If her husband died or was killed, she and her children needed others to protect them. Girls and women evolved a pattern of behaviour that allowed this relationship with other women to develop and become permanent.

This has been common throughout history and different cultures with women sharing child-care, washing clothes, labouring in the fields, gathering food and collecting water as a group. In the world of today young women go to baby groups, meet friends for coffee, and join support groups for a host of things to do with them and their children and various other activities.

Older women socialise with each other in service clubs that once were men only, wine and food clubs, quilting, other craft groups and of course meet for coffee with friends for their birthdays. Perhaps this is all about the secondary gain of belonging to the group. Maybe there is a thread here with predominance of women in the older age groups of our society compared to men. Maybe the companionship women seek with their female friends is genetic and is responsible for behaviour from the past. Once it was protection if their men didn't return, now it is perhaps consciously or subconsciously seeking companionship for the lonely years of widowhood that is far more probable statistically than "widower hood".

The fact that my wife has just left me at home to make tomato soup, from our yummy home- grown fruit and gone to afternoon tea with one of her friends to celebrate her birthday is a coincidence---or is it? Soup cooked, and decanted through a mouille mill that was old when my wife bought it 49 years ago, kitchen tidied. Interestingly my wife readily admitted that she liked belonging to these groups for the very reason mentioned -just normal behaviour!

In his book "Triumph of the Nomads" Geoffrey Blainey cites a contemporary source who studied aboriginals in Arnhem Land in the late 19th century. He describes a bucolic life of groups of women chatting and laughing together, often by a river, gathering food from animal and plant sources and having time to play with their children and tell stories. They were the main providers of food compared to the male hunters. Blainey to my surprise writes that "If one of these aboriginal people was transported to a restaurant in Paris in the late 1800s, they would have been surprised by the lack in the variety of food the diners could choose." Not all of Australia has such a rich food supply as Arnhem Land but everywhere the women certainly were the main providers of food while the men did protect them and hunted with their various weapons and traps. In the modern world this has morphed into the man striding out in front of his wife, hands free and ready for action, ever alert and tense, to protect her and the grocery order she is carrying.

How does this relate to little girls' shoes? School age girls sit on the ground in a circle facing their friends with their legs crossed and the outside of their shoes resting on the ground. Their shoes soon show the wear that this posture causes. These interactions teach girls, the importance of and how to behave in a group and this behaviour continues into adult life at work and play. I have attended hundreds of meetings with women at work and they almost always reach agreement by continued dialogue and listening to the opinions of others. I well remember my late sister-in-law who was a teacher and a nun and an expert at getting her way at a gathering. If she wanted "A" to happen and everyone else wanted "B" she would go around and around the table listening intently, nodding, smiling and making agreeable comments until like magic everyone thinks "A" is the way to go. OK I am exaggerating a little but I am sure the reader understands what I mean.

I went to a conference in 2015 when I was working for the Australian Army and attended pertinent sessions that included the management of infertility, a common problem in the army. There were two very erudite 40-year-old women running the session and the question of fertility in women of that age and intervention was a hot topic.

The two lecturers were both childless and shared their regret of that fact with the audience and I must say I thought it was inappropriate at the time but I have thought about it since.

These women were sharing their innermost feeling with the audience and there was a sense of empathy and understanding emanating from the women there. The lecturers were taken into the bosom of the audience just like women have been taken in from time immemorial. I doubt I have experienced similar bonds between an audience and a lecturer before.

When I was a medical student there were about 10% female students now there is 60% or more and in veterinarian science in excess of 90% of students are girls. About two months ago I sat next to a women veterinarian who trained in Edinburgh where there were 100% girls in her year.

Interestingly she did not think that girls were smarter than boys but that they were better organised and clearer in their aims because they matured earlier. Not long before that conversation I read an article in my old boys' school magazine and it said the same thing.

Modern women communicate and plan well as one might expect with the genes they have inherited and with reproduction controllable they no longer suffer the consequences of a lifetime of babies or early death from that same cause.

Women have clearly improved their positions in the job market in the last 50 years. I suspect that the corpus of knowledge gained when they were in the minority in the workplace is now exploding through the female workforce and has left the guys standing flat footed.

Men and boys are on a slippery slope. There are likely to be few if any male primary school teachers in a few years. When I started work the first six hospitals were managed by men the last six were half and half and of course there are far more female doctors. Perhaps it is right and proper for women to "own" health care.

The success of appeals for breast cancer funding are testament to the influence of women and the reality that breasts are much nicer than the equally dangerous but unromantic and un-championed prostate. Men are proud to stand up for breast cancer support but I am yet to see many women raising the flag for prostate cancer

It is interesting that some women still grizzle about a glass ceiling. Women now ride racehorses, drive trucks, tractors and the like, manage companies, are police and ambulance officers, pilots, bus drivers, real estate agents, lawyers, accountants, veterinarians, engineers and play cricket and football in its various forms, are the majority of television presenters and play as many or more "macho" and police roles in films as men.

I know of no roles where men have taken traditional jobs of females except a few nurses and airline stewards.

Shakespeare has Hamlet saying "Nothing is good or bad but thinking makes it so." We will just have to see what plays out for the sons of today's mothers and who will care.

SHE MATTERS

By Jenny Podorozhnaya

In a small tent made of a games table and blankets and sheets is where her boundaries were breached for the umpteenth time. It wasn't that she didn't know how to say no so much as she didn't know she was allowed to. The message so far had been clear to her, not in what was said but in what was not. It was never said that she mattered, it was never said that she counted and when she was hurt, afraid or upset there was no-one who gave her comfort or showed her how to be soothed. In order to say no, there would have to be someone or something that mattered to enforce. This was not something she knew about herself. A boundary, of course, is only as strong as your belief in it. It needs to have life breathed into it, to be reinforced with strength of will and determination. It is a tricky feat for a small girl who doesn't yet know that she counts.

It was because of this she had the experience when looking in the mirror, staring for eons into the pools of eyes staring back and wondering who it was looking from behind the eyes. Quite deep for a six-year-old, but then, she was a strange sort of child who regularly had dreams about things other people couldn't see and made comments about the things she could see clearly that shocked adults when she said them out loud. Saying things like 'She is sad; it is because her husband doesn't love her' didn't endear her to others. She had a strange kind of knowing that to her was so obvious she never understood why she incurred the shame, shock and even physical punishment from adults for saying them out loud. Nonetheless, she was accurate and uncanny in her observations and the adults around her came to dread her opening her mouth.

Perhaps it was her realisation of this dreading of her words that led to her staying quiet about the morning visits. The morning visits where she was taught repeatedly that her body was not hers, because if it was, she would never have allowed that to happen. The perverse and unintended gift of these visits being that she learned she was more than just a body, a reflection, a shell. She discovered there was a part of her that was beyond the reach of groping hands, and for now she kept that part safe and secret. She would later find that this was the part connected to all things, the place where she gained her knowing from, but for now it was defended and hidden - the bit that couldn't be damaged if she didn't show it to anyone. It was protected but isolated, safe but alone. It would take great courage and vulnerability to reveal, but when she did she would learn about the unlimited power and reserves of energy that came from allowing herself to be authentic.

Years later when she found the courage to uncover her past and found the boxes and compartments in which she had hidden the many aspects of herself, she gave them the nourishment and compassion they had been starved of previously. By then she had everything she needed to search, recover and rescue the younger parts. They were ready. Arms outstretched, they had been waiting. They spoke and she heard.

She laughed, she loved, she forgave, she healed. Her body became her own. She matters.

SISTERS AND THE SILENT MESSENGER

By Peter Harvey

The revolutionary woman must know her enemies, the doctors, the psychiatrists, health visitors, priests, marriage counsellors, policemen, magistrates and genteel reformers, all the authoritarians and dogmatists who flock about her with warnings and advice. She must know her friends, her sisters, and seek in their lineaments her own. With them she can discover co-operation, sympathy and love. (1, p19)

At one time, and in many ways still today, an unspoken contract existed between the clergy and the poor and frightened devotees of the faith to whom they ministered. It was given that devout followers of the faith would accept all kinds of advice and spiritual guidance from the men of the cloth and their handmaidens simply because these people were, relative to themselves, so learned and knowledgeable; so elevated and mighty and so righteous in their being. They were also, by definition, directly in touch with the almighty and therefore well placed to provide guidance to lead the lower forms of humanity to a higher and better plane; something beyond the mundane nine to five drudgery, poor food and mindless adherence to the soap operas served up on the idiot box.

The poor, humble families huddling in their bulging

homes and run ragged by tribes of mysteriously bestowed offspring that they could not control, depended on the church and the state for help and guidance because as simple citizens they could not nurture and educate, let alone control their unruly rabble themselves. They did not have the necessary sophistication, knowledge or skill for such a role so they looked, rather pathetically, to a higher authority for this commodity. Consequently, they sent their children willingly to the schools and the churches for pastoral care, mentoring and teaching and, if they could afford it, they sent them to schools that were actually run by the church. This provided total security of mind and spirit all in the one place. What could be better? What social solution could be so all encompassing, right and proper and offer such confidence that the next generation would be so ably assisted on their way in life?

What lurked beneath the surface of this informal and unspoken social contract, however, was an insidious power that served to manipulate and control communities and give tacit permission to the men and women working in such institutions to exercise total control over the individuals whose care they were charged with and whose lives they totally dominated. So ubiquitous was this cloud of unknowing, and so revered were the executives of these places, that it was inconceivable that they would do anything other than what was right and good in relation to the education and nurturing of the innocent young people sent to them to be educated and trained in the ways of the Lord. Children caught in this process could not complain about being ridiculed, beaten or abused by their mentors and if they were beaten by them, they clearly deserved what they received and would likely receive even more of the same from their parents when they returned home if they questioned the goings on. The teachers had the best interest of the pupils at heart and their methods were designed to help their students grow into fine human beings.

As highlighted by recent enquiries into sexual abuse in the churches (2), any sexually motivated interference by the clergy would be denied by the faithful as an impossibility. Father would simply never do such a thing, so if a child were to report such actions their parents would not deem these reports credible, the child would not be trusted and the secret of their oppression and abuse would be covered up by an insidious complicity between family and church that would serve to endorse and condone such conduct; give it permission and legitimacy and perpetuate it for coming generations. In many cases such abuse would occur in the homes of families and in the parishes where weak and vulnerable people would go in good faith seeking genuine help and support with their daily existential and economic struggles.

The church did provide teaching, after a fashion, and selected the odd pupil, who turned out to be smarter than most of the teachers, to go on to higher things; to join the church perhaps or if they were truly fortunate, to attend university and begin to get a liberal education that might eventually free them from their oppressed state of being. A hierarchy of ignorance pervaded this culture and it was only the changing needs of a burgeoning post WW2 society that demanded a more educated and informed workforce and freed more people to complete secondary school and pursue a tertiary education. This new workforce was constrained and limited in its own way, but it was still more free and liberal than its predecessor.

As this new approach to community, culture and work emerged, the old-world order, like the old human brain, still worked away within and beneath the layers of the neo-cortex and still very much influenced the behaviours and the values of the new generation of people who were, ostensibly, on a bolder life path, but essentially still controlled by the myths and legends of their old world. They still wondered about the existence of God, about virtue, right and good and although they enjoyed the spoils of sexual freedom, cars, travel and good food and wine, they were still constrained by the outmoded rituals of marriage, the glass ceiling at work and the inevitability of violence and warfare as the ultimate means for resolving important disputes. Mary was grateful for all she received and to help out a little she worked as a volunteer at the local church second hand shop. All was good and God was in his heaven, but it wasn't god that Mary should have been worried about.

When she had time to think about it, she developed a concern that something odd was happening to some of her children as they grew older. Initially she dismissed this as it did not seem possible to her that such behavioural differences could emerge in the family. All the children were treated equally. They were all treated the same and all were loved equally well. The family lived and prayed and went to church together and behind their daily lives stood the solidarity of the church providing support and guidance for them all. She must have been exaggerating these behaviours and her concerns. Fleeting though they were, must have been imaginary.

*****

Father Solomon visited the Hennessy house every Thursday evening to enjoy a simple meal of low-cut meat and boiled cabbage and to discuss the spiritual needs of the family. His regular visit was also to check on the education of the children, their progress at school and to ensure the family attended church on Sundays to hear the word of God and to make a small donation to the parish.

Often, after his humble meal of overcooked cabbage and boiled mutton he would withdraw to a private room to discuss upcoming church events with various members of the family. As the children's confirmation ceremonies approached one by one and in quick succession, he provided extra counselling sessions to prepare them for this momentous event, even raising the prospect with the boys of their becoming priests and the girls becoming nuns in the service of Jesus. His mentoring was earnest. Mary and Paul were grateful for the time he put into guiding and helping the young ones and had great hopes for their brood in a humble way as long as they did not entertain ideas beyond their station. One should never presume to be above one's place in the order of things.

The family was relatively poor for the times and supporting seven children placed great strain on Paul's modest means. Even so, they managed to pay school fees for all of the children, make regular donations to the church and meet their obligations to the parish. In return, they received spiritual guidance, schooling and free clothing from the church poor box to make up the shortfall when Paul's wages from the sausage factory could not stretch to meet the inexorably expanding family requirements.

As the children grew older, the mentoring and grooming followed them like a sycophant, pressing them mercilessly into the limitations that they were bound to personify. The priest spent long and exhaustive sessions with all of the girls initially until he despaired that the older one was never going to accept the way of God into her heart. It appeared that Constance was lost to the fold; slinking quietly out of the back door whenever she had the opportunity and simply taking her chances on the streets with the criminals and deviants that roamed outside of institutions; outside of the church, the psychiatric clinics and the mental health hospitals. She was free to roam, free as the Chief from Cuckoo land once he was given a voice.

The younger girls, however, showed much more promise. Solomon seemed relieved and fulfilled on the nights he spent in deep and meaningful discussions with them. Come closer my dear, he would say to Ellen as he held her hand and ran his fingers along her arm and across her budding breasts. This is something very special between us and God and you must never say anything about it to anyone else or the magic spell that we have will be broken. Your parents know that our time spent together is in your best interests, he added, as his hands moved effortlessly elsewhere and his tongue explored the recesses of her neck and mouth.

The education and mentoring sessions went on for years and as one thing led to another, Ellen, the one with the most promise, became pregnant with God while the secret of father Solomon remained tightly held between them. Ellen was overjoyed and yet deeply worried about the priest's probing, gesticulating and ejaculating during their meetings together, but she was not able to discuss any of this with her parents or even with her sisters or brothers. To break the covenant would impede her path to Jesus and she did so desire the white confirmation gown and to be with Christ forever in the way that father Solomon had explained through his guidance.

> 'The commonest result of the dark warning system is that when little girls do meet an exhibitionist or do happen to talk to a stranger who does something odd to them, they are too frightened and guilty, as well as too worried about the effects on their parents, even to tell them. It is a contributing factor in the pattern of child violation that little girls think of themselves as victims and cannot even summon the energy to scream or run away.' (1, p76)

This conspiracy of silence, as it happened, served to keep each of the younger girls innocent of the activities of the others. Father Solomon was systematically preparing both of them for damnation in his own, awkward way and no-one in the family or even in the broader family of the church was aware of the gravity of things. From time-to-time Mary would imagine that the girls looked, acted or even smelled strange, but she always dismissed these fleeting impressions, along with the slight flutter of fear in the pit of her stomach, as figments of her imagination, going about her business and obsequiously thanking father Solomon for his devoted work as she saw him gratefully to the door. She never mentioned these women's intuitions to Paul and with time they faded even though the girls became more and more remote from her and complained of the frequency and monotonous regularity of father Solomon's visit, especially when he was accompanied by Father Antonio, the rat, as they so aptly named him.

Solomon would bring other priests to the house for meals from time to time and to help him in his education sessions with the girls. He had not taken much interest in the spiritual salvation of the boys at this stage as one was too old and probably beyond the susceptible, impressionable age and the other too young, or so he thought at the time. His main helper was father Antonio, a slender and weak looking man with pointed features and eyes that would not settle calmly, unlike those of other priests who had learnt the virtue of patience. He had a slight tremor in his right hand while his dark priest's clothes smelled of astringent native plants or other strange foreign odours not usually present around members of the clergy. As the younger priest, he appeared more comfortable working with Jerome, the five-year-old boy, who he said showed natural promise in relation to the spiritual life.

There is something special about this young man, he would say to Mary, something very unique indeed. I have no doubt that the lord has a grand plan for him in the church. He will not be like the other boys, I feel sure. I will humbly guide him on his way.

One Thursday night, after a counselling session with Antonio, Jerome appeared pale and frightened taking himself to bed oddly and without saying good night to anyone. In the morning he was monosyllabic and walked off to his pre-school class as though he might never return home; off on a wood path somewhere some might say.

Shortly after this, Father Antonio was moved to another parish when it was revealed that some of the young boys in the pre-school had complained about how he worked with the children and said that they thought he smelt bad and made them feel sick. For Paul and Mary, the alienation and life changes of Jerome were unfathomable. Something had taken possession of him like a plague or a disease that could not be remedied and he became withdrawn, furtive and almost autistic in his behaviour until, at the age of twelve, he was found dead in his bed. He had eaten a packet of rat sack that Paul kept in the shed to control vermin about the house. It was a tragic accident Mary said and she questioned Paul about leaving poison around where the children might find it, suggesting that Jerome must have thought it was a box of sweets, otherwise he would never have eaten it.

The family fell into shock with the loss of Jerome and the younger girls became more distant and removed from the day-to-day family activities than usual. Not even the church was able to placate them or ease their strange behaviour and when Ellen was expelled from school at 14 years of age for drinking alcohol and smoking in the school toilets she left home to find a job somewhere and was never seen again.

This departure of Ellen prompted Judith, the next youngest, to confide in Mary that her sister had been in trouble for some time and that when she went to stay in the country with Auntie Tess, father Solomon had driven out there to pick her up and take her to the local town. When she came back later to Aunty Tess's place she was as white as a ghost and did not speak much to anyone. She spent the rest of the week in bed before Tess put her on the train home to her family. Not long after this she disappeared.

Jude said that something had happened to her during those priest visits and private counselling sessions with father Solomon, something that she never spoke about, but something that both the girls almost intuitively knew and shared, beyond words. They both knew of the visitations, but were unable to convey the meaning of them to each other, let alone to their mother and father. They were locked in a sad cycle of sin, their mother would say. One day the lord will release them from their melancholia and they will be happy, care free young girls again. One day the evil spirits that possessed them would be exorcised and, with the help of father Solomon, that day would come sooner rather than later, god willing. While praying earnestly for that day Mary and Paul, along with the support of the indefatigable father Solomon, battled on doing the very best that they could!

References

1. Greer G. The Female Eunuch. London: Paladin; 1971. 354 p.

2. The Guardian. 4,444 victims: extent of abuse in Catholic church in Australia revealed 2017.

Part 13 Travel

A DAY TO FORGET BECAME UNFORGETTABLE.

By Terri Christensen

It was described as a trip of a lifetime, 14 days of cruising and touring thru Belgium, Netherlands, Germany, Luxembourg and Switzerland. Col and I met new friends and explored new places. It really was a great trip. We departed the ship early morning in Basel at the end of the cruise to start our independent journey to France and Britain.

Our plan was to depart Basel for Metz which would involve a train transfer but we allowed plenty of time. We had a car waiting at Metz for us to drive to Verdun where we had made reservations for two nights.

What could go wrong....everything? The train to our first transfer stop was on time and we welcomed the early start of the day. We met a new friend, Sam, a resident of Hong Kong of Indian descent who was much smaller than the suitcase he was carrying. Needing assistance to lift his case on board he quickly struck up a conversation that was only interrupted when the train stopped. It was early morning, a cloudless sky with a bright sun warming up the track, the perfect day to commit suicide. Why does someone have to pick our train to throw themselves under?

We waited inside the carriage for over an hour and eventually we were instructed to disembark with our luggage and walk to the other side of the track via an underpass. Standing in the now blazing heat with Sam in tow we met another new friend, Sebastian, a doctor and professor of psychology at the university in Strasbourg and he kindly translated the railway conductor's instructions. A special train had been sent to ferry us to the next station to make connections. Sebastian kept track of the train schedules and assured us that we would have no problem in getting to Metz before the rental car firm closed at 5:30 pm.

Naturally a round of beers was warranted when we reached the transfer station and then we proceeded to the downstairs trains, no less than 50 steps. The boys went first; struggling with Sam's and another bag while I remained on top of the stairs to oversee the manoeuvre. Suddenly a young woman appeared on the stairs attempting to assist with the bags, only to cover up her real motive of slipping her hand into the pocket of Col's cargo pants where his wallet was located. I yelled out "She's got your wallet," loud enough for all in the station to hear. Luckily, she dropped the wallet and ran and luck seemed to be on our side now.

Sebastien and Sam escorted us to the next train for our connection to Metz and we boarded with a big sigh reflecting the events so far. We waited patiently, only to find this train had broken down and it would be another thirty minutes before we departed. Finally, on our way from the transfer station, we were getting worried about the time. I had secured a reservation for one of the few automatic vehicles available for hire in France and failure to arrive could forfeit my request.

We arrived in Metz with 30 minutes to spare before the rental agency closed, but where were they? Across the street from the station was the answer. More good luck. Thank goodness we made it!" A sign on the door in French.....what does it say? Back in 5 minutes." We waited our turn and got the keys. Neither of us had eaten during the day and we were becoming cranky. In France they drive on the right side and having more driving experience on that side of the road I became the designated driver.

It was only another hour to our destination of Verdun but our GPS continued to take us in circles when trying to locate our hotel. It is at this time we realised that the town is quite busy and there were cars parked everywhere. Of course, it was the 100th Anniversary of WWI and Angela Merkel was attending the opening ceremonies. We finally found the hotel from a small sign down a narrow laneway. Col was not impressed with the outward appearance and locked door but we had no choice and knocked. Finally one of the owners opened the door and said that our reservation, although old was valid, a strange comment we thought. Col unloaded the luggage and the other owner, accompanied me to find parking. It is a struggle to communicate when I speak no French and he speaks no English! We finally must settle on parking in a restricted area and a note is left explaining where we are located if the car needs to be moved.

Exhausted we make our way to our room to freshen up and pleased to know that the owner had made a dinner reservation for us just around the corner at a nearby restaurant. A wonderful meal washed down with two bottles of wine or should I say two wonderful bottles of wine washed down by a meal! The expression "falling into bed" is fitting. Both of us have never slept so well in such a comfortable bed. But the story isn't over yet. This small boutique hotel provides a continental breakfast of delicious croissants and fruit. We make our way down the narrow stairway to the breakfast room, Col leading the way, looking every bit the big strong, pleasantly chunky, silver haired handsome man that he is. He was wearing fashionable colour coded slacks, shirt without a tie and an open leather jacket with hand-made alligator skin elastic sided boots that matched the clothes. He was an elegant colossus on those stairs and "owned" the room -------- and those in it.

The room lit up and radiant smiles like the sun turned to him and I definitely heard the sudden intake of many breaths. The atmosphere froze and a low keening could be heard when I appeared from behind Col. I was the only female in sight. This hotel was normally used only by the happier chaps of France.

BOB AND THE TWITCHER CHICK AKA ON GOLDEN POND

By Bob Hutchinson

What to do when touring Australia, or travelling with a twitcher i.e. a bird fancier who twitches when he or she ticks off a new species from a bucket list?

My wife Jane and I had owned and operated a fishing tackle and camping shop in Port Lincoln open seven days a week for 23 years when I was strongly encouraged to retire by that certain female person mentioned above. I must admit I was somewhat reluctant to face that milestone as I still loved the job, the customers and the fishing and outdoor industry.

"Don't worry most of these stores take years to sell, you know that," she said. So we advertised and within a week the first person to look at the business bought it.

What do I do now screamed in my head. Both of us had health challenges and the thought of a future not working and earning was daunting. But, as we both say, this life is not a rehearsal, so we pushed ahead searching for options. Can't go fishing every day, useless as a handyman and gardener but enjoy the outdoors so maybe gold detecting was an option.

This activity almost always takes place in remote places and at this my dear partner Jane really perked up. Travelling in remote areas would allow her to continue her passions of photographing, drawing and painting birds and other bush life. This all sounded great so we put some plans in place.

All we had to do was get a new four-wheel-drive car and suitable caravan with both properly kitted out for a long trip to various goldfields preferably in Western Australia.

This took a substantial bite of our savings but we have no regrets. Many people wish to leave a healthy inheritance for their children but our view was that we had supported and raised our children to adulthood and it was now our time. Both our son and daughter unreservedly supported our decision.

Essential to my plans was to fill our car freezer with whiting fillets and squid tubes to smooth the way as "gate openers" into gold detecting properties as necessary.

This of course gave me the opportunity of a few last boat fishing "fixes" before heading away for a few months from my favourite pastime.

I should say that Jane's obsession with native birds turned her into a "twitcher" prior to leaving home. She had bought herself a large telephoto lens and another camera that shattered our tentative travel budget and Jane wandered near and far locally practicing her developing photographic skills.

By early May 2015 we had organised a trusted house sitter and were locked and loaded heading for Western Australia.

We soon found out that our holidays of the past were different. They were all about the destination by whatever means but not the journey. This was much different to our current venture but more about that later.

All went well for the first 1000km or so but near Cocklebiddy in Western Australia Jane yelled out "Stop, stop, quickly!" There were two magnificent adult Wedge-tailed eagles on the roadside. One crouched with outspread wings covering some fresh road kill, the other eagle waiting to pounce. Now travelling at 90km /hour and pulling up a 3-tonne van quickly is not easy especially as there was a road train right up our clacker so on I drove. I did not need to use the air-conditioning in the car for some time.

I am a quiet thoughtful person and suggested to Jane that there was a caravan park at Cocklebiddy where people unhooked their caravans and drove their four-wheel-drive vehicles down a steep sand hill and across a few kilometres of sand dunes to the Eyre Bird Observatory, an old Telegraph Station, right on the coast.

Guests can stay there for a small charge and help the volunteer staff count and describe the birds on this internationally recognised bird migration route. These data are then sent somewhere and finish up in publications that are as accurate a measure of Australia's bird life as possible.

I promised the twitcher chick a stop there next time we passed that way and that helped – I think.

Half way between Caiguna and Norsemen on an isolated stretch of highway we noticed a car and caravan pulled up on the roadside. For some reason I stopped to check. Luckily I did because there were a mature age lady and her sick mother who had been waiting for help since the previous afternoon and we were the first to stop.

They had made a 000 emergency call on her mobile telephone the previous evening that had reached the control centre who had contacted the Automobile Association to arrange a recovery vehicle but no one had turned up. A repeat 000 call was made a few hours before our arrival and she was told by the Automobile Association that for some unknown reason yesterday's callout had been cancelled. They were almost out of water and food which were able to re-supply.

Just as we were talking about fitting them both into our

car a very grumpy truck driver arrived on the scene to load their car and tow the van back to Norseman.

It is a small world. Both ladies were from Albany and the only person I knew there was Jim Allan a tackle shop owner. He was their best friend's neighbour and they knew him well.

Jane and I stopped for a few days in a caravan park at Kalgoorlie to have a look around, get the car freezer checked out and generally play the tourist. For some reason my freezer had not been getting enough current to keep the seafood frozen and kilos of whiting fillets and squid ended up being deeply buried half way across the Nullarbor.

It was 20 years since we had visited the vast open cut gold mine known as the Super Pit. It was awesome then but now breath-takingly huge and well worth a visit.

At the top end of Hannan St in Kalgoorlie and less than eight km from the Super Pit look out there is a "Museum of the Goldfields". It is easily identified by the large red steel mine head structure standing proudly higher than the surrounding buildings. As the tourist brochure says, "Visitors can discover the unique role the town and mining has played in WA's development". Perusing the various displays and replica nuggets fed my desire to get out gold detecting. If you ever get a chance to visit this museum look at the photographs and read the stories about the timber cutters supplying timber to the mines. Wagon and train loads by the hundreds were delivered, it's a wonder any trees are left.

Re-watered and provisioned, with an empty car freezer now working, we meandered north towards Menzies and soon settled into a nice bush camp at Niagara Dam. At first light next morning I received a sharp elbow in my side accompanied by "Did you hear that? Listen! Did you hear it that time?"

Now I am a deaf old bugger who doesn't wear hearing aids when sleeping and enjoys a sleep-in to at least 8.00am especially after a day's driving. Ignoring my grunts and groans, Jane quickly slipped on her favourite purple leather boots and still in her nighty was out the door, camera in hand chasing the originator of the sound. I am not sure if she did find the answer to that question but she did give fellow campers something to talk about.

How to choose our next camp site? Jane commented that birds need water therefore hopefully if we camp near water, we are sure to see birds. She had been told that Malcolm Dam east of Leonora would be a nice place to camp.

The dam was almost empty but she did meet a local character who had been checking his stock and on the way home drove up to where she was painting and said g'day.

He was also interested in birds so they had a wonderful talk and walk and took many pictures.

Turned out this chap was a local councillor involved in the current local Shire art exhibition that had some healthy prize monies. After looking at some of Jane's drawings of local birds and scenes, he positively encouraged her to enter.

Jane appreciated the suggestion but politely declined and commented that she draws and paints for herself. My response, "Jane, it could be good fuel money or we could use it for tourist excursions" but no.

Fast forward to Derby in the far north where Jane had heard the nearby sewage ponds were a good place for birds. Down the dirt road we went with the road narrowing as each kilometre passed. Cyclone boundary fence in sight and Jane jumped out of the car and sneaked up to the ponds while I waited in the heat, smell and insects.

Sometime later a tired Jane returned very happy with beautiful photographs of birds on the mirror surface of the pond with trees silhouetted against the setting sun.

I thought then and still do that they were some of the best pictures that she took on the trip but back to reality.

She then told me that there was no room at the end of track to turn around with our twenty-two-foot van connected. Not willing to reverse several kilometres I managed to do about a 30 plus point turn on a nearby small partial clearing at the side of the track.

If you could prise Jane away from the camera and easel I'm confident she would have numerous incidents she could relate about me Yes I am picking on Jane but these are just some of the little asides that have made our 47-year marriage so memorable. I still wouldn't swap her for the world.

Travelling then to Kununurra, Jane happily suggested the caravan park with the most trees for birds would be a good stop-over. It was but full so we stayed with other travellers in the pleasant grassed over-flow area but that didn't stop Jane walking around the park, her neck craned backwards matching bird calls with actual birds high in the trees.

Topping up supplies at the nearby supermarket I spied a note on the community noticeboard about a guy who was a native bird enthusiast wishing to meet other like-minded people. Jane rang and arranged a quick visit to his house.

He was a real bush character with a wealth of knowledge and stories about birds. This gentleman lived in a simple house but had turned the backyard into the environment of a small tropical rain forest.

There were no bird cages but plenty of bird baths and an untold number of different species of native birds noisily enjoying this little patch of paradise. Jane was invited to climb the rickety ladder to the top of his garden shed where she could see a bower bird in his bower.

Jane has never been too keen on heights but this opportunity wasn't to be missed. Tentative step by tentative step she carefully worked her way upwards balancing fear and camera as she inched closer and closer to a much sought-after target.

Damn! The bower was too close for the telephoto lens but by leaning backwards with nervous husband waiting to catch her she got the shot. "Best shot of the trip," she excitedly explained. She had reached the twitchers' Promised Land.

At this chap's suggestion early next morning we collected him and drove around many irrigation channels and waterways where he showed us many bird species.

He had so much knowledge about this area that his predictions about what birds we would find where proved very accurate. Jane has since referred other twitchers to him.

While we were in this area, we started talking about what we had learned about our time on the road and it was interesting to put it all together.

Firstly forget about doing big distances every day. The caravan slowed us down and then at each camp there is the settling in and the leaving all of which takes time. Every rest stop means opportunities wandering the nearby scrub looking for new bird species and of course taking photographs.

Early morning starts and travelling at dusk also out, not because of the danger of animals on the road but because, you guessed it, they are good times to look for birds. On a positive side, windy days are no good for bird hunting so we can, in theory, travel then but towing a van when it is windy is not much fun. So it all takes time but we did get into the she'll be right zone eventually.

Enjoying fish and chips, a wine and a spectacular sunset turning the waters of Lake Argyll into a giant golden pond we reflected on our journey thus far. We are delighted to say that we grew closer to each other. The new places, new experiences, new friends all have made this change in lifestyle a wonderful and very positive experience.

Will we do it again –you betcha!

POSTSCRIPT

Oh! I hear you asking about gold detecting? Well we did a 10-day tag-a-long and I was the only person to miss out finding gold. Turns out both hearing aids were busted and needed replacing so $9400 later, I have booked in for another tag-a-long next year. Jane hopes to increase her tally to well over 400 birds and visit even more sewage ponds in this wonderful country.

Jane has suggested that after our 10-day tag-a-long trip in the Laverton and Leonora goldfields we visit the south west corner of Western Australia. Why? Could it be that different birds abound in this area?

Goodbye Pilbara gold fields, goodbye Kimberly gold fields, perhaps the year after?

DIVINING: MYTH OR MAGIC OR MADNESS?

By Bob Hutchinson

After a few weeks bush camping in a Western Australian goldfields area Jane & I needed supplies so we drove into a small mining town that had been through some tough times and now was having an injection of new money from travelling nomads and gold seekers armed with strange devices for finding the elusive metal.

After picking up essentials from the general store we wandered down the street to the local butcher. The butcher has cattle and does his own killing and processing. The result was excellent sausages and steak out of the cold room, vacuum packed and wrapped in butchers' paper for us.

The butcher's brother wandered in and we were soon chatting with him about our unproductive gold chasing exploits and so on.

The conversation sort of ran out. He was leaning against the wall and tipped his dirty old Akubra back and gave me a searching look from what were unusually piercing eyes as though he was making his mind up about something. He then asked "Do you believe in divining?"

"Yes, I certainly do and I can find water with wire divining rods but I can't tell the flow, depth or salinity". I was accepted and invited by this brother to see how he divined water and GOLD!

We zigged and zagged along the footpaths and across and along the main street of town swinging a gold ring on a string or using divining rods. I'm sure we mapped every water main and branch pipe within a couple of hundred metres of the butcher shop. His technique was to ask the ring or divining rods questions. Is the water deeper than 10 metres, is it deeper than 50 metres, no? Then next question, is it deeper than 40 metres, 30 metres etc. until he had the depth. Salinity and flow he gauged by action and strength of the movement of ring or divining rod. A very close watch of his hands looking for any tell-tale from skin or tendon movement, not even the faintest twitch.

Now that he showed me how to divine water he said he could do the same on gold but had run out of time to show me! We were invited to contact him on our next visit to learn this art.

Should he be believed, that's up to you but one would think an old bomb of a Commodore would not have been the chosen transport of a successful water and gold diviner but hey, you never know what he had home in the shed.

My dear Jane was hiding in the small supermarket across the street avoiding and denying any connection with her mad husband. When I told her about our future appointment with the gold diviner her comments were along the lines of three card trick, thimble and pea trick, con man and some other stuff as we drove out of town..

The next town wasn't far away, only 240km, where we met a friendly gold miner at the servo who invited us out to his lease to try our luck. Now this was about the time of the Wolf Creek horror film and some real prospectors had gone missing in this area and only one body has been discovered. A woman is still missing.

I called in to the local cop shop and asked if this guy is OK to visit? Sorry sir that is confidential information we cannot release.

What? Even if he is a suspect of vile deeds? That's the law came the reply. Where do I go from here? A rare brainwave saw me calling into a store selling gold detecting equipment and I asked them. "Excellent guy, quite successful at gold mining, you are very lucky to be invited out there," was the response. I called our new friend and arranged to meet in a couple of weeks as we had commitments elsewhere.

We contacted him in due course but rain prevented a visit to the lease but we called into his home to drop off some better-than-cash King George Whiting fillets as a thank you.

Talking around the kitchen table I mentioned our divining instructor and his alleged ability to divine gold and I sat bolt upright when he said "Yep I can do that I'll show you".

He excused himself for a minute and returned with two wire divining rods and a bag of gold nuggets that he spread on the floor in little heaps.

He walked back and forward showing me how the rods work and how to hold them. I walked backwards and forwards watching the wires bend as I walked over the little piles of nuggets. I must say holding that gold in my hands felt quite wonderful and I can believe how some folks do get gold fever.

So next year if you see someone walking around goldfields with waving fence wire wands around stop and say hello. I usually have a drink or two back at camp to share along with some stories.

DOUG WADE'S KNEE, U2 FLIGHTS, ME AND THE USAF

By Peter Morton

Doug Wade was a legend who kicked 1057 goals, the fourth best in the Victorian Football League (VFL) and /or the Australian Football League (AFL) that was formed in 1992.

He played 208 games for Geelong and was cleared to the lack lustre North Melbourne Football Club when a new rule was brought in that anyone who had played 10 years for a club would be cleared to another club if he wished. He played a further 57 games, including a premiership in 1975 with North Melbourne.

Under the leadership of club president Allen Aylett, North Melbourne obtained the services of several champion players from other teams and became a champion team.

I lived and worked in Victoria at this time and saw North Melbourne play in person or on television quite often

In 1976 I went to a medical conference in Toronto and after we flew to Colorado Springs to stay with Burley and Loretta Vandergriff. Burley and I met in Woomera where I was a doctor and he was a Colonel in the United States Air Force (USAF) and Commander of Narrungar a USAF facility nearby.

My job in Warrnambool involved disaster planning and Burley was able to arrange for me to attend a multi service US Defence Forces disaster planning seminar in Colorado Springs.

He also arranged a reunion of our Woomera poker school that was celebrated with great enthusiasm until two o'clock or later the next morning. I had to get out of bed at six o'clock to get to the seminar that started at seven o'clock - a challenge indeed.

On arrival I swallowed coffee and doughnuts, registered and sat at the back of the hall by myself and was the only person not in uniform.

I do not think I fell asleep but had great difficulty in not doing so, resorting to sticking my pen into my hand to keep awake. Somehow, I got through until lunch time and joined the queue outside to be fed.

I had a badge with my name and Warrnambool Australia written on it and a man in a Colonel's uniform spoke to me and said he was a doctor and had worked at Geelong. He told me that he was the first surgeon to operate on Doug Wade's well known bad knee.

I asked him what he was doing in Geelong and the answer stunned me when he replied, "We had a U2 base there". The U2 was a surveillance aircraft that operated at or above 70,000 feet that is twice the height large commercial jets fly. There were no satellites in those days. It was a spy plane with excellent cameras.

They flew from Laverton or Avalon near Geelong or East Sale RAAF bases from 1960 to 1966 and "ya gotta believe it" the missions were called "Crow flights".

The height was supposed to protect the U2s from planes, which it did, and missiles which ultimately it did not. On May 1 1960 Gary Powers, the pilot of an U2 was shot down in Russia attempting to cross that vast country from take-off in Pakistan to landing in Norway.

I well remember the cause celebre that followed, including

the Russian President Khrushchev cancelling a meeting with the US president Eisenhower and later banging his shoe on the desk while haranguing the United Nations.

Soon after this seminar Burley took us to Cheyenne Mountain, the headquarters of NORAD that watches over the USA for aircraft, satellites, rockets and missiles that might threaten America.

Of course, to do that they have to watch those same things that are normal commercial or military traffic.

The place is extraordinary. It is a building of seven or eight stories inside the mountain entered through two steel doors that would admit a large bus. There is a gap between the building and the road and kneeing down I saw that the building was supported by large springs about a metre in diameter with the "wire" 10cm or more in diameter.

Looking up, the whole side of building could be seen as there was a gap between the building and the mountain that was covered in giant "chicken wire" held by bolts shot into the rock.

We were taken into a room and welcomed by a USAF officer who told us that they watched 150,000 internal and 3000 international flights a day and 4,200 satellites, about half Russian and half USA, with a handful from Britain and France. He made us laugh when he said "Sure is a SOB when those damn satellites break up".

There were maybe 20 other people mostly couples of service personnel and our host was asking where they came from and telling the weather conditions at the time.

He asked Leonore and she said "Woomera Australia". He

replied

"I am sorry ma-am we have no information on that".

Burley muttered "Bullshit" in my ear.

We had one final treat and that was to see a game of gridiron at the USAF Academy that is a beautifully designed white building at the base of the Rocky Mountains. If the Adelaide Oval is the best Test Cricket ground in the world then this must the best ground where any of the many brands of football are played.

It was a spectacular panorama and outside and inside the Academy was magnificent, an architectural masterpiece, blending inside and out with the omnipresent Rocky Mountains.

The USAF team were trainee officers and the opposition from another university that had a cheer squad of nubile athletic girls, just like the movies. The USAF had a team of male youths as a cheer squad. Every time the USAF team scored; they did push ups. If the team scored five points, they did five push ups. If they scored another five points, they did ten push ups and so on.

Sadly, the USAF team lost by a big margin but the contents of the Colonel's hip flask and coke (Coca Cola not the other stuff) helped ease the pain. Seriously, it was a magnificent and unforgettable spectacle and a great day out.

IT STARTED WITH A HAT

By Peter Morton

One of the best family holidays we ever had was the last with our four children before the girls 18 and 20 finished their tertiary studies and moved on in their lives and the boys 10 and 12 got serious about school and all that those brief comments entail. And it started with a hat.

We were living in Port Lincoln and saw Graham Tabe, our plumber, in the early 1990s wearing a cap from the USAF defence facility, Narrungar, near Woomera.

I had worked at Woomera almost 20 years before and wrote to the Commander, Colonel Hess who was on his third posting as he climbed the ranks from Captain to Colonel and remembered me in a strange way really. His roommate Gary Scharnberg, later a Doctor of Space, played in the same poker school as me and according to Colonel Hess did not cash a pay cheque in the two years he was posted to Woomera. Hmm!

He included a cap in his reply and also was very complimentary about a book I had written called "Fire across the Desert." It was in fact written by a Dr Peter Morton but this one had a PhD in history from Flinders University in Adelaide. Before I had time to correct him, I received an invitation to the usual July fourth celebration. I rang him and told him my error but he was happy for us to go because we were part of that world for three years.

We had planned a trip to Western Australia at about that time so we were able to go to Western Australia via Woomera

Three of our children were living in Adelaide. With our

fourth we left Port Lincoln with trailer full of camping gear and supplies, picked up the others en-route and drove to Woomera.

It was a formal occasion so the girls wore their best dresses and were very pleased to have their pictures taken with the ceremonial guards in their magnificent, impeccable uniforms with their peaked hats tipped over so low that it appeared that they could not see past their mirror like shoes.

My fellow guest of honour was the famous Len Beadell, the surveyor, road builder and raconteur who did more than anyone to take Woomera and its testing range and atom bomb sites from desert to what it became.

In 1962 he took his baby daughter and wife on one of his road building ventures and named the road the "Connie Sue Highway" in her honour. He was taking her back to that road for her thirtieth birthday.

It was a wonderful night and I did know a few people there. As the night wore on the years seemed to fall away and I saw people of certain ages and ranks that for fleeting moments I thought were my friends of long ago.

At 0300 we were up, packed and on our way via the Stuart Highway to Kingoonya and Ceduna and the Eyre Highway that we would take us to Perth.

Just north of Ceduna we saw a mob of camels in the early morning light. I am not sure who got the bigger fright, them or us

After a very long day we camped west of Eucla and settled down for the night after Leonore and I had a glass or two of port as a night cap. We woke at 0300 and started to pack up to be greeted by our daughters growling about us still being up drinking port. They were not impressed when we gave them the bad news.

The next day was long but uneventful and we camped near Norseman, where it was very cold. Leonore had to shine a light on the ropes when I was loading the roof rack and tying things on because my fingers were so cold I could not feel what I was doing. I had to look.

We got some food at Balladonia and I noticed we had a leak from a fuel pipe that I fixed. Somewhere between there and Norseman we got a flat tyre on our trailer and I changed the wheel. At Norseman we stopped and I had a good look at the changed wheel. I felt uneasy about something but all seemed OK.

Sarah had just got her driving licence so she drove and I sat next to her when out of the corner of my eye I saw wheel rolling on and then off the road at speed. I thought it had come off the roof rack but I then realised we did not have any wheels up there. It was the near side wheel of the trailer. Sarah handled the crisis with aplomb and later said "You didn't yell at me Dad". My comment was "Sometimes it is important not to yell".

It took a long time to sort this out but when I had changed the wheel, I let down the jack too soon and remembered a sort of squishy feeling when I tightened the nuts. As we went along the nuts were not tight against the wheel, which moved back and forth wearing both the nuts and the hole the bolts went through.

With making the nuts smaller and the holes bigger the wheel jumped off the trailer and the extraordinary thing was that had no effect on the handling of our Nissan Patrol. If we had not seen the wheel rolling off the road I doubt we would have noticed it missing.

We wandered around and found a nut or two that were cone shaped and amazingly one or two were still on the bolts; the wheel had jumped over them.

We put the wheel with the flat tyre on it, pumped it up, pinched a nut or two from the good wheel, made do with the damaged nuts, put on the hazard lights and tootled off. We had a couple of stops to blow up the tyre.

We had a CB radio and the boys made a few contacts. We then helped someone behind keep in touch with their travelling mate ahead by relaying their calls. Next thing we got a message along the lines of "Mike Charlie Alpha this is Oscar Bravo X-ray. We have White Nissan and trailer with hazard lights driving slowly west in front of us. Will talk later good buddy. Out"

We identified ourselves and they asked if we were ok and could they do anything for us. I asked if they had any Holden wheel nuts that were and probably still are the standard for trailer wheels. "Yes, I have", came the reply, "Pull up at the clearing just ahead and I will give them to you". His wife, who drove a Holden, kept getting her wheels pinched at super markets so he put some locking nuts on the wheels and tossed the old ones in the spare wheel well later. The odds on that must be very high indeed.

Put the new nuts on, had the wheel and tyre sorted, drove to Phippard's home and all was well.

Next was an uneventful drive to Exmouth, a favourite spot of ours and we met Dick and Cathy Stedman and Rod and Sue Smith and their children, as arranged.

We snorkelled and fished at Ningaloo Reef, which was not particularly productive but as always beautiful. Sue, Peter and I went on an overnight trip with Chris May, a prawn boat skipper, who I knew from previous trips as his dad was a friend and patient of mine in Port Lincoln. That was, as usual, exciting and interesting particularly to see and eat what was in the net then and later.

Tim, the keen fisherman of our family, was ill but recovered in time to go on a charter boat and caught some decent fish. Recalling this I suppose Leonore and I were a little sad that the girls were grown up and this was probably our last family trip, but we did have a second "family" coming along in the boys.

The other thing that was seriously sad was that out good friend Dick Stedman was seriously ill and in pain from throat cancer and the burns on his skin from radio therapy were obviously uncomfortable but I do not recall him complaining. Sadly, he died soon after.

In retrospect, I think I was unbalanced about this because I had delivered Tiffany Stedman, Emily Smith and our son Tim and neither shutterbugs Rod and I or anyone else took a damn picture of the four of us.

On the way home we pulled in to get fuel on the outskirts of Carnarvon and while the man was filling the tank, he grabbed the front of the trailer and wriggled it and it moved. Some welds had given way which he fixed. I asked him how he knew there was something wrong. He replied that he "Always check because my hobby is fixing trailers". I can think of half a dozen times we have had trouble in the bush that has been detected at a petrol station or some other place. The problem was almost inconsequential at the time but had the potential for real trouble.

Our return to Adelaide and Port Lincoln was relaxed and pleasant and we enjoyed the company of our grown children very much.

Gee that reminds me. Our oldest grandchild is not much younger than Sarah was when the wheel fell off. The waters surely are slipping away.

MEMORIES OF STREAKY BAY PLUS

By Peter Morton

I was in a pleasant mood sitting at home in Port Lincoln in September 2017, basking in the joy of the Sturt Football Club's victory over Port Adelaide in the South Australian National Football League Grand Final, the day before, daring to dream about the Adelaide Football Club repeating this feat the next weekend in Melbourne against Richmond, although by a lot more than the solitary point victory of Sturt.

A friend, John Granger, rang and interrupted my reverie to tell me that the day before he had met a friend of mine from Woomera who, like me, had worked there in the 1970s and together with our wives we were good mates. His name was Chris Lightowler and he had recounted a trip we had made on the Anzac weekend in 1974, 550km south west of Woomera to Streaky Bay.

We all are beset by real and imagined worries but this and another trip to Streaky Bay made me think just how good simple things can be. Chris and his wife, another Australian couple and a USAF Colonel from Woomera and his wife came with us. There were about 15 people altogether, including assorted kids and some dogs.

We arrived in Streaky Bay but the caravan park was too crowded so we moved across the road and camped in the showgrounds, where left over wood from the recent log chopping competition made excellent firewood later.

I had made arrangements for a Bob Bennett to take us fishing the next day. I met him in the pub as instructed, had a beer and returned to camp.

A council chap was there and pleasantly told us we should be in the caravan park. We said that we would be happy to pay the fees and this, together with the impression he somehow got that the sand fly bites on one of the children were the very contagious spots of measles, meant we were allowed to stay in the showgrounds.

But it got better. Bob appeared with a bucket of 19 big King George Whiting that we cooked in our new Bedourie camp oven. A simple, kind and generous thing to do and they certainly were enjoyed.

Next day we went fishing. A lady asked Bob to take her son's lunch to where he was fishing. This we did and tied up for a yarn. The fishermen were teasing our American friend about him having trouble using a hand line that was their stock in trade. He just clamped his teeth firmly on his pipe and puffed away holding his line in the narrow gap between the sterns of the boats.

The local guys were mainly talking and drinking beer and were quite annoyed when our mate caught five whiting in as many minutes right underneath us. He removed his pipe and gave them a piercing look from his very blue fighter pilot eyes and then a huge smile.

In 1975 I delivered the daughter of Sue and Rod Smith in Woomera. We are still friends and what's more that daughter, our son and their spouses and children now live in Shepparton and have become friends. (*I spoke to Sue earlier this evening three days after the launch of this book on 23April 2018 and a week ago they visited their offspring and ours in*

Shepparton. Ed)

In Easter 1975 they joined us for another trip to Streaky Bay, where we camped in the sand dunes. Rod and I went down the street to hire a little fishing boat at the local garage and chatted with the owner about the boat.

He looked at us somewhat quizzically and then interrupted our conversation by saying "Would you like to come out with me in my big boat".

We got heaps of whiting and other fish including snapper and he gave us plenty to keep, which we cooked on the campfire in the same camp oven as before with the same enjoyable result.

On another trip from Woomera to Port Lincoln we experienced similar acts of kindness. Jack Reece from the Boston Hotel sent me to see a Wilson Hissey about some fishing and Wilson literally dropped his tools and said that would be ok. We grabbed some food and beer, rowed out to his yacht and had a lovely evening on the water. He later became a friend and patient of mine.

These stories are not about going to the Melbourne Cup or the Grand Prix, it is about simple pleasures and the kindness of people that I am sure influenced our decision to move to this part of the world. The old song says it all in the words 'Little things mean a lot"

This is my world and where I want to be. I hope that I have justified the privilege of living in this lovely part of Australia for what has been, this year, half my life and more than half Leonore's life.

PS: Last week I took a friend of my best mate in Adelaide fishing - the first time I have been out for more than 12 months. In two trips we caught 40 whiting and about the same number of other beautiful garfish, trevally and tommy ruffs that we cooked over two meals, with fish left over to take home.

Three days later another guy and I caught 10 large blue crabs that he doesn't particularly like so he gave them to us. That same man, Bob Hutchinson, the day before we drove to Melbourne for Christmas knew I was unable to get out fishing to catch some fish for our children, so put his boat in the water and went 20 miles to Thistle Island in rough conditions, caught his bag limit and brought them around for us to take to our family.

It doesn't get any better than that and what goes around comes around. We made the right choice to live here, no doubt about it.

PPS The 80 people and who they were at the launch of the book certainly confirmed those thoughts I wrote about so many years ago. We made the choice to settle in a beautiful part of Australia with people to match.

PPPS –Just last night i.e. 25/4/18 Bob Hutchinson rang at about 4.00 PM. He had broken down at sea and asked would I launch my boat and come and get him. Of course I did –that is what we do.

THE DAY I GOT ON THE WRONG SHIP

By Robin Dutton

Many people have caught the wrong bus, but I managed to get on board the wrong ship.

Dad left the Army in 1963, joined ELDO (the European Launcher Development Organisation) and moved to Paris. I was 17 years old, nearing the end of my penultimate year at a boarding school in a small town called Sandwich, located in the South East of Kent. Instead of going to Paris for the Whitsun half term holiday, I chose to participate in the Ten Tors Expedition, which involved navigating and hiking for 50 miles across Dartmoor in two days.

At the end of that summer term, I went on the traditional school cadet camp, which was held near the Lake District in the North of England. After the camp I hitchhiked to Bury in Lancashire to visit relatives, and then on to Ramsgate in Kent, where I stayed with my good mate Patrick Wroe. The next day I travelled by train to Dover, where I was to catch the ferry to Calais, and then the train to Paris.

Not wishing to miss the ferry, I made sure I was early. I arrived at the ferry terminal, went through the passport check point and onto the wharf where there were two ferries moored. I went to the gang plank of the nearest one, showed the guy in uniform my ticket and he waved me on. The ferry left in due course, and about one hour later I decided to exchange the five pounds that Dad had given me for the trip. As an aside, I thought he was crazy giving me that amount of money, the same amount as my pocket money for the whole term, and with which you could buy a Harris Tweed sports coat.

I started to suspect that all was not right when the ship's money exchange bureau refused my request to change the five pounds into French francs. My suspicions deepened further when, after the scheduled trip time to Calais of 90 minutes, there was no land to be seen anywhere. Then I saw that the ship's life rings all had Ostend written on them! Bugger I thought, I'm going to Belgium. Sure enough, an hour later the ferry docked in Ostend. I followed the crowd off the boat, saw a railway worker in uniform and explained my predicament – should I try and get to Calais as I had a ticket from there to Paris. Luckily for me, he was a British Rail worker on exchange to Belgian Rail, and in a broad cockney accent, he advised me to follow the crowd, pay the conductor on the train and get off at Brussels Central and find a train to Paris from there. I got on, gave the conductor 5 pounds, got about 800 Belgian units of currency in change and duly arrived in Brussels about one hour later.

I walked along the underpass, saw a sign that said Paris and up I went. Waiting at the platform was an elegant silver and blue train, the Trans European Express. I explained my situation again to a porter on the platform, who told me to get on, and sort it out with the conductor on board as the train was about to leave. I got on and sat down in the sumptuous red leather seats, as the whole train was first-class only. The train left Brussels Central, and it was soon evident why it was called an express, when it went around curves, the only sensation was that the whole landscape tilted, not the train. The rails were all continuously welded, so there was none of the normal clickety click sounds. The conductor finally came along, so once again I explained my situation and was told that I would have to buy a first-class ticket to the French border, and then up-grade my Calais/Paris ticket to first-class. I gave him all my money and he gave me some French money back.

I sat back and enjoyed the scenery flashing past, and in due course arrived at Paris Gare du Nord railway station. Little did I know that I walked past my Father and two brothers who were by now waiting for the second train from Calais. I lined up and got a taxi to 33 Avenue Paul Doumer, my parents' address in Paris, watching very carefully as the meter was racking up the francs! I was almost at the point of running out of money when we arrived. I paid the driver and received one and a half new francs change, the equivalent of less than two shillings. And I thought my father was crazy giving me so much money.

In spite of travelling via Brussels, I was only two hours late arriving in Paris. Dad and my brothers were extremely surprised to find me at home when they returned because they had watched the passengers coming off the trains from Calais so carefully and could not understand how I had slipped past them. They had not been watching the trains from Brussels!

The remaining trips to and from Paris were uneventful.

Part 14 Is a SOB my least favourite character?

WHAT IS A SON OF A BITCH?

By Peter Morton

A question in an e-mail recently asked "What is a son of a bitch?" followed by a picture of two bomb technicians in their Michelin Man protective suits. One was defusing a bomb. The other was standing behind with a blown-up paper bag in one hand and the other ready to explode the paper bag. The caption said "That is a son of a bitch."

I chuckled and pondered whether I have met anyone who would truly be considered a son of a bitch. I remembered one candidate from a trip to Western Australia in the 1970s and another in the 1980s soon after we moved to Port Lincoln.

In the 1970s our mates Ian and Lyn Phippard invited me to Karratha for a camping and fishing trip at the nearby Withnell Bay. As we were in the area, so to speak, I decided to also visit friends in Broome.

The late Dick Coxon, who used to fly me around in Royal Flying Doctor Service aircraft, was crop spraying south of Perth and was keen to join me. We met in Perth and flew to Karratha in his boss's crop spraying aircraft. Hell, it was noisy.

We were warmly greeted by Ian and Lyn who had everything organised. Next day six blokes with three four-wheel-drive vehicles, three small boats and a pallet of beer set up camp on the beach at Withnell Bay.

We had a great time but there was one minor annoyance; a friend of one of the Karratha guys often visited us and strutted around with beer belly and high-powered rifle proudly displayed. He bragged about shooting kangaroos and what a good diver he was, which he demonstrated by diving into very murky water, a real no-no for a diver.

What annoyed us most was his belittling of women. I suppose we have all said things like "This is all good men's stuff-nice to get way" or "The girls wouldn't like this" but he went on and on.

My mate Dick, nick named "Bambino," was a big, strong, portly gentleman of few words and he was sick of this motor mouth. He put an empty beer can on the ground with the open end towards us and asked if he could borrow the guy's rifle. He put his cigarette on the ground, sat in a chair about 20metres from the can, wrapped the rifle strap around his arm, put his right foot on his left knee and rested his right elbow on his right knee, took aim and fired.

When we looked at the beer can there was a nick of no more than two mm in the side of the old style opening not the newer glugging openings. In other words, it had passed almost exactly through the hole.

When he saw the nick, without batting an eyelid, Dick jerked the shell out, left the bolt open and slapped the rifle into the guys waiting hands macho style, picked up his cigarette, sat down and had a puff looked at the guy and said "The sights are out".

Old mate's eyes and mouth opened wide. He was stunned. His beloved rifle was unable to "cut the mustard". He frantically adjusted the sight up, down and sideways, each time test firing and used about $50 worth of ammunition.

I actually started to feel sorry for him and even sorrier

when I found out that he hung the washing out every morning at five am. He certainly was not a son of a bitch.

Before we discuss the second SOB candidate, our trip to Broome turned out to be more interesting than we thought.

After the camping trip we flew to Broome in that noisy bloody aeroplane and settled into Michael McMahon's home. Michael was a Catholic priest I had worked with and a fine, hospitable and dedicated man. We mentioned going for a walk on the famous Cable Beach and he told us it was divided into clothes to left and clothes optional to the right.

We turned to the left and soon walked past a naked woman lying on the beach. We stopped and sat down about a hundred yards further with no one else in sight.

Very soon a man and woman stopped at the water's edge about 20metres away and directly in front of Dick and me. He was small with a trim muscular build aged about 50 clad only in very brief underpants or bathers of some sort and a black Greek fisherman's cap. He had a camera around his neck.

She may have been Samoan and was a big girl in her 30s, maybe 90-100kg, and dressed in a white caftan which she removed in one silky action. She was absolutely naked, chubby with gorgeous coffee coloured skin and lots of it.

While we digested this, the man started taking pictures as she lay down, sat up and rolled over one way then the other at the water's edge. Finally, she lay on one side and raised her uppermost leg in the air. The man was "In like Flynn" with the beady little eye of his camera clicking away very close indeed to what my granddaughter would call her "woo-woo".

The second candidate to be considered as a son of a bitch or not was Seamus, an Irish computer expert I met in Port Lincoln in the late 1980s where he worked for one of the large fishing enterprises.

He had studied and worked in that field in the USA in the late 1970s and gained a doctorate in computer science. He was looking for a quieter life and decided to see what Australia had to offer.

I was impressed when he told me that he had never failed any exams and he emphasised the point by telling me his younger cousin, who was following in his footsteps and in Australia, had failed the final exam four or five times.

We became friends as we both played squash and cricket. One day at a barbecue we were chatting and I told him that I had worked at Woomera in the 1970s when there was lot going on and I had spent some time unsuccessfully trying to find opals at Andamooka, but I knew people who were successful.

He seemed quite interested in this and we decided to visit Woomera for a few days. By an incredible coincidence his cousin was working at Woomera as a storeman, still trying to pass his exams studying by correspondence. I asked a mate to organise some friends and Seamus' cousin Jimmy to meet at the ELDO mess, as the good old Senior Mess had closed, at a time to be arranged.

I also arranged to meet an opal miner at Andamooka.

We duly drove to Woomera and had a look at the old rockets and other memorabilia in the Woomera Village. It was sad for me to see what had happened to such a vibrant community of 5000 people but Seamus found it interesting.

We soon were on our way to Andamooka and met Bill, an

opal miner. I bought about 10 opals for myself and on behalf of some friends in Port Lincoln. Seamus bought two or three.

After a look at the opal mines and the town we returned to Woomera and the party at the ELDO Mess. The venue and the people brought back a lot of very pleasant memories and time passed quickly.

Early in the evening Seamus introduced me to Jimmy, who seemed a really nice guy and in the conversation that followed Seamus remarked that Jimmy was doing computer studies the same as he had done. He then turned to Jimmy in front of a group and said "By the way how, did you get on with your last exams?'. "Oh, you failed, sorry I forgot" and something about the number of times he had failed. Seamus was bloody rude, mean, unkind and impolite. Poor Jimmy must have wished the floor would open and swallow him.

Later Seamus interrupted me while I was reminiscing with someone and asked to borrow my opals. I gave them to him and soon after curiously followed him to the bar area.

He was a personable sort of guy and he was talking about his wonderful job and how much money he was earning and soon Jimmy would be doing the same. "For instance, look what I just bought in Andamooka" and, like a magician, produced a handful of opals most of which were mine. I walked away and he returned my opals. I said nothing to him about his contemptible conduct or indeed anything else ever again.

Dear reader you are the judge and jury. I submit that Seamus was a son of a bitch.

Part 15 Woolongong dreaming

DAD'S NEW CAR

By Colin Gamble

My father was a cattle dealer and a good bloke. He was a very good judge of cattle, horses and especially rum. He loved horse racing and was known to have a bet or two. He had a particular regard for the hard men who drove trotters.

He was brought up in difficult times during the Great Depression, joined the Australian Infantry Forces when he turned 21 and fought in World War Two in New Guinea. He was shot through the ear lobe near Kokoda and hand grenaded at Shaggy Ridge. He was proud of his service and rightly so. He is still the toughest man I have known and I have known plenty of them.

Dad wasn't a vain man but had one glaring weakness. He loved flashy cars and the flasher the better.

When I was very young, he had a black Plymouth that was a great car until my mother reversed up the driveway with my door open and hit a wall, damage was excessive, especially to me as she blamed me for leaving the door open. The car was repaired but it was then damaged goods and had to go.

I have never found out how he heard about or why he wanted a particular car in a second-hand car lot in a distant town, but off we went one Saturday morning. It took about two hours on a very hot windy day and of course we had no air conditioner in those days and it did not help that the Mum, two sisters and a stranger were in the car. I had never met the stranger nor did I again after this trip. I suspect he was a car whisperer mate of Dad.

When we arrived hot and bothered at our destination it took ages to find the particular address in the midst of a great many nondescript car lots. We eventually found it hiding in plain sight amongst its siblings.

The salesman's name was Murray. He was wearing a white Pelaco brand shirt with little plastic wing tips in the collar. He also wore a wide, bright green tie with a yellow horse's head painted on it and was smoking a cigarette. At one stage he pointed to his tie and said to Dad "I'm a good horse trader mate, a bit like you are with cattle". I thought it was a strange thing to say for someone who sold cars.

Dad said later that "He could have talked underwater with a mouth full of marbles". The car in question that took my father's fancy was a second hand 1959 Holden station wagon two or three years old. The car was two toned, grey with a pink flash down the side, if you were alive in that era you would remember them.

After looking all around the car, having a cursory inspection of the engine, kicking the tyres and whispering knowingly, Dad wanted to take it for a spin. The stranger, Murray the salesman and I went with Dad and that made me feel grown up.

We turned left out of the yard and left again onto a road between paddocks. About 200 yards, sorry metres, down the road smoke belched from under the bonnet. Dad stopped the car, got out and opened the back door for the car whisperer and I to get out as quick as we could in case the bloody thing exploded.

Murray also jumped out and gingerly opened the bonnet that made the smoke worse and we could not even see him. When the bonnet was fully open Murray grabbed handful after handful of long green, wet grass from the side of the road and chucked them somewhere into the engine compartment.

Eventually he put out the fire. We really were lucky to find that green grass growing in an overflow from some irrigation.

After about a minute or so Murray closed the bonnet and said that all was under control. Dad told Murray to drive and without any further trouble we went back to the yard.

When we pulled up Murray and Dad got out and Murray offered Dad a cigarette that he refused with a polite "No thanks". Murray lit his own cigarette, turned to Dad and said "Whad do ya reckon mate-we gotta deal?"

Mum and the children were nearby and although Dad was furious, swearing or belting someone in front of women or kids was just not done.

I was so proud of him. He said "No thanks," and shook Murray's hand who returned Dad's firm grip with a "She's apples mate," comment. But she certainly was not apples.

Dad was immensely strong and did not let go of the handshake but increased the force of his grip. Murray resisted for a while but soon was standing on his toes, jaw clenched with eyes popping and his fingers going white. Dad whispered something to him without opening his mouth much and squeezed a little bit harder. I had seen it in a cartoon before but never in real life but his tie rolled up like a blind when the string is let go and that is what Dad did. He let go and turned away.

The trip home was long and boring and we didn't get the

lemonade Murray had promised us on arrival.

We didn't get a new car for some time after that incident, as you could appreciate, but eventually he sold the Plymouth and got another vehicle from somewhere else.

Every time I drive past that car yard I think of Murray and his tie rolling up like a blind. I remember it like it was yesterday but no one else does. I suppose Dad was turning away, Mum was getting the two girls into the car and the car whisperer was whispering to the engine. So maybe I was the only one who saw it happen.

THE COACH – Part one

By Colin Gamble

I was working in Sydney and being from the country yearned to return so when I was asked to transfer to Wollongong I jumped at the chance. Being still relatively young and fit I decided to join a rugby union club and this club will remain nameless but is prominent in the northern suburbs.

To state the obvious, a good team and good coach complement each other and if one is absent success is rare. It quickly became evident that our coach was quite brilliant. He watched other teams play noting their strengths and weaknesses and placed his team accordingly. He also engaged a fitness guru to flog our team into fantastic fitness. As the season continued winning was the norm as our team was really firing.

Opposition teams were very competitive and played with great tenacity but lacked the polish of the three top teams. Eventually the teams were sorted out and the two best teams were to play each other in the grand final. We were one of them and the opposition team was equally as good as we were and were also addicted to fitness so the game promised to be unforgettable.

Instructions were given days before the game. What to eat the morning of the game, what time to assemble at the ground and things like that. When we arrived at the sheds the assistant coach told us to change and go to the warm up area as Harry the coach would be a little late. When we returned to the rooms just prior to kick off Harry was sitting there with tears in his eyes. He told us he struggled to come to the game as he had driven over his dog on the way to the game and was very upset but owed it to the team to come.

As he was addressing us, behind closed doors as usual there was a knock on the door. It was pushed open by club president, Frankie Henderson, who was holding a large brown paper bag. Harry asked what was in the bag, Frankie said he didn't know but it came from the president of the opposition. Harry tore open the bag and gasped when he saw it was full of cream puffs. He screamed to us that they considered us cream puffs and threw them at us in a rage.

With a full head of steam, we tore into the opposition and after a hard game were victorious by three tries. As with all winning in Australia celebrations were boisterous and always included grog.

Later at the club I noticed Angela, Harry's wife, arrive and I approached her and offered my condolences for the loss of their dog. She looked at me stunned and said "What dog?" I told her what Harry had said about the dog and Angela said she had had enough of Harry as they had no dog and she had spent the previous night making cream puffs which were not eaten and to cap it all Harry had threw them at you lot. You all should grow up."

As I said earlier good teams need good coaches and vice versa and I realised that Harry Staggers was indeed a good coach and my team mates agreed. Surprisingly Harry was a mathematics teacher at a local college so he was certainly intelligent but above all he was a consummate actor and con man.

THE COACH – Part 2

By Colin Gamble

When we last heard of Harry Staggers, he had just trained our premiership football team in a country competition but since then Harry had gone to bigger things. You may recall Harry trained a good team and used standard and obscure methods: namely fitness, diet, planned strategies and psychological ploys. Harry was transferred as a mathematics teacher to another college. When Harry settled in the new place again trained a winning football team with similar methods to the ones he'd used with us.

Because of his records with country teams Harry was invited to abandon his teaching career and coach a metropolitan club. The added incentive was a hefty retainer which would keep him and wife Angela very comfortable. Harry was no fool and realised that the position was tenuous as clubs very quickly replaced unsuccessful coaches. He knew clubs at city level had very good players, employed trainers, dieticians, psychologists and good managers but the winning edge was sometimes found in an obscure place usually in the minds of players because all top-grade players had the physical attributes to succeed.

Harry had friends in the army and with his father, a retired Army Colonel, Harry understood the machinations of this organisation.

Harry took his players to the nearby army training base and they completed the advanced training obstacle course. Being young and fit all the players finished the course in very good time which impressed the army instructors. Harry and the two instructors became very close and the football club invited them to a club barbeque. All coaches involve their players in motivational activities nowadays including paint ball fights, white water rafting, bridge climbing, visits to Las Vegas etcetera but Harry was one of the first to do this. At the barbeque Harry agreed to go for a spin on the Warrant Officer's Harley Davidson on condition that they both were naked. The story goes that when stopped by highway police they booked the driver for not carrying his licence and Harry for not wearing a helmet. It is believed that the cop said he wasn't game to mention their attire. Of course, this story has been embellished and who knows what really happened.

Back to coaching, Harry was having some success and won enough games to believe a finals berth was possible. Still looking for the edge he devised a plan which included his army mates. On the last training night Harry gathered his players into a huddle for what they believed would be a talk on strategy. All they heard was a strange woop, woop, woop sound getting louder and louder and an army chopper landed 50m from the players.

When the blades stopped rotating a figure emerged from the fuselage in full combat gear even to face camouflage. It was Harry's mate, the Warrant Officer who began a loud and emotional talk on going over the top, doing it for your mates and so on.

This was the Harry's edge. The Warrant Officer did his best and the players were bouncing around, yelling, gritting their teeth and looking for polar bears to fight. Harry was happy. The soldier called ATTENTION and ANY QUESTIONS at about the same decibel level as the helicopter flat chat and glared at the players with a look that said, ANY DUMB BASTARD THAT ASKS A QUESTION WILL DO 400 PUSH UPS AND RUN 10 KM WITH A FULL PACK BACKWARDS.

Standing at the back of the crowd was front rower Tommy Magee a good player but not overly smart or good with non-verbal clues and put up his hand. The soldier yelled out "WE HAVE A QUESTION, WHAT IS IT?" Silence and the offer repeated. Magee asked "CAN I GO FOR A RIDE IN YOUR HELICOPTER PLEASE? The mood was lost, the whole exercise blown.

The team lost the semi-final by 50 points and at season's end Harry was let go by the club as he appeared to have become withdrawn and lethargic. Harry moved to northern Queensland and was last heard of coaching a girls' soccer team. Harry was indeed a character and a good teacher and coach but as we said before coaching is a hard game.

THE ROCK

By Colin Gamble

The day was hot and uncomfortable as the fierce westerly off the land had flattened the surf and made it too dangerous to enter the water. As patrol captain at the surf club I decided to close the beach early so we could go for a beer and my mate and fellow patrol member Ranga agreed especially as he lived in the direction of the pub and loved a beer. The beach was closed, the gear put away in quick time and we raced through the strong winds to our cars to drive to the nominated hotel, Hooper's Royal Hotel of Woonona, otherwise known as the Hooper's Hilton.

Life in the mid1970s was different to today. No one had a computer, engineers still used slide rules, .08 was the alcohol maximum and there was no State Emergency Services (SES). The SES is a great organisation and has volunteers to help during accidents and disasters and now is nationwide. In the seventies if there was a problem the police or fire brigade were called and they turned up whenever they had the time. People generally helped each other if they could in dangerous situations.

The way to the pub was from the surf club down The Avenue and up Campbell Street to the highway and then a right and the pub was there on top of the hill. This route had been travelled by many fellow lifesavers over the years but I don't think any of them encountered the problem faced by Rang and myself that day.

Woonona is a suburb north of Wollongong and for years

housed miners from the many local coalmines along the escarpment that parallels the coast. These houses were built in the 1930s and constructed of weatherboard and had three bedrooms, kitchen, laundry and an enclosed veranda in the front. They were durable but with time were becoming fewer and outdated.

As I was in the lead car, I was first into Campbell Street and I had to avoid debris blown around by the fierce wind. As I neared the end of the street ,I saw an elderly man, perhaps in his eighties, on the roadway dressed in an old suit pants, vest and white shirt waving frantically for me to stop. I stopped as did Rang behind me and we left our cars to see what was bothering the man who was gesticulating wildly. He eventually told us that the roof over his veranda was about to be blown away.

As we were studying the situation a bloke from across the road whom Rang and I knew came on the scene. We decided that if we had some wood and nails, we could somehow secure the roof, alas the old bloke had no nails or timber or anything else we could use.

I then spotted a very large rock in the garden, being used as a decorative feature. We decided the rock would do fine as it had a flat side and weighed at least 50kgm. It wouldn't rock in the wind and we could place it on the corner of the roof on the side which was lifting.

We struggled and boy did we struggle to hoist the rock onto the roof. I stood on an overturned steel garbage bin and the other two worked to lift if to me then climb onto the roof to pull it up and position it in the right place. I forgot to mention that Rang got his nickname because of his long arms and great strength and even though we were young and fit it really took some effort.

When we returned to the ground, we studied our work and were very pleased to see that the rock was holding the roof down even in the strongest gusts of wind.

We gathered on the street and the old bloke came and thanked us for saving his house. We told him he should get professional help to do a permanent job when the wind had subsided in the following week. Old bloke assured us it would be done and again thanked us.

Over the years things change, I moved away from the Woonona area, joined a surf club in the city and sadly Paul, known as Rangatang, died at an early age. I often think about the past and sometimes get very sentimental.

Forward 25 years and I was in Woonona I decided to see how the surf club looked and as I turned into Campbell Street the memories of the day Ranga, the old chap, the neighbour and me put the rock on the roof came back to me.

I looked at the old bloke's house and noticed it had been smarted up, different fence, new paint job and more colourful flowers and a large rock sitting on the corner of the veranda roof. I stopped the car and looked again; laughter came. The bloody rock had stayed in the same position for 25 years.

Part 16 Ulysses would have had them

THE STORY OF THE LINSELLS

By Ruth Linsell and Peter Morton

INTRODUCTION

Leonore and I moved to Port Lincoln in 1979 and soon after we bought a farm near Frenchmans, north of Coffin Bay, walking distance from Noel and Ruth's farm, Mena Grange. We later bought and leased land in Port Lincoln adjoining Winter Hill, a property overlooking Port Lincoln, they bought in 1984.

We sold our last rural interest in Port Lincoln about 10 years ago. For 25 years Noel, Ruth, their son Scott and sometimes Byron have helped us with these properties and at home removing old trees and the like.

They killed and cut up cattle and sheep for meat, looked after our property while we were away for years, organised shearing and some cropping, built yards, helped with fencing and calving, planted shelterbelts of timber, mended our windmill and made their shearing shed at Port Lincoln available for family functions. Noel has mended dozens of pieces of gear for me, shown us where mushrooms are, let us leave a few cattle for meat on his farm and so on and last but not least we raised 90 poddy calves together.

It is not surprising that we have become good friends in fact they are the closest we have in Port Lincoln. We are enormously grateful for what they have done for us and our family and it has not only been for us.

They have helped more people than I could count in big and little ways. Ruth has written about the charity work they have done and still do. The Tunarama Festival is held on the long weekend in January. Noel was the site manager in 2018 and that meant he had to get up at 5-30 am and make sure all the exhibitors were in their allotted places and deal with any problems plus sell raffle tickets and food to raise money for the RFDS.

Ever since I have known Noel, he has had a pronounced limp from a childhood injury. How he has done what he has physically I do not know He has been laid low several times recently but can get around on his "Gopher" or in a fork lift.

Ruth is also troubled by arthritis but still has a huge work load as President of Probus and Secretary of the RFDS auxiliary.

This all sounds busy enough but when they have Country and Western singers, weddings or other functions in their large shearing shed, in aid of the RFDS it means preparing sit down dinners for 100-150 people. This is their story:

RUTH AND NOEL 1939-1962

They were both born in Wagga Wagga in 1939, Ruth on 20th March and Noel 25th December.

Ruth's father Archie was born in Camperdown Victoria in 1896 and mother Vera in Melbourne in 1915. Archie served in the First Light Horse and was at the Battle of Beersheba. He died at 95 and Vera 80.

Ruth was the eldest of 4 children and attended primary school at Tarcutta and later Woodstock Presbyterian Girls School in Albury. She grew up on a farm but had a very sheltered upbringing that will be very relevant in her life to come.

Ruth left school at 15 and worked at Radio Station 2WG, Riverina Broadcasters as receptionist and later was the Secretary to the Assistant Manager and the Chief Engineer. She worked there for about five years and then became a permanent member of the Commonwealth Public Service working for the Department of Social Services in Wagga for two years before she and Noel were married.

Noel's father, Reg Linsell, was born on the banks of the Murrumbidgee River in 1912 and his mother Irene was born at Yerong Creek in 1918. She is well and will be 100 on the 29th March 2018. Reg was general stockman for the Scottish, Australian Investment Company who owned Bulls Run Station on the Murrumbidgee River but interrupted this to enlist in the Australian Army and served as an Engineer in World War Two. Irene worked as the housemaid at Bulls Run while he was away.

When Reg returned home, he acquired a Soldier Settlement block at Humula about 40 km from Tarcutta. Reg and Irene had two boys and a girl.

Noel had anything but a sheltered life. He was almost brought up by the manager of Bulls Run who took him out to the paddocks in a utility very day. In the 1945 drought, cattle often became stuck in the river mud and at six years old Noel had to paddle in the mud with a light cable and attach it somehow to a beast dead or alive that was stuck in the mud, so it could be towed out. If this was not done the dead animals would foul the little water there was for the remaining stock.

Another job for Noel was to be lowered into a well with a

five-gallon bucket (20 litres) that he would fill with water from a tin and then pulled out, tipped on the garden, and the process repeated. Eventually Noel was lifted out of the well.

When Noel was eleven he was butted by a ram and dislocated his knee cap. It was put in plaster but they missed the hip injury that occurred at the same time. This was a slipped femoral epiphysis and resulted in a shortening of his leg and limited him playing contact sports but he did play golf. He spent nine months in rehabilitation without schooling and left school when he was 12 after his father had a confrontation with a Railcar and almost broke his back. Noel then had to run the farm and dairy with his mother for about 18 months and understandably is very close to her.

It is not surprising that Noel is poor reader but his mother never gave up helping him. AS a teenager he was able to complete two short courses in Animal Husbandry at the Wagga Wagga Agricultural College.

To digress: when I first met Noel, I noticed Ruth often read things to him but he compensated with a photographic memory particularly for cattle. In recent years his son Scott has been investigating the reduction of underground water available at his Terre Station near Lock. This has generated a mass of paper work from SA Water and other government departments. Noel told me recently that he has markedly improved his reading by wading through these documents. That, as much as anything else he has done, shows the measure of the man.

They certainly had a tough time in those days at Humula. Rabbits were endemic and were attacked with phosphorus bombs, rippers, guns and dogs. Mr Linsell had a dozen dogs, big ones for kangaroos and small for rabbits. He even trained a couple of foxes as well. There was an upside though in that rabbits fetched a good price for their meat and skins and could be caught literally in the hundreds.

Noel's main recreation and first love was helping an old neighbour in his workshop. He has a remarkable knowledge of mechanics, electricity and plumbing and in summary can fix anything on a farm except----'bloody lawn mowers!'

It is highly likely that he only survived financially on occasions in years to come when he kept gear going that many others could not.

When Noel was quite young, he gathered produce from Tumbarumba, the South Coast of NSW and the Murrumbidgee Irrigation area of NSW, such as honey, grain, wool, eggs, cheese, fruit and vegetables and helped to make displays for the Southern District of NSW at the Royal Sydney Show. His forte was making displays with grasses and cereals.

This was before he had a driving licence! When he went for his licence he was surprised not to do a driving test. When he asked why, the police man told him he had seen him driving for a very long time so it was quite unnecessary.

The town of Humula was a very small village with no amenities so the people of the district decided to build a Hall for social events. This is when Noel's ability to raise money and make things happen was born. Many events were held but the most enjoyable for Noel was the boxing that was held in the Humula creek when dry. Seats were carved in the banks and the ring built in the middle of the creek bed. Once, Australia's first world champion boxer, bantamweight Jimmy Caruthers, from Sydney, gave an exhibition match.

Noel was very involved with Rural Youth and in 1959, aged 20, he won a trip to represent the Southern Riverina district as their Star Junior Farmer at the Adelaide Royal Show and to tour the mid-north and Eyre Peninsula regions of South Australia to help establish Junior Farmer groups. At the time he met a Byron MacDonald, who I know, from the South East of South Australia. His nick name is "B-MAC" and he is a real goer as that name would suggest. Noel was so impressed with this guy he later named his first son Byron. I told B-MAC this in Robe at Easter 2017 and naturally he was very pleased to hear that piece of news.

This trip was a watershed in Noel's life as he fell in love with the West Coast part of Eyre Peninsula and later when a Bill Brown offered him the job of managing The Grove at Elliston, he could not wait to take Ruth to check out this wonderful place. They scooted over and back on the Easter weekend 1961 and Ruth was just as excited as Noel.

They were married on December 2nd 1961 at St Columba's Presbyterian Church, Tarcutta. I have seen the photographs and Noel could have been Tom Cruise.

On January 4 1962 they set out for the promised land with their worldly possessions of personal items, wedding presents, a car, a trailer, a dog and a budgie and entered a new world, The Grove, at Elliston.

THE WILD WEST COAST 1962 -1984

They were both 22 without much in the way of possessions or cash.

Noel was a tough, strong man who had been working hard for 10 years doing a man's work. Not tall but with heavy shoulders and chest, with black hair and dark skin thanks to his Cornish genes and he had an artistic bent.

Ruth came from a farm but had a private school education, was not allowed to wander around near the farmhands or in the shearing shed unaccompanied by her father or to watch milking. Strangely perhaps she and the other children were allowed to watch sheep being killed for their meat.

She was red haired, tall with near alabaster skin and had worked in an office in a senior secretarial job.

They were 1500 km from their families and friends and lived near a tiny town 160km from Port Lincoln but they had each other and a firm belief in what they were doing.

Ruth tells how it was for the next eight years. I find this an extraordinary tale from and about an extraordinary person.

We settled in at The Grove and Noel enjoyed the responsibility of being the manager and share farmer. Even though I was raised on a cattle property I had a very sheltered life and knew little of farming and had only seen a cow milked once before meeting Noel, who came from a dairy farm, so the new life style was an amazing change.

Within three months of moving to Elliston Noel contracted pneumonia. He had just finished preparing 800 acres for cropping so I, a very inexperienced tractor driver, with the help of neighbours and halving the bags of seed grain so I could lift them to tip the grain into the seed box, put in 800 acres of crop.

For years I helped with the cropping and harvesting, as in driving tractors, shovelling grain, bagging and sewing bags, maintaining a house, learning to cook, feeding shearers and helping with the sheep work. Oh yes, I became Secretary of the

Elliston Show Society and a member of the Elliston Branch of the Country Women's Association.

One other little thing I did, that I had never heard of. Noel was quite happy to go down wells to clean them out and one day had to go down 320ft. The workman and I took an hour to pull him out. It was so deep Noel could see the stars. Another time he shinnied 100 feet or more down the water pipe to repair a pump at the bottom of a well only to meet a brown snake coming the other way. He said that he was faster than the snake but his arms were "bloody sore" when he got to the top.

Maybe his forays into the well at Bulls Run when he was six had something to do with his willingness to do what must be an unpleasant job.

We stayed at The Grove and nearby Springvale until July 1964 and with good seasons we made enough money to put a deposit on a property of 2000 acres of scrub, rabbits and some cleared land at Coulta, known as Rocky Vale and the Frenchman, about 100km closer to Port Lincoln.

For some time we had to rent accommodation in the village of Coulta while I travelled to Rocky Vale to remove a coating of bird droppings with an egg slice before we could occupy our home. The accommodation was basic but we did have a good wood stove, a kerosene fridge, 32volt power and a fantastic old stone fire place. It was very cosy in the winter with the fire blazing and listening to the roar of the nearby surf.

To get cash to live I milked four cows once a day and sold the milk to friends at Coulta. Noel and I also shot rabbits three nights a week with the help of a spotlight. Noel shot and I drove over some of the roughest ground imaginable.

We shot and trapped rabbits and even kept some to fatten

in cages. Some we had to gut and skin for sale to local businesses. We travelled to Port Lincoln every few days to sell the rabbits, others we left the skin on with their back legs tied together so that they could be hung over a wire. They were then taken to cold storage at the Port Lincoln meatworks and later to Adelaide for export. Frequently we took them direct Adelaide. We made good money from the rabbits and used the money to buy food and farm necessities.

To find the funds to farm this property Noel continued to share-farm various properties between Coulta and Sheringa including The Grove, Springvale Talia, Lairg Station, Lake Hamilton, Sheringa & Mount Hope.

Oh yes, I almost forgot we had two children, born in Port Lincoln while we lived at Rocky Vale. Fiona was born 20th July 1964 and Andrea 9th March 1968

I looked after our farm and also helped with the share farming often camping with the girls in the caravan and driving tractors, trucks and headers and there were always the cattle and sheep to look after at home. When I drove a tractor the children either stayed in a vehicle at night in the middle of the paddock or in a playpen under the truck for shade with a couple of dogs for protection and I stopped every second round to check on them.

By this time, I was quite resourceful and would face any challenge. One day when I tried to cross a causeway, I hit a rock and jammed the car in reverse gear. Instead of waiting for someone to come along I drove 10 miles in reverse. I also drove gruin trucks and towed farm machinery nearly as wide as the road that I had to move from when cars came along that became quite tiring for any length of time.

In 1970 we sold Rocky Vale and Frenchman and purchased Mena Grange at Coulta 10km away. It was a good property with underground water but badly eroded that contour banks later helped repair. We had cattle, sheep, crop and a few pigs and were able to build a trucking business carting sheep for the live export trade, cattle, grain, other stock, timber and other things. At last we were reasonably comfortable financially.

The girls went to the Lake Wangary Primary School and then boarded at Woodlands in Adelaide.

We duly had Byron 9 January 1974 and Scott 31 May 1975 both born in Cummins when we lived at Mena Grange

After moving to Coulta, I transferred to the local CWA and eventually became Marble Range Group Secretary and held this office for three years and with no Presbyterian church I became a member of the Church of England and the children were baptised in that faith in Coulta

THE WHEEL TURNS AGAIN AND AGAIN
1984 –PRESENT

Noel and Ruth purchased Winter Hill in 1984, after 14 years at Mena Grange, from Metro Meats so that the boys could go to school in Port Lincoln and the two workmen and two truck drivers they employed could live with their families instead of Ruth having to feed and look after them at Coulta.

It is in a wonderful spot on a hill overlooking Port Lincoln to the east and the sea to the south and their home is one of the most majestic stone homes on Eyre Peninsula.

The large woolshed, extensive undercover sheep yards and other shedding was also an attraction. They had two trucks running between Port Lincoln and Adelaide carrying sheep and cattle from the market to the Abattoirs. Quite often the two boys and Ruth would help load the trucks in the middle of the night if they were running late for the curfew at the Abattoirs or for Dublin where they had a very strict closing time. The live sheep trade was in full swing at this time and about 45,000 sheep were needed from Eyre Peninsula for a ship to load here.

They loaded the last two boats from Winter Hill. Australia had an embargo on sheep going out of Australia with any more than one inch of wool so all sheep had to be shorn in the eight stand Shearing shed at Winter Hill and injected against Scabby mouth. If agents could not put together a load of 45,000 sheep for the boats, they would not load at Port Lincoln.

The live sheep business ended sooner than expected in Port Lincoln because Eyre Peninsula farmers were changing from the dry land farming that they had been practicing for decades using rotating sheep, grain and clover and turning to continuous cropping, even pulling down fences to gain a few more acres. There were simply not enough sheep.

Yards and other facilities were built at Dublin north of Adelaide so that became the place where the sheep for export were taken.

Noel also carted sheep, pine from a forest that had been opened up near Coffin Bay, cattle to Adelaide and sheep to the MV Trowbridge for shipping to the Abattoirs on Kangaroo Island. The forest closed. The Trowbridge ceased.

Interest rates exploded to 24%. Once more Ruth had to not only help on the property but find a way to earn some cash so she returned to TAFE to update her skills. Ruth commenced work at the Eyre District Education office as a relief assistant clerical officer to the Regional Supervisor and stayed there for about eight years.

She joined the Penguins club to boost her confidence and joined Leonore as a member of the Crippled Children's Association

Things continued to deteriorate financially and more diversification was needed. They started a new project bottling, selling and delivering their own underground water and Winter Springs was born and became very successful. It became apparent that Schweppes could provide water much cheaper and Winter Springs closed as a spring water business but the name continued with the property selling cattle & sheep. The good news was that Noel became the Schweppes man on Eyre Peninsula until about 2008.

In the early 1990s Leonore and I and Ruth and Noel as a partnership raised and sold 90 baby calves we picked up from Adelaide in an old horse float Noel had turned into a double deck calf transporter that could carry 30 calves.

We had an ideal place in the large holding yards behind the shearing shed where we set up tubes and teats and sections where we could feed 15 at a time.

We were very lucky in that we could turn the calves out on the grass when weaned and then sell them direct to the prison adjoining Winters Hill to ultimately feed the prisoners. No freight, no fees, no commission. About the only time I did a good deal.

Noel of course being from a dairy knew all about sick calves and I thought I could tell but Leonore and Ruth were miles ahead of us. These calves are big awkward things as they grow rapidly but they were still babies.

Leonore or Ruth would notice that one might look a little bit unwell and next day it would have diarrhoea. It is no coincidence as they both had four children and were observant with babies.

One way another Ruth and Noel have battled after the initial hammering they took when they moved to Winter Hill. Ruth working, the spring water, Schweppes employment, the omnipresent trucks and cattle. It all came in very handy indeed.

Noel and Ruth have been helping the RFDS for 16 years with Ruth secretary for 12 years and Noel vice President for many years. Noel has also been President of the Port Lincoln Tunarama three times, a member for 25 years and is now a Life Member. The work and efforts Ruth had made were recognised and she was a finalist in the ABC Rural Woman of the Year in 1995, a well-earned recognition.

They have held functions in the wool shed such as weddings, birthday celebrations, dances, country and western concerts and even four or five rodeos in the front paddock for Tunarama that raised a substantial amount of money.

Country singers Adam Brand, Beccy Cole, THE BC BOYS, Beatles tribute group and the Bob Cats have performed there. I thought that the last named was a singing group but it was a performance by real bobcats the little earthmoving machines.

They deserve congratulations for raising $39,000 for the Royal Flying Doctor Service with their team of helpers at Winters Hill and being an integral part of the local auxiliary that in 2017 raised a total of $150,000 for the RFDS.

All things come to an end though. They have had the property surveyed and the beautiful old stone house and a few acres have been subdivided and are for sale. Noel will farm the remainder as long as he is able and then it will revert to Scott.

In closing I should add that their children and in laws have all been very helpful to them and in the main successful in their own lives. Fiona does not enjoy good health but not surprisingly faces life with extraordinary courage and maintains, somehow, a large and beautiful garden and is very artistic. Genes will out!

Time is running for all of us. Ruth and Noel are both 80 next year and we are only a few years behind them so it somehow seems appropriate that this is the last tale in this collection.

Only an hour before I wrote this, I realised that we have known these lovely people since I was 37, I am now 74 so knowing them for half my life seems to have a nice symmetry and another reason for it to be the last hurrah.

When I reflect on what I have written and what I haven't I cannot help but think of Tennyson's character, Ulysses, in the poem of the same name when he exhorts his crew "To strive, to seek, to find and not to yield".

Noel and Ruth in their lives have striven, sought, found and never yielded.

CONTRIBUTORS

Steve Ballard – Doctor.
A loyal friend and one of the best doctors I know. He tells some great stories simply and his caring nature comes through. He has tackled a very complex situation in his contribution with a degree of clarity that I could not dream of achieving.

Rory Barnes – Author and Co-editor of this book.
I have only recently met Rory, a lifetime friend of John Granger. He is a writer and has really done the heavy lifting in turning my efforts into something much more readable than I could do.

Terri Christiansen – Terri is originally from California, USA, and has been in Australia since 1992 and Port Lincoln since 2002. With a background in business and employment she has directed her management skills into a variety of community projects since retiring in 1990. Terri has been involved with the Port Lincoln Bendigo Community Bank as Director/Secretary, served on the Eyre Regional Health Board, the Port Lincoln Health Advisory Council, is a past member of Zonta, Rotary (Illawarra District), and has been a mentor at the Port Lincoln High School for 9 years. In 2007 she was appointed by the SA Attorney General as a Special Justice and conducted bail hearings, criminal court sessions and served as a Visiting Tribunal at the Port Lincoln Prison. Currently, Terri sits on the District Council of Lower Eyre

Development and Assessment Panel, retains her appointment as a Justice of the Peace, a Life Member of Community House and is president of the Port Lincoln Chicken and Chablis Club. Terri has earned a Bachelor of Arts Degree (Business) and has post graduate studies in Criminal Justice. Travel is one of her favourite pastimes having travelled to 33 countries so far.

Robin Dutton – Civil Engineer.
He explains our relationship very well in his stories. He is irreverent, funny, a bon vivant, highly articulate, a successful business man, incredibly good with his hands, an adventurous traveller but a modest man. I recall him telling me, "Peter I am actually bone bloody lazy"- I am glad he is not energetic. Once I got him motivated he produced his stories in a couple of weeks, faster than any of us and they required almost no editing

Colin Gamble – Colin Patrick Gamble was born and raised on the South Coast of NSW and worked for Australian Iron and Steel (BHP) as a metallurgist and waterfront supervisor. Colin retired to Port Lincoln in 2002 to raise beef cattle. He has served as a board member of Community House and currently mentors at the Port Lincoln High School. Colin has degrees in Metallurgy and Arts and other qualifications in history and criminology. And he is a hell of a story teller.

John Granger – Veterinarian.
John worked in Port Lincoln for more than 40 years and we developed a strong professional relationship in the early 1980s that blossomed into a rich friendship between our two

families when our children were young. Our paths widely diverged in the late 1990s and beyond but in the last few years our friendship has been well and truly rekindled. The encouragement by John and Margaret has been very important to me in this project.

Gillian Harris – English social worker and soon to be nurse I worked with in Tennant Creek. One of the really nice people I have come across in our travels and very adventurous. She will be riding her bike in the Scottish Highlands about the time this book is launched and heading for somewhere exciting soon after that.

Peter Harvey – University professor in the health field.
I have written about Peter. He is a renaissance man in a modern world and again has been a great support to me in the production of this book and in many other things. Probably the most articulate and intelligent person I have met. I have used the phrase left brain–right brain person----that probably says it all.

Bob Hutchinson – Public Servant and fishing expert.
We have had a professional and family relationship for decades and this has developed into a strong friendship. We have spent much time together working on his stories and he has been unfailingly co-operative and encouraging. Perhaps, no definitely, more important is that we have started fishing together and he is amazingly generous with his time and distributing the fish we catch—mostly I get it. A big thanks Bob-all around.

Greg Jenke – Major hospital CEO.
There is an article about the times we shared in Port Lincoln and Greg has gone on to be a very successful Hospital Administrator and in the course of this book I found out about his love of motor cycles and he has contributed mightily to the colour of the book with his motor bike stories in Australia and Africa

Margaret and Bob Kretschmer – Bob is a Naval Marine Business-Architect and Margaret is an accomplished businesswoman.

Shaun Kurovec – Ex-Policeman and now FIFO worker.

Ruth Linsell – Farming background ETC aka wonder woman.

Ken Martin – Sculptor.
Ken is a giant of a man, recognised in Australia and overseas as a sculptor and I am proud to say is a friend of many years. He has allowed me to quote verbatim from the wonderful book he wrote and I have recorded some of the discussion we have had about his work. I hope you enjoy my well-meaning but minuscule efforts to convey the magnificence of his work and his description of a work that inspired Michelangelo-breath taking stuff.

Leonore Morton – Wife in a million.

Jonathon Newberry – Doctor and educator.
It is well known that people who have grown up or have had positive experiences in rural areas are more likely to love and work there than people without those experiences. For 20 years initiatives have been made to provide a significant part of undergraduate training for medical students in rural facilities. Jonathon has been very much part of this.

James Paltridge – International horse transporter.
Lives in the UK. Jimmy must be about 20 years younger than me and I knew him when I worked on his dad's farm when at university. That was a big influence on my choice of career. His dad died in 2008 and the upshot of the funeral was a visit to the UK where Jimmy runs an International Horse transporting business in Newmarket. He looked after us like royalty, tossed us the keys to a Volvo Station wagon to use, served Grange Hermitage and the like wines, had his driver take us to the airport in London and I nearly forgot. He met our son Peter and gave him the job of managing the farm he inherited.

Jenny Podorozhnaya – Jenny is a practicing psychologist from the UK. She moved to Port Lincoln with her GP husband Dimitri and four children a few years ago. Despite that load she is a leading light in the Chicken and Chablis club and good friend of Leonore's. I felt very, very cold and still when I read the story she wrote.

Bevan Roberts – Hotel broker and lover of rural Australia.
Bevan lives in Adelaide and we have seen little of each other

in recent years but I am pleased that he contributed his story.

He is my cousin and I well remember the red, raw lesions on his heel when he played sport, they must have been very painful.

He is well versed in our world here as our family, particularly Bevan and his dad, have been friends with the Agars and Robertsons at Elliston for generations.

Christine and Phillip Stain – Loyal and generous friends. Leonore has known Christine for 54 and I Phillip for 62 years and as a foursome we have been close friends since 1982. They are the only people who have visited us everywhere we have lived in our wanderings. Their yarn says it all.

Ann and Chris Watts – Teachers and community activists. Retired teachers who we met when they were teaching at La Grange Mission where I visited as a Medical Officer when I worked in Broome in 1970. We had a lot of fun then and have kept in touch ever since. They are both fanatical sports fans, devoted to their family and community. They encouraged me in this book project and have come from Melbourne for the launch. Thanks so much.

Geoff "The Duke" Whitehead – Local man, ace mechanic, footballer, fisherman, philosopher, acute observer, loyal to family and friends and available for audiences and blessings 0800 every weekday morning at the Edinburgh St Hall of Grace.

www.ingramcontent.com/pod-product-compliance
Lightning Source LLC
Chambersburg PA
CBHW051417290426
44109CB00016B/1333